PUBLISHED BY
Aspen Professional Services
63 Duffers Drive
Linn Creek, MO 65052

Psychology of Disability
[Edited by] Andrea Perkins Nerlich, Ph.D.
          Kathleen M. Glynn, Ph.D.

Includes bibliographical references
ISBN 978-0-9853389-9-2

TO SECURE ADDITIONAL COPIES, CONTACT

ASPEN PROFESSIONAL SERVICES
63 DUFFERS DRIVE
LINN CREEK, MO 65052
JANDREW@SOCKET.NET
573.286.0418 (CELLULAR)
573.317.0907
ASPENPROFESSIONALSERVICES.COM

TABLE OF CONTENTS

ACKNOWLEDGEMENTS

It is a daunting task to undertake the work started by a veteran scholar, and we knew we had some big shoes to fill in stepping in for Dr. Joseph Stano to make this book come to fruition. We hope the finished work on this edition does justice to the work Joe started in the original version. We are sincerely grateful to Joe for having faith in us to bring this text to the finish line as he transitioned into his well-deserved retirement.

We would like to heartily thank all the authors for their thoughtful and detailed chapter revisions. Many of you are colleagues with a Springfield College connection where the original text was born. Your pride and dedication has shone through in these chapters. It would be easy for an author to update a few references and sentences to bring a chapter up to par for a second edition; however, it is evident that each author made substantial revisions to the chapters to reflect relevant and contemporary issues necessary for counselors in training. Thank you for your diligence in getting materials completed when called upon. Your expertise and commitment are evidenced in your work. You are truly valued, inspiring colleagues, and a pleasure to work with.

Special thanks to Dr. Cherie King for guest editing chapters we wrote. Your "extra set of eyes" were incredibly valuable. We would especially like to thank Jason Andrew for his patience and guidance in working with us through the transition of assuming editorship and helping us through our first project. It is also a bonus for us to have a rehab insider as a publisher. Thank you, Jason!

We have grown through this experience and are thankful for our time to work together on writing and editing this text. Any time you take on a project that is above and beyond the typical responsibilities of an educator, it can be challenging to maintain work-life balance. Couple that with being working mothers of young children and it can make for some late nights or grabbing editing minutes between nap times. We are grateful for the journey, thankful for the friendship that resulted, and proud of the finished product. Please enjoy!

ANDREA AND KATE

EDITORS AND CONTRIBUTORS

EDITORS

KATHLEEN M. GLYNN, PH.D., CRC

Dr. Glenn is an Assistant Professor in the Rehabilitation and Disability Studies Department at Springfield College where she also serves as the Rehabilitation Counseling Graduate Program Director and Fieldwork Coordinator. Dr. Glynn earned her Ph.D. in Rehabilitation Counselor Education with a Doctoral Portfolio in Disability Studies from the University of Texas at Austin, the M.S. in Rehabilitation Counseling from The University of Massachusetts Boston, and the B.A. in Legal Studies from the University of Massachusetts, Amherst. She is a Certified Rehabilitation Counselor (CRC) with experience working in state-federal vocational rehabilitation.

Dr. Glynn has presented at the local, state, and national level on the topics of ethics, public vocational rehabilitation outcomes for transition age consumers, implications of WIOA for transition planning, best practices for supporting student veterans in higher education, online learning for students with visual impairments, implications of social media use in counseling, as well as rehabilitation counselor burnout prevention and self-care. She has published articles on predictors state-federal vocational rehabilitation outcomes for transition age individuals. Her research interests include state-federal vocational rehabilitation outcomes utilizing RSA-911 data, best practices for working with transition age individuals, counselor burnout, self-care, and issues related to higher education for students with disabilities, as well as stigma surrounding substance use disorders.

Aside from being actively involved in a multitude of service activities at Springfield College, Dr. Glynn also consults with state-federal vocational rehabilitation agencies providing professional development/continuing education trainings for counselors. Some of her community service activities include involvement with the National Council on Rehabilitation Counselor Education (NCRE) as a proposal reviewer and awards committee member, serving on the board of directors for Community Options, a non-profit agency, a member of the Springfield Coalition for Opioid Overdose Prevention, and a previous board member for the Texas Rehabilitation Association.

ANDREA PERKINS NERLICH, PH.D., CRC, CVE

Dr. Andrea Perkins Nerlich is an associate professor in the Rehabilitation Counseling Program at Hofstra University. She teaches courses for students in rehabilitation counseling and mental health counseling related to medical aspects of disability, psychosocial response to disability, assessment, transition services, and career counseling. She has presented numerous times at the national, state, and local level on topics related to rehabilitation counseling and education, and published book chapters and journal manuscripts in the areas of assessment, psychosocial response to disability, substance use treatment, and collaborative education. She serves as editor of the *Vocational Evaluation and Work Adjustment Association (VEWAA) Journal* and on the national boards of directors for VEWAA and the Rehabilitation Counselors and Educators Association (RCEA).

Dr. Nerlich consults with school systems related to transition curricula, and community rehabilitation agencies for the innovation of their vocational evaluation units. She is the advisor to the Rehabilitation Counseling Student Association and the chairperson for VOICE Day, a community and professional education event centered on disability, mental health, and at-risk populations. She also regularly coordinates a review course for students and professionals studying for the CRC examination. She previously served as the regional representative for the National Council on Rehabilitation Education (NCRE), serving as co-chair for proposal review at the 2017 annual conference. She also serves as a site reviewer for the Council for Accreditation of Counseling & Related Educational programs (CACREP).

Dr. Nerlich completed her doctorate in rehabilitation counselor education from Michigan State University and received a Bachelor and Master's degree in rehabilitation counseling from Springfield College (MA). She has worked in the private non-profit and for-profit systems as a case manager, program coordinator, and vocational evaluator. In 2017, she was awarded the "40 Under 40" award from Springfield College for exemplifying leadership and the mission of the College, as well the President's Award from NCRE for service to the organization and profession. Her research interests include transition services for students with disabilities, ecological assessment and vocational evaluation, collaboration models for service, and student and professional development. She is a competitive triathlete, field hockey player, wine and food enthusiast, and enjoys spending time with her husband and amazing son.

CONTRIBUTORS

MICHAEL P. ACCORDINO, D.ED., CRC, LMHC

Dr. Accordino is a professor in the Rehabilitation and Disability Studies Department of Springfield College. He worked in the field of psychiatric rehabilitation (community residential rehabilitation and partial hospitalization programs) for eight years and has been a rehabilitation educator for 20 years. Dr. Accordino has published articles pertaining to treatment outcomes of psychiatric rehabilitation facilities, vocational rehabilitation of people with psychiatric disabilities, and has conducted communication skills training in community mental health and prison settings. He has also presented nationally and internationally on the same topics.

MELISSA MANNINEN LUSE, PH.D., LPC, CRC

Dr. Luse is an assistant professor and the coordinator for the Online Rehabilitation and Human Services Minor at The Pennsylvania State University, in the Rehabilitation and Human Services Program. Dr. Luse is a licensed professional counselor by the State of Michigan and is a certified rehabilitation counselor. Her work/interest includes ethical dilemmas counselors face in rural and small-town communities, and the development and effectiveness of online counseling programming.

MICHELLE MARMÉ, PH.D., CRC, LCPC

Dr. Marmé is a lecturer at Northeastern Illinois University in the Counselor Education Program. Additionally, she is a consultant with the ChangeLearning Alliance, developing training materials and scholarship related to varying issues and audiences concerned with optimizing the integration of people with disabilities in society. She is a member and/or held leadership positions with Coalition of Illinois Counselor Organizations, Council on Rehabilitation Education, National Rehabilitation Counseling Association, and National Council on Rehabilitation Education.

JAMIE S. MITUS, PH.D., CRC, LMHC

Dr. Mitus is an associate professor at Hofstra University in the Rehabilitation Counseling and Rehabilitation Counseling in Mental Health Programs. She currently serves as the Department Chair of the Counseling and Mental Health Professions Department. Prior to her role

vi

as Department Chair, she served as the Program Director of the Rehabilitation Counseling Programs for 10 years. In this role, she routinely performed program evaluation as part of university, accreditation, and grant-related requirements. She also carried both programs through the CORE reaccreditation process and the initial accreditation of both programs by CACREP. Dr. Mitus joined Hofstra University in 2003 and has taught several courses including; Philosophy and Principles of Vocational Rehabilitation, Multicultural Counseling, Group Counseling, Case Management, Job Placement, Practicum, and Internship.

ROXANNA N. PEBDANI, PH.D., CRC

Dr. Pebdani is an assistant professor in the Division of Special Education and Rehabilitation at California State University, Los Angeles. She completed a bachelor's degree in psychology at the American University of Paris. Her master's degree in Rehabilitation Counseling was earned at Syracuse University, and she has a Ph.D. in Counselor Education from the University of Maryland. After completing her education, she began a Post-Doctoral Fellowship at the University of Washington. Dr. Pebdani's research focuses on women's issues in disability. She focuses on pregnancy and fertility for women with disabilities, as well as sexuality and disability. She also conducts research on quality of life for individuals with disabilities, pedagogy in rehabilitation counseling, and writes widely on cultural competency in rehabilitation counseling.

SAGE ROSE, PH.D.

Dr. Rose is an associate professor of Research at Hofstra University, teaching graduate-level courses in research methodology, tests and measurement, motivation and emotion, and multiple levels of statistical analyses. Dr. Rose's research focuses on Hope Theory and goal-directed perceptions that facilitate academic motivation and achievement among struggling students. Within Dr. Rose's research, the use of positive psychology constructs, like hope, help identify student strengths and weaknesses in academic areas, and has the potential to develop educational interventions that support student well-being.

STEVE ZANSKAS, PH.D., CRC

Dr. Zanskas is an associate professor in the Counseling, Educational Psychology, and Research Department at The University of Memphis. Dr.

Zanskas is the Chair of the Commission on Rehabilitation Counselor Certification's (CRCC) Ethics Committee and President-Elect of the Rehabilitation Counselor and Educator's Association (RCES). Dr. Zanskas is the Co-Director of the Center for Rehabilitation and Employment Research. He was listed as a faculty "Research Millionaire" by The University of Memphis and an Alumni Association nominee for Teacher of the Year in 2013. In 2017, Dr. Zanskas was awarded the 2017 Earl Crader Award for Outstanding Teaching, Service, and Scholarship by The University of Memphis' College of Education. Dr. Zanskas is the Graduate Coordinator of the Rehabilitation and Clinical Rehabilitation Counseling concentrations and the Co-coordinator of the doctoral program in Counseling at The University of Memphis. Dr. Zanskas is a certified rehabilitation counselor and is an LPC in Wisconsin and Michigan.

CHAPTER 1

UNDERSTANDING DISABILITY FROM A PSYCHOSOCIAL AND PSYCHOLOGICAL PERSPECTIVE

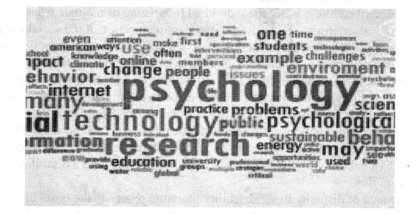

ANDREA PERKINS NERLICH

Although the world is full of suffering,
it is also full of overcoming.

Helen Keller

The term *disability* conjures up thoughts of disease, illness, medical staff, and hospitals. Diagnoses are coded and classified, within the medical model, to determine the most efficacious course of treatment. While a disease focus may be appropriate in the acute phases of treatment, this perspective is insufficient to meet the social, psychological, and emotional needs of those who will experience chronic conditions.[38] The field of rehabilitation has for decades embraced the philosophy that individuals with disabilities must be viewed holistically and uniquely within their environments and communities to assist with maximizing potential and growing in the experience.[50,61,91]

The experience of living with a disability is constructed differently for each person depending on several factors. Some of these are internal, psychological factors (e.g., personality characteristics or coping skills). Others are external, psychosocial factors inherent in the structure of society and nature of interactions between individuals. Drawing on the theories of Kurt Lewin, Dunn[21] described that it is not the individual (consisting of biological and psychological determinants) or the environment (comprised of the social world of the person) on its own that determines how a person will perceive, think, or behave in a situation, but rather the interaction of the person *and* the environment that determines how a person will respond at any point in time. "Thus, the focus should always be on the person *in* the situation and not just the person's qualities or those attributed to the situation."[21,p. 6] Furthermore, even if factors or situations appear to be nearly identical between two individuals with a disability, the lived experience can be vastly different; and the experience for each individual can vary from day-to-day. As such, living with a disability is a process in flux.

One area of disparity in the disability literature relates to the onset of disability—whether a person is born with a disability (i.e., congenital) or acquired the disability at some point along the lifespan. It is typically opined that individuals with a congenital disability have known disability since birth, with no adjustment demands,[77] whereas individuals who experience a traumatic injury/illness undergo a process of reconstruction in which they attempt to make sense of the world following the event. The outcomes of both groups are varied.[59] However, two common issues do emerge for both groups: acceptance of disability and devaluation in the eyes of others.[67,86] People with disabilities are impacted on a societal level through stigma, prejudice, and lack of access; however, central to the issue of public acceptance is the degree to which individuals see disability as part of their self-identity.[22] The crux of navigating the disability experience, therefore, is moving toward positive outcomes, beliefs, and goals. Recognizing that interpersonal and intrapersonal circumstances impact on the disability experience, this chapter will investigate both the internal and external perspectives relevant to the disability experience.

INTERNAL PERSPECTIVES

INPUT—PROCESS—OUTCOME

This framework is used to describe and evaluate the functions of computers, organizations, work flow, teams, and many other contained systems. Essentially, conditions are present, or information is added into a system; information is processed or analyzed; and outcomes result from the conditions and processes. Livneh[48] used a similar structure of Antecedents-Process-Outcomes to describe the conceptual framework of his model of psychosocial adaptation to chronic illness and disability (CID). This general framework will be applied here to understand the process of psychosocial adaptation to CID.

If a person with a chronic illness or disability is considered the "system" in question, the input to the system will be comprised of the sociodemographic variables intrinsic to the person, his/her psychological and coping mechanisms, and variables related to the disability itself. The process consists of the responses a person exhibits because of the disability experience, as well as its impact on the conception of self. Finally, the outcomes can be a few variables that reflect positive response to the disability, including quality of life, recovery, and meaning. Larsen expounded upon the idiosyncratic nature of this system:

> *Adjustment can only be viewed from the perspective of the individual. Physical changes and function may or may not be pertinent to the individual. As the lived experience of illness is different for each individual and family, so is the psychosocial adjustment. The process and outcomes differ because of past experiences, age, gender, ethnicity, socioeconomic status, and other variables that science has yet to identify.*[38,p. 45]

In the following sections, each of these constructs will be reviewed in greater detail.

INPUT

The factors and conditions present within and around a person are potent determinants of his or her psychosocial adaptation process. Miller[62] identified several power resources that facilitate a person's ability to cope with chronic illness, including physical strength, psychological stamina, social support, positive self-concept, energy, knowledge, motivation, and a belief system (hope). When certain resources are compromised by an illness, the remaining resources are used to compensate, and coping strategies are developed to prevent or overcome powerlessness.

In their review of literature, Livneh, Martz, and Wilson[52] identified the following as predictors of psychosocial adaptation to CID:

> ➤ specific socio-demographic variables;

> ➤ disability-related variables;

> ➤ measures of psychological adjustment, personality attributes, and coping strategies; and

> ➤ perceived social support and the availability of appropriate community support systems.

The first three of these variables will be reviewed below as "input" factors in the process of psychosocial adaptation; the fourth factor—external supports— will be discussed later in the chapter.

SOCIO-DEMOGRAPHIC VARIABLES

Socio-demographic variables are the characteristics of individuals; they are what make us unique from or like one another. Livneh[44] identified level of physical maturity, gender, chronological age, religion, and ethnicity as contextual, biographical antecedent variables in the process of psychosocial adaptation. Other socio-demographic variables include marital status, family size/birth order, level of education, spirituality, and income level. Goals, interests, and preferences are also salient, as the disability may impact a person's ability to continue to enjoy valued activities.[59] These specific characteristics, and their combinations, can have a significant influence on the process of psychosocial adaptation. For example, choice of coping approaches and the effects of encouragement differ substantially depending upon gender and age.[39] In a sample of individuals with progressive disabilities, Chen and Crewe[11] found that life satisfaction was higher in those who were married, female, and employed. Among those with mental illness, females are less stigmatized[37] and those who are older are better able to develop resilience to stigma.[23] Pande and Tewari[69] found that perceived distress was negatively correlated with socioeconomic status and education, and positively correlated with age.

DISABILITY-RELATED VARIABLES

Disability can be the result of genetic or hereditary conditions; birth trauma; accidents or injury; diseases and illnesses; and conditions associated with aging, lifestyle, and climate change.[35] However, it is not merely the presence of disability that necessarily impacts the quality of a person's life, but rather the nuanced way in which that disability manifests itself and disrupts

4

participation.[25] Variables that determine the nature of the disability for the individual include the time and type of disability onset, functions impaired, severity and visibility of the disability, its stability over time, and the presence of pain.[59] As a product of the various etiologies, the experience of living with a disability is unique for each person. For example, those whose conditions are acquired,[66] more visible,[10] more physically restricting,[69] and unpredictable[47] demonstrated more difficulty with positive psychosocial adaptation.

Several factors contribute to the perceptions others hold regarding disability and disease, impacting individuals living with those conditions. Traditionally, individuals are stigmatized based on the visibility of their condition; its origin, course, and impact on beauty; the degree to which it causes difficulties in interpersonal relationships; and the perceived danger posed by the person with the condition.[59] These represent value judgments on the part of society against people with disabilities. For example, those who are seen to contribute to the cause of their disability are treated more harshly, as in the case of two people with traumatic brain injury; the veteran will be viewed as a hero, while the intoxicated driver is disregarded as receiving a deserved punishment, despite the same condition. Similarly, those with Type II diabetes, lung disease with a history of smoking, and heart disease from an overindulgent lifestyle are not met with equal sympathy to those not seen as contributing to their condition.[35] This holds true, as well, when the condition is associated with an already stigmatized group, as in the case of HIV with gay men, intravenous drug users, and those involved in prostitution.

Legitimacy is another value-laden criterion for how disability and illness is perceived. This relates mainly to the fact that most people believe only what can be seen with the eyes, or that medical science can explain. Those with an invisible disability or one with periods of remission can cause confusion in the minds of onlookers when they cannot function to expected standards. Health is assumed, but limitations may be present even when visible "proof" of a disability is not available. Legitimacy also comes into play when the condition has not yet been accepted as real or well-understood by the medical community. Conditions stemming from climate change and environmental causes (i.e., respiratory conditions linked to air pollution, vector-borne diseases like Zika virus), multiple chronic illnesses following disasters (i.e., cancer and respiratory conditions in 9/11 responders, high morbidity in post-Hurricane Katrina communities), and conditions not easily diagnosed and medically debated (e.g., fibromyalgia, multiple chemical sensitivities, chronic Lyme disease) are met with skepticism, claims of faking and malingering, and the potential for not meeting eligibility criteria for needed services.[35] "Institutionalized practices seldom account for invisible illness and intermittent disability. Those who cannot meet taken-for-granted norms experience their subsequent marginalization as ranging from being ignored to being degraded and deprived."[10,p. 8]

PSYCHOLOGICAL VARIABLES

The psychological resources and self-perceptions of a person prior to the onset of a disability can serve him or her substantially throughout the psychosocial adaptation process. While there is an expectation from society that individuals who acquire a disability need to manage their disability and persevere,[21] this post-disability management is usually most successful when there was a strong core of psychological resolve in a person's pre-disability self-concept. Core self-evaluations (CSE) is the term used to describe this fundamental, global perception people have of themselves as worthy or capable.[79] CSE is composed of self-esteem, self-efficacy, emotional stability, and locus of control. These pre-existing psychological characteristics are important, but not necessarily the sole determinant of positive outcomes,[57] as we will see. Below are examples of some of these salient psychological variables: body image, coping, and sense of coherence.

Body image. Body image, as an aspect of self-concept, represents a person's love and appreciation for the unique appearance and function of one's body; this impression is also impacted by society-prescribed ideals.[84] Those born with a disability demonstrate the same process of body image, ego, and self-identity development as those without disabilities; however, the experience of acquired disability can shake a person's perception of body image and overall self-concept. The impact of disability is highly subjective, but incorporates the views of others, societal expectations, and the degree of importance placed on the body part or function that was changed. Changes in body image may be perceived as more distressful to some people than the disability itself because of the first impression physical appearance makes and the negative feedback that may result.[69] An outcome of successful adaptation is typically the integration of limitations and disability into one's reconstructed body image and self-perception, and perhaps an appreciation of factors that deemphasize physical appearance.[84] Additional information related to the impact of disability on self-concept can be found in Chapter 5.

Coping. Coping is an effort to diminish the impact of a threat or loss, or reduce the distress associated with it, often generating positive outcomes from the experience.[13] Coping may not necessarily mean a person will choose the strategy that will work the best, but it is a tentative effort to deal with stressful situations.[80] The function of coping is not to avoid stress, but rather to respond in a way that will increase resilience and allow the person to gain perspective over the situation. "Coping responses contribute to resilience and, in turn, likely emerge from resilience."[21,p. 114]

Approaches to dealing with stress will differ depending upon the context of the situation encountered, previous success with strategies, and the perception of the predictability of the situation.[63] Early conceptions of coping identified two sets of cognitions associated with the process—primary appraisals concerned with the significance of a stressful event and secondary appraisals related to assessing the availability of resources or options for dealing with the stress.[89] Recent conceptualizations classify coping skills along the lines of problem-focused vs. emotion-focused strategies and engagement vs. disengagement approaches.

In problem-focused coping, a person's attention centers on what can be done to change the situation to attenuate stress. With emotion-focused strategies, no effort is made to change the situation, as this will not be likely to succeed. The emphasis is on dealing directly with the emotional distress.[89] In other words, problem-focused strategies seek to manage the source of the problem, whereas emotion-focused strategies attempt to change the meaning assigned to the stressful event. Engagement and disengagement strategies differ in their function, the former for approach and the latter for avoidance.[50] Engagement coping strategies include problem focusing, active planning, information seeking, cognitive restructuring, seeking social support, and expressing feelings; disengagement coping strategies include denying, wishful thinking, self-criticizing, socially withdrawing, using alcohol/drugs, and engaging in cognitive distraction. Additional discussion of coping can be found in Chapter 6.

Sense of coherence. Considered an overarching construct of coping, sense of coherence can be conceived "as a personality characteristic or coping style—an enduring tendency to see one's life space as more or less ordered, predictable, and manageable."[2,p. 214] Sense of coherence (SOC) creates the point of view to see the world as comprehensible, manageable, and meaningful. Comprehensibility, the cognitive component of SOC, is the extent to which an individual can make sense of adversity and crisis; manageability, the behavioral component, is related to how clearly an individual perceives resources are at his or her disposal to meet challenges.[50] Meaningfulness is defined as the extent to which individuals feel that the challenges faced are worth engagement and energy.[25]

Sense of coherence is not a coping strategy, but rather a global coping orientation that allows individuals to select the appropriate strategies.[85] As such, those with strong SOC are less likely to perceive many stressful situations as threatening and more likely to activate necessary resources to meet demands. Lustig[56] cited thirteen different studies that identified a relationship between adjustment and positive attributes, such as internal locus of control, coping strategies, social support, and purpose of life, recognizing these factors could be encompassed under the umbrella of sense of coherence. Livneh and Martz[50] found that greater use of hope and sense of coherence was linked to better adaptation among people with spinal cord injury. In a sample of individuals with cystic fibrosis, those with higher sense of coherence were better able to take advantage of support and had a better relationship with their treatment team.[25] Sense of coherence, along with time since and age at injury, was attributed to higher life satisfaction in individuals with traumatic brain injury.[32] Now that the personal "input" characteristics of the system have been investigated, we will turn to a discussion on the process of psychosocial adaptation to chronic illness and disability.

PROCESS

Historically, there has been lack of consensus about what constitutes the process of psychosocial adaptation to chronic illness and disability.[4,21,59] Early literature used the words adjustment, adaptation, and acceptance to describe the process.[41,42,43] However, there has been some debate regarding the utility of such words, with researchers advocating the use of the word *response*. Olkin[68] contended that the choice of the word *response* is favored, as it does not imply a specific trajectory; *adjustment*, on the other hand, implies a series of steps toward a plateau. As a person with a disability, she felt that living with a disability forces a continued response where on any given day the condition can be relegated to the background, one of many factors with which to deal, or a prominent force. Smart[77] is the most prolific advocate for using the term *response*:

> The word response is more accurate because it communicates more fully that (1) it is not disability itself, but the meaning that the individual ascribes to the disability that will determine the response to the disability; (2) there are many types of responses or adjustments to disability in addition to the psychological adjustment, including occupational and social adjustment or response; (3) the words adjustment, adaptation, and acceptance pathologize the experience of a disability, meaning a disability is automatically assumed to be an undesirable state (we would not say that a person adjusts to being a woman or a person of color); and (4) the individual, including those individuals with stable disabilities, copes with disability and makes adjustments throughout his or her lifetime, and, therefore, acceptance is not a one-time event.[77,p. 233]

Despite the debate, there has been relative consensus among the models on the fact that adaptation is a multidimensional construct *and* a subjective process. Indicators of the multidimensional nature of adaptation include demonstrated skills and participation in valued roles, awareness of assets, and successful negotiation of the physical environment.[59] In terms of its subjective nature, increasing attention has been paid to the lack of prediction that can be made through the objective analysis of factors related to the person and his/her environment; rather, "the individual's personal and subjective analysis of his or her total situation appears to be the most important factor in guiding his or her response."[4,p. 7] According to Livneh and Parker,[53] theoretical frameworks share the following common features:

> they are a dynamic, unfolding temporal process;

> they integrate both interpersonal elements (e.g., coping mechanism, past experiences, cognitive appraisals) and transpersonal elements (e.g., influence of social networks, encountered environmental barriers); and

> most individuals appear to move toward transformed personal growth and functional adaptation.

Apropos to the second point, most models that address response to disability emerge from a biopsychosocial perspective, integrating the various processes and pathways that contribute to a person's recovery and adaptation—bio-medical, social, and psychological. The bio-medical pathway represents the illness itself and its course, including ways to manage the condition and restore function; the social and psychological pathways represent how a person and those around him perceive the situation.[34] A biopsychosocial perspective assimilates these personal and environmental factors with coping processes in a holistic way, including the participation of the person and his support network, to maximize health and well-being.[63] Change in one domain will result in changes in subsequent domains, therefore interventions that simultaneously address all of the pathways will fare better than those aimed at a single one.[38]

Models of response to CID have unfolded over the years to incorporate a more holistic, biopsychosocial perspective. The earliest models included a predictable progression of linear phases, which may or may not overlap; the attainment of latter phases was contingent upon the traversing of early ones.[53] The second genesis of models followed a linear or temporal structure, but accounted for the complexity added by disability-related characteristics, personality attributes, and environmental influences. These factors were seen to have a predictive, mediating, or moderating effect on the outcome of the process. A third iteration of models focused on the reorganization of oneself following a chronic illness or disability. Similarly, models also conceptualized value change as a transition resulting from the adaptation process to an enhanced quality of life. Newer theories conceptualize the adaptation process as a non-linear or cyclical experience of interacting with internal and external forces. Below is an expansion on some of these extant theories.

PSYCHOLOGICAL RESPONSES TO DISABILITY

The experience of trauma and disability triggers a process of loss and mourning for the individual. The term *chronic sorrow* has been used to describe this experience of grief,[47] as daily events can serve as a reminder of lost function, goals, and dreams. The literature has pointed to a series of psychological and behavioral responses prompted by acquired disability. These reactions have been classified into short-term or early reactions, intermediate reactions, and long-term reactions.[45] Although a stage-like model has not been

9

empirically demonstrated, there are patterns of reactions indicative of movement from more negatively-connoted reactions to ones that are more positive.[49] Critics of these models warn that the full complement of responses should not be anticipated or expected by counselors, as a person may never experience all stages or emotions.[59] Additionally, the stage model only truly addresses the individual response and not the added stress of dealing with the societal response of prejudice and discrimination.[77] Below is a broadening of the typical early and intermediate reactions.

Shock. As an early reaction, shock is typically perceived as the individual's initial reaction to the onset and realization of a physical or psychological trauma.[59] Individuals may describe being overwhelmed, confused, and unable to feel.[77] Psychic numbness, cognitive disorganization, and decreased mobility and speech are hallmark reactions at this stage.[46]

Anxiety. Anxiety as a state-like (situationally-dependent) reaction should not be confused with a trait (enduring) condition of the individual with a disability. As a phase in the psychosocial response to disability, "anxiety is viewed as a panic-stricken reaction upon initial sensing of the magnitude of the physically or psychologically traumatic event. This state-like reaction is signified by confused thinking, cognitive flooding, numerous physiological correlates (e.g., breathing problems, rapid pulse rate), and purposeless overactivity."[46,p. 20]

Denial. Denial has been seen as a protective psychosocial mechanism to defuse early periods of intense anxiety and to buffer the self from being overwhelmed by the looming adverse consequences of loss.[52] It is an attempt to temporarily escape the reality of the situation. The opposite and proactive reaction, vigilance, is an attempt to confront the threat to maintain control over what is happening.[39] Denial has been positively associated with a perceived strengthening of sense of coherence following disability and better overall adaptation.[63] This may be a sign of the adaptive properties of denial to negate or downplay the consequences of the injury. It has been argued, however, that beyond its initial usefulness, denial can interfere with rehabilitation efforts and increase psychosocial distress. Marini[59] advocated for "healthy denial," where a counselor can assist a person and her family in moving forward, while not closing off hope for a medical advance or cure in the future.

Depression. As the feelings of shock and denial give way to the realization of the permanency of the condition, individuals may begin to manifest feelings of despair, hopelessness, and isolation.[47] Whereas denial is a reaction of a person clinging to one's former self, depression is a future-oriented reaction of trying to struggle with the uncertainty of the things to come.[77] There is a widely-held societal belief that individuals must/will continue to mourn their disability. This is often referred to as the *requirement of mourning*; however, this is merely a projected value judgment of how people might feel if they themselves were to experience a disability.[59] Depression is not considered to be a universal reaction for people with disabilities, although it is a typical reaction to the loss of body integrity, social participation, and function.[46]

Internalized Anger. The reaction of internalized anger results from self-directed feelings of resentment, guilt, and blame. This often results from the self-attribution of responsibility for the condition or failure to achieve successful outcomes.[47] Self-injurious behaviors, suicidal ideation, and bitterness may be behavioral manifestations of this phase of reaction.[59]

Externalized Hostility. Conceived as a contrasting reaction to internalized anger, externalized hostility is the outward blame or aggression directed toward other people, including family and medical staff.[47] This retaliation against imposed functional limitations may manifest itself as antagonistic behavior, passive-aggression, and demanding attitudes.[59]

REFORMATION OF SELF

Self-concept is the organization of personal attributes that have been consistent over time, with this context being the key to understanding the self. Chronic illness has a disruptive effect on self-concept, requiring a reconstruction to integrate an accurate perception of the altered body into an overall positive concept of the self.[22] As an outgrowth of the social nature of the self, a person with CID tries to reconcile the self-concept by integrating past and present conceptualizations within both the physical and social realms. The task of this response is to change the cognitive perceptions and beliefs—or schemas—a person has about oneself, others, and the world at large. The move should be from negative schemas about the disability experience to more positive ones through which a person can derive meaning and attain control.[59] Three scholars have adopted frameworks to describe the reconceptualization of self after chronic illness or traumatic injury.

As an earlier investigator into the process of adapting to impairment, Charmaz[8,9] conducted in-depth and longitudinal interviews with individuals living with chronic illnesses. Common experiences that challenged the development of meaning for those individuals included:

➤ living a restricted life;

➤ existing in social isolation;

➤ experiencing discredited definitions of self; and

➤ becoming a burden.

As a defense mechanism immediately following a disability, people endeavored to keep their impaired body separate from self-concept to protect from the unsettling feeling this alteration of self brings. Charmaz[9] contended that, following a disability or illness, people expect to resume life unaffected by their limitations; but, as their bodies are tested, they realize they must make trade-offs or lower goals until their goals match their lessened capacities. Individuals will eventually begin to integrate new experiences and realizations into their self-concept. Charmaz postulated, "Until they define the changes as chronic and experience their effects daily, ill people look for recovery and can keep illness, and therefore their bodies, at the margins of their self-concepts. Subsequently, they continue to objectify their bodies and distance themselves from them."[9,p. 663] Decreasing this objectification meant that individuals were more in tune with the cues of their bodies and were able to extend more control over their lives by protecting their health.

In researching individuals with spinal cord injury, Yoshida[92] described the process of identity reformation using the analogy of a pendulum, as respondents recounted how they moved back and forth between their pre- and post-disability identities until they came to adopt a concept of self that integrated both. These individuals identified "self" as a reflexive process that incorporates the appraisals of the individual and others, and the shared meanings that arise from social interactions. In her research, she found five predominant identity views emerged from the accounts of the respondents, conceptualized as five points along a pendular arc (from left to right): the former self, the supernormal identity, the middle self, the disability identity as part of the total self, and the disability identity as the total self. (Disability replaces the original term, disabled, in the current description)

At the beginning of the disability experience, the position of the pendulum begins at the far extreme of the *former self*, which serves as the basis for identity reconstruction, but can never be totally recaptured. As the permanency of the situation is realized, the person will shift to the opposite extreme of *disability identity as the total self*, which is taken largely as a negative view. The hallmark of this identity is heavy reliance on the assistance and expectations of others, which can engender anger, depression, and resentment on the part of the person with a disability. This resentment spurs another shift in the pendulum to the position of *supernormal identity*; this identity is characterized by engaging in activities of an extraordinary nature or refusing any assistance from others. For study respondents, the purposes of these activities were to prove they "were no worse off than other people."[92,p. 226] and produce a personally and socially-credited identity. The high time and energy demands necessary to sustain the supernormal identity cause individuals to set the pendulum in motion back toward their disability identity, coming to the point *disability identity as an aspect of the total self*. At this point, both the disability and former identities are considered part of the self to varying degrees.

The final resting place of the pendulum, theoretically, is the *middle self*, a term coined by one of the respondents in the study. Yoshida posited that individuals "may or may not experience all of these identities; or a person could be situated at any one of these identities with relatively little movement to any other identity view(s). If individuals reach the middle self, they still carry the other identity views with them."[92, p. 223] Barring other crises or trauma, the middle self is an identity that incorporates the former and disability identities as one's true self; individuals acknowledge how things are and how they will be, understanding that there are limitations associated with their condition. At this time, individuals may also acknowledge they are part of a collective disability consciousness and understand the social implications, and possible disadvantages, of such a status in larger society.

Finally, Kendall and Buys[33] put forth a recurrent model of adaptation that considers the continuous process of schema adjustment resulting from setbacks throughout the lifespan. As one encounters a setback following disability, the person may again experience vacillation between sorrow and acceptance; the person then engages in a process to reorganize one's conception of self and return to homeostasis. The authors postulated that an individual will develop schemas throughout one's life to filter experiences. Individuals will continue to use existing schemas, following injury, until they conclude that they no longer "fit" their current reality.

When disability or illness causes a disruption in the understanding of self in relation to existing schemas, the person must develop a new schema so that a "more realistic stance towards life can be adopted, together with a brighter outlook on the future and fresh involvement in the community."[33,p. 17] Schemas are revised and restructured as a person assimilates a new understanding of self, abilities, relation to others, and relation to the environment. This modification of schemas is guided by three themes:

> the search for meaning in the disability and in post-disability life;

> the need for a sense of mastery and control over the environment, the disability, and the future; and

> the effort to protect and enhance the self and one's post-disability identity.

These result in a shift in the person's conception of self between what was and what is, tending toward a center point over time, with no limit to the number of times this shift can occur. These changes are akin to those in the Resiliency Model, where individuals utilize resilient qualities developed from previous disruptions to self to cope with new stressors and maintain homeostasis.[57]

VALUES CHANGE

Like transformation of self-concept, the realignment of an individual's value system to incorporate his or her disability-related changes should be considered an important rehabilitation process. Beatrice Wright,[90] who pioneered the study of response to disability, proposed the theory of cognitive restructuring, in which the person with a disability redefines his or her reality. The four main tenets of this theory are:

13

➢ enlargement of the scope of values;

➢ subordination of the physique relative to other values;

➢ containment of disability effects; and

➢ transformation from comparative-status to asset values.

Essentially, Wright[90] postulated that individuals need to shift their values to focus on strengths and new aspects of personal worth. The value change that takes place is one in which a centrally important domain becomes less important and a more peripheral and previously less important one becomes more central to accommodate a person's current abilities. Value change "represents an awakening interest in satisfactions that are accessible, and facilitates coming to terms with what has been lost."[90,p. 163] The process of value restructuring is aimed at normalizing the disability experience or regarding the disability as non-devaluing.[64]

More recently, Bishop[4,5] developed the disability centrality model to reflect the change in values and construction of meaning that result from adaptation to disability. This model is an extension of Devins'[19] illness intrusiveness model. Centrality refers to the importance individuals assign to an area of life altered by the onset of CID.[5] According to the model, the illness impacts subjective quality of life (QoL) in that it reduces opportunities to experience satisfaction in central domains, increases the frequency of negative emotions, and reduces feelings of personal control.[6] Enhanced QoL, through greater opportunity and control, is the desired outcome of the adaptation process. To accommodate for decreased opportunity and control, the individual with a disability will begin to internally renegotiate the centrality of certain values and activities.[48] Peripheral values may become more central if formerly central values can no longer be fulfilled.

People responding to disability actively work to achieve and maintain maximal life satisfaction by closing perceived gaps between present and desired levels of QoL. A perceived reduction in quality of life may trigger one of three responses in a person: (1) change the importance assigned to the domain; (2) change behaviors or circumstances to increase control in that domain; or (3) attempt no change and continue to experience negative effects.[5] When a person perceives control and satisfaction over a life domain, then the impact of the disability over that domain decreases; when the impact decreases, QoL increases.[58]

NON-LINEAR MODELS

The process of adaptation to disability incorporates physical, cognitive, emotional, and psychological changes for the individual, experienced within the contexts of one's environment. As suggested earlier, this response does not occur neatly along a linear or temporal plane, with prescribed and predictable reactions. Three theories relevant to psychosocial adaptation to disability embrace one's need to continually respond to the environment, crises, and disruptions to progress in a cyclical, flexible way.

Building from Lazarus and Folkman's transactional theory of coping, Moos and Holahan[63] introduced the Crisis and Coping Model, a biopsychosocial model of coping with CID. This model incorporates five sets of factors that influence the choice of coping skills in each situation. The first three sets of factors—personal resources (e.g., sociodemographic and personal characteristics), health-related factors (e.g., onset and severity of condition), and social and physical contexts (e.g., support, personal space)—provide the information from which a person will engage the remaining two factors, subjective cognitive appraisal of the health condition and formulation of adaptive tasks (like secondary appraisals). The function of cognitive appraisal is to determine how controllable, threatening, and/or manageable the condition will be, in addition to the extent to which one feels personally responsible for it. Adaptive tasks relate to how one attempts to manage the effects of the condition, such as managing symptoms and maintaining relationships. These factors shape the choice of coping skills, which then mediate the relationship between the factors sets and health-related outcomes.

Moos and Holahan[63] postulated that, although illness and treatment can be traumatic, most individuals cope relatively well with the crisis and recover to a new state of equilibrium, though some do not. In this mutual feedback cycle, coping skills are enacted to enhance health-related outcomes; positive health outcomes in turn alter the additive five factors of the model to promote future health outcomes. For example, as in a study with individuals with cystic fibrosis, Findler and colleagues[25] found the positive health outcomes of social adjustment and life satisfaction were achieved when greater sense of coherence, closer relationship with the treatment team, and lower ratings of subjective illness severity were indicated.

A newer inclusion to the theories of psychosocial adaptation is the application of chaos and complexity theory (CCT) to the fields of counseling and human behavior. Chaos theory is the study of turbulence and natural disorder, which paradoxically has a sense of beauty and order to it.[70] Although no unified definition exists for this theory, it has been described as nonlinear, interactive, dynamic, and self-organizing in nature. A nonlinear system is one in which the input does not equal the output, where a minor change to the system may result in a catastrophic consequence, referred to as *sensitive dependence on initial conditions*.[59] There is no repetition or predictability inherent in the effects on the system. In describing the behavior of these systems, Livneh and Parker noted:

Nonlinear systems typically contain as part of their operational space, referred to as phase space, critical junctions of instability that

15

are termed bifurcation points. A bifurcation point is located where the system encounters two separate choices (often portrayed as a fork in the road). When a system reaches a bifurcation point, its earlier stability has already been compromised because of internal or external forces. Immediately beyond this point, the system's properties undergo abrupt and seemingly unpredictable changes. Following the bifurcation, or crisis point, the system increasingly adopts new behaviors and gradually becomes more stable as it reaches more adaptive levels of functioning, until the next bifurcation point.[53,p.20]

Because of bifurcation points, patterns of behavior within the phase space, or *attractors*, develop with varying levels of chaos and unpredictability. The system is influenced by its internal factors, by the context or environment in which it is situated, and the interaction between the two. Human systems are considered open systems because of this interaction and susceptibility to external forces. Conceiving of these systems as holistic and non-linear is intuitive, given the unpredictability of disability and the influence of innumerable psychosocial and psychological factors. To return to a more stable and adaptive state of self-organization, the person requires information, resources, and support from the external environment. In the context of psychosocial adaptation to CID, following a traumatic event, a person will decompensate for a time until eventually a new pattern of self-organization emerges to bring the person back to psychic balance.[59]

A final theory related to the process of adaptation to CID is the recovery model; although recovery will be explored as an outcome of successful adaptation, it is also a process that influences it. Corrigan and colleagues demonstrated the dynamic process of recovery:

Regardless of whether personal goals have been attained, recovery as a process is achieved when the person has replaced despair with hope, with the idea that achievement is possible even in the face of distress, dysfunction, and disability. Viewing recovery as a process does not mean people need to demonstrate certain benchmarks such as symptom remission or expected goal attainment. Instead, this view asserts that people can live with disabilities and achieve personally meaningful goals that still lead to a life with personal dignity.[15,p.39]

The Substance Abuse and Mental Health Services Administration (SAMHSA)[82] is at the forefront of defining recovery as the process for those with mental health and substance use disorders. They posited their working definition of recovery as "a process of change through which individuals improve their health and wellness, live a self-directed life, and strive to reach their full potential."[82,p.2] Support for individuals should be given in the areas of home, health, purpose, and community to facilitate this process. Recovery is viewed as a hopeful, person-driven, and holistic process, based on respect and culturally responsiveness, while supported by quality relationships. Recovery can take on many paths and forms, as it is a personal journey recognizing that continued growth and improved functioning might involve setbacks.

Supporting individuals within the process of recovery requires a paradigm shift to where the client is involved in or directing treatment, with providers still having a prominent role. At its essence, recovery is supporting a client's self-determination, the belief that the person is empowered and competent enough to make decisions. To do this, providers may need to move away from merely monitoring *adherence* to a treatment plan, and toward efforts to understand the processes that affect the behaviors and decisions the client makes.[15] The recovery process seeks to discover a way of living a fulfilled life and a more positive, hopeful personal identity apart from behavioral health issue: "individuals learn what is necessary to care for a changed self, take slow steps to reconnect with what is left of the old self and to refine a new self, and ultimately solidify a recovered self that finds the daily struggles less overwhelming."[74,p. 49] By understanding where a person is on this journey of self-discovery, a counselor can tailor approaches to match specific needs and develop connections in the client's community to facilitate support.

Whether seemingly straightforward or more circuitous in presentation, the processes of adaptation described above honor the deeply personal nature of this journey. The following section describes common goals and outcomes of a person's response to the experience of disability.

OUTCOMES

In the current literature, the words adaptation and adjustment have been deemed as acceptable terms to describe the process, but not necessarily the outcome. The idea of adjustment as a final stage has been rejected for being unrealistic,[33,70,77] since there will be consistent changes that occur across the lifespan. Bishop described adaptation as "a process of responding to the functional, psychological, and social changes that occur with the onset and experience of living with a disability, chronic illness, or associated treatments."[4,p. 6] However, he contended

the desired outcome of this process was enhanced quality of life. Other indicators of a positive response include independence, positive self-concept, sense of personal mastery, and engaging in valued relationships and activities.[21] The following is a discussion of five positive or desired outcomes of the response to disability.

MEANING MAKING

Vash[86] described a model for *levels of acknowledgement* when adjusting to a disability, including:

- ➢ recognition of the facts;
- ➢ acceptance of the implications; and
- ➢ embracing the experience.

As reflected in this third level, the outcome of the process is that a person understands she would be different without her disability, and this is not necessarily desirable. Vash referred to rising above the limitations imposed by disability to a position of neutrality, or positive regard, as *transcendence*. Once thought to be a person's inability to acknowledge or accept disability, it is now recognized transcendence occurs because of disability, not in spite of it.[77] This transformation is more than a victory over illness, but rather a new way to understand and address it.[10] Finding some positive meaning from disability enhances well-being,[21] although in the process of seeking meaning, people may also encounter negative emotions along the way.[60] Positive reinterpretation of disability include seeing it as a challenge to overcome or a chance to prove oneself against adversity,[69] a desire to avoid representing disability as a weakness or something to be pitied,[28] and considering disability as a source of potential.[77] A person may be able to find benefit from the disability experience, as crises present opportunities to reconstruct one's personality and develop greater coping capabilities.[38] When a person achieves growth through transcendence, he or she is able to proceed with a more positive outlook on life.

QUALITY OF LIFE

While influenced by both internal and external factors, quality of life is a construct *unique to each person*, although researchers have attempted to codify and define its key domains. Attempts to measure QoL in people with disabilities tend to speak to the priorities and orientation of the researchers more so than the subjects.[31] Internal desires and values are the driving forces in the determination of subjective quality of life, but society at large also provides expectations of its citizens against which their successes and failures will be judged. Typical areas that comprise quality of life include physical health, psychological or emotional health, social support, level of independence, employment or productivity, personal beliefs, and economic or material well-being.[26] Related to disability and illness, health-related quality of life (HRQoL) comprises how an individual's well-being might be affected over time by the condition.[54] Miller best described the comprehensive nature of quality of life:

> *Quality of life encompasses being able to engage in roles that are important to individuals: to perceive themselves as worthwhile; to achieve a sense of independence; to feel satisfaction with self, accomplishments, and relationships; to have sense of wellbeing despite the limitations imposed by illness; to give and receive love; to have*

energy to enjoy life's special pleasures; to cope effectively; and to have hope.[62, p. 8]

Crewe[17] identified quality of life as the ultimate goal of rehabilitation. It has also been put forward as the desired outcome of the psychosocial adaptation process.[4] Within the field of rehabilitation counseling, quality of life has come to be associated with successful efforts to return to psychosocial homeostasis following the advent of a disability, as well as the attainment of person-environment congruence. QoL offers counselors and consumers the opportunity to look more holistically at the consumer's life and context to incorporate the interactions of personal, social, and environmental domains.[26] However, measurement of quality of life should not begin with the areas of life impacted, but rather the importance the individual ascribes to those areas of life.[5] Subjective well-being, taking into account life satisfaction and the amount of positive and negative affect an individual generally experiences, has been suggested as a more meaningful assessment of QoL.[78] The continuous nature of the scores on many QoL assessments indicate that personal progress can occur on a spectrum, without the need to set a threshold or requirement on the construct.[12]

RECOVERY

Recovery is another alternative outcome for the psychosocial adaptation process. Bishop described recovery as "a deeply personal process of changing one's attitudes, values, feelings, goals, skills, and roles. It is a way of living a satisfying, hopeful, and contributing life even within the limitations caused by illness. Recovery involves the development of new meaning and purpose in one's life as one grows beyond the effects of disability or illness."[3, p. 48] The concept of recovery does not mean that the person has been cured of her condition—it means that the person has found a way to reframe her reality to continue to live a purposeful life. In addition to a reduction in symptoms, the person experiences optimism, empowerment, interpersonal support, and stigma reduction.[12] One can recover from the condition, but the memory of the process and the fact that it exists does not change. Professional intervention is a purposeful, but not necessary, condition to realizing recovery.[3] Paramount to achieving this outcome is that people take personal responsibility and an active role in managing their lives, consistent with the philosophies of consumer empowerment and self-determination.

RESILIENCE AND GROWTH

Resilience and growth can be viewed akin to bouncing back following trauma, maintaining equilibrium in the face of loss, and thriving amidst adversity.[60] While a person can be resilient by nature (i.e., trait), the process of resilience is a state-like construct in which the person is able to mobilize cognitive, emotional, and behavioral skills to overcome challenges. Adaptation to disability calls upon the person to develop such skills to move toward the outcome of personal growth; to paint resilience as a stable personality trait a person either does or does not possess would be dangerous, as the person could be seen as personally responsible for his or her problems.[88] As the basis for resilience interventions for people with disabilities, Stuntzner and Hartley[81] identified factors for interpersonal resilience, including positive emotions and hope, internal locus of control, active problem solving, and the belief that things will work out. Interpersonal resilience was impacted by peer and family support. Cumulatively, these factors unite to allow the person to be successful notwithstanding adversity, and move toward an experience of post-traumatic growth.

Post-traumatic growth is the positive personal changes that result from the challenge of disability. Post-traumatic growth signifies the person has gone beyond pre-disability levels of psychological functioning to demonstrate enhanced personal strength, improved relationships with others, an appreciation for life, spiritual change, and embrace new possibilities.[83] The emotional struggle that results from the trauma spurs cognitive rumination and a processing of the event, allowing the person to make positive changes, derive meaning, and move past to growth.[18]

DISABILITY IDENTITY

An outcome for the response to disability is the formation of a disability identity. Identity refers to conceptions of self, expressions of individuality, and accounts of group affiliation.[22] As stated earlier, a person's numerous identities compose self-concept; disability identity is one such component for those who live with disability or disease. While not always the primary status of the person, disability identity can be activated when a person is confronted with a limitation, real or imposed. The nature and visibility of a person's disability are going to influence its impact on a person's life, especially in how others view the person.

According to self-identity theory, how a person chooses to identify oneself, including group memberships, can have positive implications for self-worth, political action, and collective action.[67] It is assumed individuals would avoid being associated with stigmatized groups, when in fact, individuals who express their disability through social activism feel less defined by external labels and work toward social justice for all people with disabilities.[66] Therefore, embracing one's disability identity, as part of the total self, allows for the person to view his or her disability positively, engage with a collective for social rights, and take pride in the experience. The concept of disability identity will be further explored in Chapter 4. Now that we have investigated the internal, psychological perspectives, we will delve into the influence of external factors on life with a disability.

EXTERNAL PERSPECTIVES

Although the adaptation process and development of self-concept are different depending upon whether the condition is congenital or acquired, the experience of social interaction and stigma may be the same for all individuals with disabilities. People may adjust well to the experience of disability and accept their disability as part of their self-concept; the general public, however, may not be so accepting. Much of the stigma and devaluation of people with disabilities is historically rooted in the structure of society and the perceptions of disability that resulted from it.

Three traditional models of disability—medical, economic, and sociopolitical—have created laws and service systems that still exist today. The medical model has its roots in the practice of medicine and physical rehabilitation, where disability is equated with a diagnosis and pathology.[77] Within this model, physicians are considered the experts and the person with a disability is supposed to "try hard" to adapt to his situation. Most public and private programs rely on this model because eligibility is based on medical documentation of pathology and role limitation, and treatment typically ceases once medical recovery stops.[76] The economic, or functional, model assumes everyone needs to be a contributing member of society, therefore the functions people can or cannot perform construct their disability.[77] Civil rights and services are provided to those with a chance to contribute to society. The state-federal vocational rehabilitation system is largely premised on this notion, as is most rehabilitation legislation. The final model, the sociopolitical or minority model, was championed by disability rights activists. Those who support this model contend that disability is a societal, rather than private, concern. The problem is not that a person has an impairment, or he cannot work, but that society is not structured in a way to offer opportunities and prevent barriers to full participation to people with disabilities. This is the model upon which the Americans with Disabilities Act (ADA) and its amendments are based. As Smart noted, "people with disabilities often jokingly refer to the intent of the ADA as 'boldly going where everybody else goes.'"[77, p. 79]

The current state of the art for rehabilitation counseling is to focus on reducing barriers and promoting inclusion for people with disabilities. For this reason, the overriding disability paradigm is that of the World Health Organization's International Classification of Functioning (ICF) model. This model recognizes the interactive process of disability as both medical and social.[69] The key components to the model are the interaction among function, activity, participation, environment, and personal impact of disability. Integral to providing medical services from this perspective is patients' understanding of health and their individual conceptions of disability.[1] From a counseling and service perspective, this biopsychosocial model allows practitioners to understand how an individual functions in his or her preferred environments, roles, and activities, using that individual's personal definition of QoL. The discrepancy between current and desired levels of functioning regarding physical, social, and community engagement will be the basis for planning and service delivery.

A counselor's focus must be on facilitating empowerment within the consumer. Frain and colleagues[27] operationalized empowerment to include control, assertiveness, competence, self-esteem, and participation in the community. However, societal structures from older models (i.e., medical and functional models) have left us with lingering discrimination and obstacles. Within this structure, several specific forces impede the attainment of quality of life and empowerment. These include:

- ➢ public attitudes;
- ➢ accessibility to resources and support;
- ➢ availability of opportunity and choice; and
- ➢ the lack of a collective identity for people with disabilities.

The following sections will elaborate on these societal forces and discuss frameworks for understanding them, as well as approaches for change.

ATTITUDES & SOCIAL INFLUENCES

One of the most substantial barriers people with disabilities face is stigma, prejudice, or discrimination from others in society. Several issues color the attitudes of others as either positive or negative. The first is perception of the cause of the condition, responsibility for the condition, or threat imposed by the condition or person.[59] Those who are viewed to have had a hand in the cause of their condition are met with harsher treatment. People with disabilities are often viewed as a threat to safety or economic well-being because of a fear of the unknown.[77] Some people disparage those with disabilities because they are perceived to be a drain on resources and welfare.

Second, negative attitudes are also generated from the fact that people perceive those with disabilities to not align with the cardinal values of American society—independence and self-sufficiency; work and productivity; and attractiveness.[29] Health and able-bodied functioning are the prescribed normative standard in our culture.[10] Citizens' own fear of losing these values fuels their negative treatment or avoidance of people with disabilities. Hahn[30] proposed that avoidance of people with disabilities was related to two types of anxiety on the part of people without disabilities. The first, *existential anxiety*, is triggered by the threat of loss of potential and function; the other, *aesthetic anxiety*, is triggered by fear of the loss of attractiveness.

A third issue related to attitudes toward disabilities is that of overgeneralization. People with disabilities, regardless of their skills and abilities, may be categorically discriminated against and devalued because they are associated with a disability group rather than seen as individuals.[21] Another manifestation of this is when others over-generalize one aspect of the person (i.e., disability) to the whole person, as when it is assumed that a person with cerebral palsy lacks intelligence. Beatrice Wright[91] referred to this effect as "spread." Others have referred to this as attribution of a *master status*,[21] where disability is seen as the defining characteristic. A broader discussion on public perceptions can be found in Chapter 3.

Approaches for change. Each of these experiences can result in the marginalization of people with disabilities. With erected barriers and created division, those with disabilities experience disconnection, devaluation, and discrimination.[10] Several actions, on the part of a tolerant and just society, can be undertaken to shift current prevailing attitudes; the most prominent of these are revising media portrayals and comfort/contact with people with disabilities. In shows and movies, people with disabilities are portrayed in demeaning and sensationalized ways, often exaggerating the prevalence of symptoms or dangerousness of individuals.[77] Popular and news media utilize these exaggerations as "click-bait" to draw readers into stories. Other stories and films portray people with disabilities as heroic for doing typical things, a practice referred to as "inspiration porn."[93] These media images burn lasting impressions of fear, pity, or underestimation of potential that are often difficult to overcome without counter information. Using actors with disabilities to portray characters with disabilities, rather than those without disabilities pretending as such, would provide a more trustworthy representation. News outlets should also create and adhere to an ethical standard of focusing on the facts of a case, rather than speculating as to the mental health conditions of those involved in crimes, when reporting breaking news.

Another form of counter information is to increase comfort and contact with people with disabilities in order to shift societal attitudes, lessen discriminatory behaviors, and improve the quality of life for people with disabilities. For example, individuals with mental health disorders from countries with the greatest comfort in talking about mental health experienced lower stigma and higher empowerment.[24] Direct contact with individuals with disabilities will create authentic perceptions to counter fear and pity. The conditions that promote constructive intergroup contact include one-on-one contact, equal status among members, explanation of expected behaviors and etiquette, and participation in cooperative activities.[21]

Resources & Support

In the face of a personal crisis, it is often helpful to obtain emotional support from others when we cannot seem to cope adequately by ourselves. Emotional support is encompassed within the broader concept of social support, which also includes informational and material support.[39] The speed and ease by which an individual moves through the process of adaptation and identity development is contingent upon the resources available to the person.[33] The availability of generalized resistance resources supports a sense of coherence and facilitates positive adjustment to the challenges associated with life. These resources include money, religious faith, family, and social support, which provide consistency, a balance of stimuli, and participation in determining outcomes.[56]

Personal, social, environmental, and financial support has been found to influence the response to disability. Kendall & Buys[33] found that individuals with higher levels of resources progressed through the adjustment cycle at a faster rate, with better outcomes and fewer recurrent problems, than those with low levels of resources. Familial, spousal, and social support hve been linked to higher perceived life satisfaction and well-being.[89] Within mental health services, peer support is seen as an essential element to empowerment.[16] However, social interactions operate as a two-way street, with the person experiencing benefits from both giving *and* receiving in the relationship.[31] For example, respondents in Shea's[74] study indicated that reciprocity based on shared interests and needs strengthened relationships.

Emotional support is psychologically the most valuable resource in times of personal crisis because it can make a person feel less isolated and provide a buffer against stress.[39] Social capital is a useful construct to conceptualize the necessity and benefit of social support for people with disabilities. In its most general sense, capital is a resource that is acquired, accumulated, and of value. Unlike physical resources, social capital is concerned with relationships between individuals and groups. Lin[40] described social capital as containing three ingredients: resources imbedded in a social structure; accessibility to those social resources by individuals; and use of social resources for purposeful actions.

APPROACHES FOR CHANGE

Counselors should assess the level and availability of resources to be used for support in times of crisis. This harkens back to the secondary appraisals individuals make during a coping response. By proactively determining the resources a person has available, a counselor can identify gaps between actual resources and potential needs. Interventions that flow from this analysis include obtaining physical and financial resources, developing skill sets, devising crisis intervention plans, and creating and strengthening supportive relationships to be mobilized in times of crisis, but also sustain the person in his or her daily life.

CHOICE & OPPORTUNITIES

Empowerment has been a key concept in the Disability Rights Movement since the 1960s.[73] As seen above, the ability of people to utilize resources, exert personal control, and attain quality of life is dependent on their access to choice and opportunities. This is in line with the concepts of consumer direction and self-determination. The following sections describe two social justice frameworks for understanding and increasing opportunities for consumer choice and empowerment.

Capabilities approach. Based on the work of Amartya Sen and Martha Nussbaum, the capabilities approach is "a broad normative framework for the evaluation and assessment of individual well-being and social arrangements, the design of policies, and proposals about social change in society."[72, p. 94] The core characteristic is what people are able to do and to be. According to this framework, *capabilities* are opportunities to achieve particular states of being or undertake particular activities; these states of being and activities are termed *functionings.* A person's *capability set* is defined as the functionings one could achieve, if he or she desired, as well as the ones the person is actually achieving.[7] One's capabilities and functioning achievement should be considered the objects of value for measuring quality of life. The ends of well-being, justice, and development should be conceptualized in terms of capabilities to function, that is, do they get to engage meaningfully and be whom they want to be.

A critical distinction in the capabilities approach is between the means to achieve (i.e., goods and services) and the freedom and ability to achieve (i.e., capabilities, functioning). The ability to use a good to achieve a specific function depends on the characteristics of the person, social policies and attitudes, and environmental conditions. Just because a person has access to a commodity or service does not mean he is going to have the opportunity to realize its benefits because of his circumstances. For example, because a person with a spinal cord injury possesses a college degree does not mean he will be readily employed, due to public or employers' perceptions of the abilities of individuals in wheelchairs. Robeyns stated the goal of ultimate importance is that people have the freedom and opportunities "to lead the kind of lives they want to lead, to do what they want to do and be the person they want to be."[72, p. 95]

Consumer-directed theory of empowerment. In order for people with disabilities to experience personal satisfaction and quality of life, they must play the central role in directing disability policy and rehabilitation service delivery essential to their empowerment. Choice and control are still lacking in current rehabilitation service and treatment systems. Kosciulek[36] presented the consumer-directed theory of empowerment (CDTE) as a model to guide the development and evaluation of disability policy and rehabilitation services. The theoretical constructs comprised in the CDTE are consumer direction, community integration, empowerment, and quality of life.

Consumer direction is based on the following assumptions: (a) people with disabilities are the experts on their service needs, (b) choice and control must be present in all service environments, and (c) it should be available to all without financial restraints. Consumer direction "refers to those activities whereby consumers with disability develop a sense of personal control and acquire the

25

opportunity to influence social and political systems."[36, p. 198] Inherent in this paradigm are the freedoms of consumers to:

> ➤ control and direct the delivery of services;

> ➤ have present a range of viable options from which to choose;

> ➤ have available appropriate information and support for choice; and

> ➤ have the ability to participate in systems design and service allocation.

Through expanded opportunities for choice and participation in the community, consumers with disabilities will be empowered toward greater personal and political control to attain life of quality.

APPROACHES FOR CHANGE

Capabilities and consumer direction are both predicated on the presence of opportunities for individuals with disabilities, as well as their freedom to make choices from these options. Empowerment of the individual flows from this. Personally, and on a societal level, empowerment is a powerful mechanism for change because it expands opportunities, rather than limits them; it prescribes what can be done to achieve goals, as opposed to what should not.[16] How systems are structured creates inherent barriers to choice and opportunities. For example, Corrigan and colleagues[15] noted system-level barriers to quality mental health care as a lack of adequate mental health benefits, problems with geographic access to services, and fragmentation of services. Political climate and collegiality among lawmakers also pose a barrier to choice, as was witnessed in the struggle to enact and retain the Affordable Care Act,[71] which offered health care options to those who might not otherwise receive them.

Individuals with disabilities can either be enabled or constrained by their physical, economic, political/legal, social, and cultural environments. In response to ethical obligations and a desire for social justice, counselors should actively engage in professional advocacy at a level to which one is comfortable (i.e., local, state, national, international) on behalf of consumers. More importantly, however, counselors should facilitate self-advocacy in each consumer to empower participation in a collective response within the disability community.

COLLECTIVE IDENTITY

Consumer direction affords individuals the opportunity for action, but political action cannot be fortified without a strong body of advocates. Lack of a collective identity has kept people with disabilities from making more substantial political strides. Disability studies scholar Paul Longmore[55] referred

26

to the quest for collective identity as the second phase of the Disability Rights Movement. Historically, one obstacle to a collective identity has been that there is more perceived differences among people with disabilities, based on functional limitations and needs, than similarities.[62] Watson[87] identified the difficulty of establishing community among people with disabilities as a lack of shared beliefs, class, and needs, creating a barrier to a sense of unity. While impairment can be the basis for commonality, this commonality is not enough to spur collective action. Two perspectives to creating this common identity are helpful in moving toward collaboration among all people with disabilities.

The first perspective is embracing disability culture. The focus of the disability culture movement is that people with disability claim the right to define the disability experience and the ways in which they respond.[76] Values the disability culture espouse are: disability should be celebrated as part of diversity; discrimination and stigma are part of the broader cultural context, not the disability; and a need to embrace interdependence.[14] Conyers[14] identified the following socio-cultural barriers to disability culture:

> ➤ high level of social isolation experienced by people with disabilities;

> ➤ the disability-specific approach to early legislation that reflected a historic lack of political unity among people with disabilities;

> ➤ limited or non-existent cross-generational transmission of cultural values, attitudes, and mores associated with disability culture; and

> ➤ people with disabilities may internalize negative attitudes of disability from the mainstream.

Another framework for understanding collective identity is Mpofu and Conyers'[65] representational theory. These scholars postulated individuals with disabilities can use three criteria to find commonality and a platform for collective motivation—restrictions on economic opportunity, communicative self-representation, and access to a preferred way of life. People with disabilities are undervalued in the workforce and subject to discrimination, which limits their opportunities for economic self-sufficiency, despite the passage of the Americans with Disabilities Act. Widespread use of disrespectful language that does not honor the principles of person-first language, and images of helplessness portrayed in the media stifle communicative self-representation. A recent example of communicative self-representation was the online movement #CripTheVote to encourage people with disabilities to get active and vote in the 2016 presidential elections.[20] Institutionalization, genocide, limited access to amenities and venues, stereotypes and stigma, being regarded as ill despite health, and pressure to acculturate all reflect denial of access to a preferred way of life. As people with disabilities rally to find commonality in their movement, they can focus on their similar experiences of oppression rather than on individual needs resulting from disability or condition.

APPROACHES FOR CHANGE

Although systemic and legislative issues present barriers to political participation for people with disabilities, the building blocks to creating change stem from one outcome previously mentioned, disability identity. Those who are willing to challenge the status quo are those who have claimed disability as a defining aspect of self.[67] Individuals with a strong sense of disability identity are more secure in aligning with the disability community. A person who identifies with the disability community will challenge externally-imposed group definitions and work to improve the status of the group.[66] Therefore, first working to enhance the individual disability identity of a consumer will pave the way for greater collective participation of that individual in advocacy efforts.

How disability identity is conceived will have bearing on the ability of the disability community to finally coalesce around common issues. Nario-Redmond and colleagues[66] suggested the Disability Rights Movement adopt a hybrid, more inclusive model of disability identity, whereby individuals do not see themselves in a disability category, but as a member of a group limited by the stigma and discrimination imposed by society. For example, while those with episodic conditions may not be subjected to consistent barriers when in remission, they can still be members of the disability movement and collective consciousness. Engaging in collective activism will provide for the reciprocal relationships alluded to earlier, as well as enhance choice and opportunities, further enhancing empowerment.

INTERVENTIONS FOR COUNSELING

The experience of living with a disability can be easier or more difficult depending on the presence and quality of psychological and psychosocial resources available to an individual. Regardless of the individual's condition or response to disability, prevailing societal structures can influence day-to-day experiences and, ultimately, quality of life. Counselors can play an integral role in assisting the individual's response, as well as work to reduce environmental barriers, both structural and attitudinal. In this respect, the following interventions will address some of these issues:

> *Defining quality of life*: To holistically understand a person's life in context, the counselor should assess salient life domains of the person to establish the basis for interventions. Rather than assuming

which life roles and domains are most important, QoL assessment should investigate subjective consumer ratings of importance, satisfaction, and perceived control in each domain.[58] This assessment should be rooted in the ICF model to incorporate a more holistic and expansive model of the factors and outcomes that encompass QoL.[26] This can be used to prioritize counseling and service interventions to address those needs that are most central to the consumer and his or her personal response process.[4]

➤ *Facilitating the response process:* Addressing psychosocial issues early in the response to disability will prevent decline and establish a path of progress for an individual.[34] The key is to meet the person where he is at in the process of recovery to tailor interventions toward integrating one's disability identity into self-concept.[74] Livneh and Antonak[47] suggested the following interventions: (a) assist consumers to explore the personal meaning of disability; (2) provide consumers with relevant medical information; (3) provide consumers with supportive family and group experiences; and (4) teach consumers adaptive coping skills for successful community functioning. Teaching self-management techniques, which address physical health, psychological functioning, and social relationships, will allow the person to take a more active role in the adaptation process.[38] Self-management applies the skills of problem-solving, decision making, resource utilization, forming partnerships with professionals, and acting to make progress across all levels of functioning.

➤ *Improving resources.* Enhancing material and personal resources will allow individuals to better cope with challenges and barriers. Specific strategies can be implemented to achieve this goal. Kendall and Buys[33] suggested the following interventions: (a) establishing a network of supports that can be activated to deal with recurrent issues in the consumer's adjustment process; (b) facilitating consumer direction by recognizing consumers as the experts in determining their own adjustment needs; and (c) devising strategies to strengthen and develop positive self-concept. Silarova and colleagues[75] proposed incorporating interventions to change one of the components of sense of coherence to improve HRQoL. Stuntzner and Hartley[81] provided concrete training curricula for improving resilience among consumers.

REFERENCES

[1]Alguren, B., Fridlund, B., Cieza, A., Sunnerhagen, K. S., & Christensson, L. (2012). Factors associated with health-related quality of life after stroke: A 1-year prospective cohort study. *Neurorehabilitation and Neural Repair, 26*(3), 266-274.

[2]Antonovsky, H., & Sagy, S. (2001). The development of a sense of coherence and its impact on responses to stress stimuli. *The Journal of Social Psychology, 126*(2), 213-225.

[3]Bishop, M. (2001). The recovery process and chronic illness and disability: Applications and implications. *Journal of Vocational Rehabilitation, 16*, 47-52.

[4]Bishop, M. (2005a). Quality of life and psychosocial adaptation to chronic illness and acquired disability: A conceptual and theoretical synthesis. *Journal of Rehabilitation, 71*(2), 5-13.

[5]Bishop, M. (2005b). Quality of life and psychosocial adaptation to chronic illness and disability: Preliminary analysis of a conceptual and theoretical synthesis. *Rehabilitation Counseling Bulletin, 48*, 219-231.

[6]Bishop, M., Shepard, L., & Stenhoff, D. M. (2007). Psychosocial adaptation and quality of life in multiple sclerosis: Assessment of the disability centrality model. *Journal of Rehabilitation, 73*(1), 3-12.

[7]Burchardt, T. (2004). Capabilities and disability: The capabilities framework and the social model of disability. *Disability & Society, 19*, 735-751.

[8]Charmaz, K. (1983). Loss of self: A fundamental form of suffering in the chronically ill. *Sociology of Health and Illness, 5*, 168-195.

[9]Charmaz, K. (1995). The body, identity, and self: Adapting to impairment. *The Sociological Quarterly, 36*, 657-680.

[10]Charmaz, K. (2008). Views from the margins: Voices, silences, and suffering. *Qualitative Research in Psychology, 5*(7), 7-18.

[11]Chen, R., & Crewe, N. (2009). Life satisfaction among people with progressive disabilities. *Journal of Rehabilitation, 75*(2), 50-58.

[12]Chiu, M. Y. L., Ho, W. W. N., Lo, W. T. L., & Yiu, M. G. C. (2010). Operationalization of the SAMHSA model of recovery: A quality of life perspective. *Quality of Life Research, 19*, 1-13.

[13]Chou, C., Chan, F., Chan, J. Y. C., Phillips, B., Ditchman, N., & Kaseroff, A. (2013). Positive psychology theory, research, and practice: A primer for rehabilitation counseling professionals. *Rehabilitation Research, Policy, and Education, 27*, 131-153.

[14]Conyers, L. M. (2003). Disability culture: A cultural model of disability. *Rehabilitation Education, 17*, 139-154.

[15]Corrigan, P. W., Druss, B. G., & Perlick, D. A. (2014). The impact of mental illness stigma on seeking and participating in mental health care. *Psychological Science in the Public Interest, 15*(2) 37-70.

[16]Corrigan, P. W., Larson, J. E., & Rüsch, N. (2009). Self-stigma and the "why try" effect: Impact on life goals and evidence-based practices. *World Psychiatry, 8*, 75-81.

[17]Crewe, N. M. (1980). Quality of life: The ultimate goal in rehabilitation. *Minnesota Medicine, 63*, 596-589.

[18]Dekel, S., Solomon, Z., & Ein-Dor, T. (2012). Posttraumatic growth and posttraumatic distress: A longitudinal study. *Psychological Trauma: Theory, Research, Practice, and Policy, 4*, 94-101.

[19]Devins, G. M. (1994). Illness intrusiveness and the psychosocial impact of lifestyle disruptions in chronic life-threatening disease. *Advances in Renal Replacement Therapy, 1*, 251-263.

[20]Disability Thinking. (2016, March). *"#CripTheVote: Notes on "crip".* Retrieved from http://disabilitythinking.com/disabilitythinking/2016/3/28/cripthevote-notes-on-crip

[21]Dunn, D. S. (2015). *The social psychology of disability.* New York, NY: Oxford University Press.

[22]Dunn, D. S., & Burcaw, S. (2013). Disability identity: Exploring narrative accounts of disability. *Rehabilitation Psychology, 58*, 148-157.

[23]Elkington, K. S., Hackler, D., McKinnon, K., Borges, C., Wright, E. R., & Wainberg, M. L. (2012). Perceived mental illness stigma among youth in psychiatric outpatient treatment. *Journal of Adolescent Research, 27*, 290-317.

[24]Evans-Lacko, S., Brohan, E., Mojtabai, R., & Thornicroft, G. (2012). Association between public views of mental illness and self-stigma among individuals with mental illness in 14 European countries. *Psychological Medicine, 42*, 1741-1752.

[25]Findler, L., Shalev, K., & Barak, A. (2014). Psychosocial adaptation and adherence among adults with CF: A delicate balance. *Rehabilitation Counseling Bulletin, 57*, 90-101.

[26]Fleming, A. R., Fairweather, J. S., & Leahy, M. J. (2013). Quality of life as a potential rehabilitation service outcome: The relationship between employment, quality of life, and other life areas. *Rehabilitation Counseling Bulletin, 57*, 9-22.

[27]Frain, M. P., Bishop, M., & Tschopp, M. K. (2009). Empowerment variables as predictors of outcomes in rehabilitation. *Journal of Rehabilitation, 75*(1), 27-35.

[28]Galvin, R. D. (2005). Researching the disabled identity: Contextualising the identity transformations which accompany the onset of impairment. *Sociology of Health & Illness, 27*, 393-413.

[29]Gatens-Robinson, E., & Rubin, S. E. (2016). Societal values and ethical commitments that influence rehabilitation service delivery behavior. In S. E. Rubin, R. T. Roessler, & P. D. Rumrill (Eds.), *Foundations of the vocational rehabilitation process* (7th ed., pp. 181-194). Austin, TX: Pro-ed.

[30]Hahn, H. (1988). Can disability be beautiful? *Social Policy, 18*(3), 26-32.

[31]Hammell, K. W. (2007). Quality of life after spinal cord injury: A meta-synthesis of qualitative findings. *Spinal Cord, 45*, 124-139.

[32]Jacobsson, L. J., Westerberg, M., Malec, J. F., & Lexell, J. (2011). Sense of coherence and disability and the relationship with life satisfaction 6-15 years after traumatic brain injury in northern Sweden. *Neuropsychological Rehabilitation, 21*, 383-400.

[33]Kendall, E., & Buys, N. (1998). An integrated model of psychosocial adjustment following acquired disability. *Journal of Rehabilitation, 64*(3), 16-20.

[34]Kendall, E., Catalano, T., Kuipers, P., Posner, N., Buys, N., & Charker, J. (2007). Recovery following stroke: The role of self-management education. *Social Science & Medicine, 64*, 735-746.

[35]Koch, L. C., & Rumrill, P. D. (2016). *Rehabilitation counseling and emerging disabilities: Medical, psychosocial, and vocational aspects.* New York: Springer Publishing.

[36]Kosciulek, J. F. (1999). The consumer-directed theory of empowerment. *Rehabilitation Counseling Bulletin, 42*, 196-213.

[37]Lannin, D. G., Vogel, D. L., Brenner, R. E., & Tucker, J. R. (2015). Predicting self-esteem and intentions to seek counseling: The internalized stigma model. *The Counseling Psychologist, 43*, 64-93.

[38]Larsen, P. D. (2016). Psychosocial adjustment. In P. Larsen (Ed.), *Lubkin's chronic illness* (9th ed., pp. 43-62). Burlington, MA: Jones & Bartlett.

[39]Lazarus, R. S. (2006). *Coping with aging.* Cary, NC: Oxford University Press.

[40]Lin, N. (2001a). Building a network theory of social capital. In N. Lin, K. Cook, & R. S. Burt (Eds.), *Social capital: Theory and research* (pp. 3-29). New York: Aldine De Gruyter.

[41]Lindemann, J. I. (Ed.). (1981). *Psychological and behavioral aspects of physical disability.* New York: Plenum.

[42]Linkowski, D. C., & Dunn, M. A. (1974). Self-concept and acceptance of disability. *Rehabilitation Counseling Bulletin, 17*, 28-32.

[43]Livneh, H. (1986). A unified approach to existing models of adaptation to disability—I. A model of adaptation. *Journal of Applied Rehabilitation Counseling, 17*(1), 5-16, 56.

[44]Livneh, H. (2000). Psychosocial adaptation to cancer: The role of coping strategies. *Journal of Rehabilitation, 66*(2), 40-49.

[45]Livneh, H. (2001). Psychosocial adaptation to chronic illness and disability: A conceptual framework. *Rehabilitation Counseling Bulletin, 44*, 151-160.

[46]Livneh, H., & Antonak, R. F. (1997). *Psychosocial adaptation to chronic illness and disability.* Gaithersburg, MD: Aspen Publishers.

[47]Livneh, H., & Antonak, R. F. (2005). Psychosocial adaptation to chronic illness and disability: A primer for counselors. *Journal of Counseling & Development, 83*, 12-20.

[48]Livneh, H., Bishop, M., & Anctil, T. (2014). Modern models of psychosocial adaptation to chronic illness and disability as viewed through the prism of Lewin's field theory: A comparative review. *Rehabilitation Research, Policy, and Education, 28*, 126-142.

[49]Livneh, H., Lott, S. M., & Antonak, R. F. (2004). Patterns of psychosocial adaptation to chronic illness and disability: A cluster analytic approach. *Psychology, Health & Medicine, 9*, 411-430.

[50]Livneh, H., & Martz, E. (2014). Coping strategies and resources as predictors of psychological adaptation among people with spinal cord injury. *Rehabilitation Psychology, 59*(3), 329-339.

[51]Livneh, H., & Martz, E. (2016). Psychosocial adaptation to disability within the context of positive psychology: Philosophical aspects and historical roots. *Journal of Occupational Rehabilitation, 26*, 13-19.

[52]Livneh, H, Martz, E., & Wilson, L. M. (2001). Denial and perceived visibility as predictors of adaptation to disability among college students. *Journal of Vocational Rehabilitation, 16*, 227-234.

[53]Livneh, H., & Parker, R. M. (2005). Psychological adaptation to disability: Perspectives from chaos and complexity theory. *Rehabilitation Counseling Bulletin, 49*, 17-28.

[54]Lo Buono, V., Corallo, F., Bramanti, P., & Marino, S. (2017). Coping strategies and health-related quality of life after stroke. *Journal of Health Psychology, 22*, 16-28.

[55]Longmore, P. K. (1995, September/October). The second phase: From disability rights to disability culture. *Disability Rag & Resource.* Retrieved from http://www.independentliving.org/docs3/longm95.html.

[56]Lustig, D. C. (2005). The adjustment process for individuals with spinal cord injury: The effect of perceived premorbid sense of coherence. *Rehabilitation Counseling Bulletin, 48*, 146-156.

[57]Machida, M., Irwin, B., & Feltz, D. (2013). Resilience in competitive athletes with spinal cord injury: The role of sports participation. *Qualitative Health Research, 23*, 1054-1065.

[58]Mackenzie, A., Alfred, D., Fountain, R., & Combs, D. (2015). Quality of life and adaptation for traumatic brain injury survivors: Assessment of the disability centrality model. *Journal of Rehabilitation, 81*(3), 9-20.

[59]Marini, I. (2012). Theories of adjustment and adaptation to disability. In I. Marini, M. J. Millington, & N. M. Glover-Graf (Eds.), *Psychosocial aspects of disability: Insider perspectives and counseling strategies* (pp. 115-143). New York, NY: Springer Publishing. [4]

[60]Martz, E., & Livneh, H. (2016). Psychosocial adaptation to disability within the context of positive psychology: Findings from the literature. *Journal of Occupational Rehabilitation, 26*, 4-12.

[61]McCarthy, H. (2014). Cultivating out roots and extending our branches: Appreciating and marketing rehabilitation theory and research. *Rehabilitation Counseling Bulletin, 57*, 67-79.

[62]Miller, J. F. (2000). *Coping with chronic illness: Overcoming powerlessness* (3rd ed.). Philadelphia, PA: F. A. Davis, Co.

[63]Moos, R. H., & Holahan, C. J. (2007). Adaptive tasks and methods of coping with illness and disability. In E. Martz & H. Livneh (Eds.), *Coping with chronic illness and disability* (pp. 107-126). New York, NY: Springer Publishing.

[64]Mpofu, E., & Bishop, M. (2006). Value change and adjustment to disability: Implications for rehabilitation education, practice, and research. *Rehabilitation Education, 20,* 147-161.

[65]Mpofu, E., & Conyers, L. M. (2004). A representational theory perspective of minority status and people with disabilities: Implications for rehabilitation education and practice. *Rehabilitation Counseling Bulletin, 47,* 142-151.

[66]Nario-Redmond, M. R., Noel, J. G., & Fern, E. (2013). Redefining disability, re-imagining the self: Disability identification predicts self-esteem and strategic responses to stigma. *Self and Identity, 12,* 468-488.

[67]Nario-Redmond, M. R., & Oleson, K. C. (2016). Disability group identification and disability-rights advocacy: Contingencies among emerging and other adults. *Emerging Adulthood, 4,* 207-218.

[68]Olkin, R. (1999). *What psychotherapists should know about disability.* New York: Guilford Press.

[69]Pande, N., & Tewari, S. (2011). Understanding coping with distress due to physical disability. *Psychology and Developing Societies, 23,* 177-209.

[70]Parker, R. M., Schaller, J., & Hansmann, S. (2001). Catastrophe, chaos, and complexity models and psychosocial adjustment to disability. *Rehabilitation Counseling Bulletin, 46,* 234-241.

[71]Patient Protection and Affordable Care Act, 42 U.S.C. § 18001 et seq. (2010).

[72]Robeyns, I. (2005). The capability approach: A theoretical survey. *Journal of Human Development, 6,* 93-114.

[73]Sales, A. (2007). *Rehabilitation counseling: An empowerment perspective.* Austin, TX: Pro-ed.

[74]Shea, J. M. (2009). Coming back normal: The process of self-recovery in those with schizophrenia. *Journal of the American Psychiatric Nurses Association, 16,* 43-51.

[75]Silanova, B., Nagyova, I., Rosenberger, J., Studencan, M., Ondusova, D., Reijneveld, S. A., & van Dijk, J. P. (2012). Sense of coherence as an independent predictor of health-related quality of life among coronary heart disease patients. *Quality of Life Research, 21,* 1863-1871.

[76]Smart, J. (2004). Models of disability: The juxtaposition of biology and social construction. In T. F. Riggar & D. R. Maki (Eds.), *Handbook of rehabilitation counseling* (pp. 25-49). New York: Springer Publishing Co.

[77]Smart, J. (2016). *Disability, society, and the individual* (3rd ed.). Austin, TX: Pro-ed.

[78]Smedema, S. M., Catalano, D., & Ebener, D. J. (2010). The relationship of coping, self-worth, and subjective well-being: A structural equation model. *Rehabilitation Counseling Bulletin,* 53(3), 131-142.

[79]Smedema, S. M., Chan, Y. J., & Phillips, B. (2014). Core self-evaluations and Snyder's Hope Theory in persons with spinal cord injuries. *Rehabilitation Psychology, 59,* 399-406.

[80]Snyder, C. R. (2001). *Coping with stress: Effective people and processes.* Cary, NC: Oxford University Press.

[81]Stuntzner, S., & Hartley, M. T. (2014). Resilience, coping, & disability: The development of a resilience intervention. *VISTAS Online, Article 44.* American Counseling Association.

[82]Substance Abuse and Mental Health Services Administration. (2012). *SAMHSA's working definition of recovery: 10 guiding principles of recovery.* Washington, DC: Author.

[83]Tedeschi, R. G., & McNally, R. J. (2011). Can we facilitate posttraumatic growth in combat veterans? *American Psychologist, 66,* 19-24.

[84]Tiggemann, M. (2015). Considerations of positive body image across various social identities and special populations. *Body Image, 14,* 168-176.

[85]van Wijk, C. H., & Waters, A. H. (2008). Positive psychology made practical: A case study with naval specialists. *Military Medicine, 173,* 488-492.

[86]Vash, C. L. (1981). *The psychology of disability.* New York: Springer Publishing Co.

[87]Watson, N. (2002). Well, I know this is going to sound very strange to you, but I don't see myself as a disabled person: Identity and disability. *Disability & Society, 17,* 509-527.

[88]White, B., Driver, S., & Warren, A. M. (2010). Resilience and indicators of adjustment during rehabilitation from spinal cord injury. *Rehabilitation Psychology, 55,* 23-32.

[89]Wilson, L., Catalano, D., Sung, C., Phillips, B., Chou, C., Chan, J. Y. C., & Chan, F. (2013). Attachment style, social support, and coping as psychosocial correlates of happiness in persons with spinal cord injuries. *Rehabilitation Research, Policy, and Education, 27,* 186-205.

[90]Wright, B. (1980). Person and situation: Adjusting the rehabilitation focus. *Archives of Physical Medicine and Rehabilitation, 61,* 58-64.

[91]Wright, B. (1983). *Physical disability—A psychosocial approach* (2nd ed.). New York: Harper and Row.

[92]Yoshida, K. K. (1993). Reshaping of self: A pendular reconstruction of self and identity among adults with traumatic spinal cord injury. *Sociology of Health & Illness, 15,* 217-245.

[93]Young, S. (2014, June). *Stella Young: I am not your inspiration, thank you very much.* [Video file]. Retrieved from https://www.ted.com/talks/stella_young_i_m_not_your_inspiration_thank_you_very_much

CHAPTER 2

ETIOLOGY OF
DISABILITY

MELISSA MANNINEN LUSE

Advances in nutrition, medicine, and technology over the last century have resulted in lower death rates for infants and children, as well as increased life expectancy rates around the world.[51] Today, the average life expectancy in the U.S. is 78 years.[6] In other countries, life expectancy rates are much higher. In Japan, for instance, the average life expectancy is about 85.[51] The health gap between industrialized and developing nations has also narrowed in recent years.

However, as longevity increases, so does the risk for the development of chronic illness and disability. In industrialized nations, heart disease, stroke, and cancer are the leading causes of disability and death. These chronic illnesses, mostly due to lifestyle (e.g., smoking, poor diet, and lack of physical activity), cause significant long-term health problems, activity limitations, and difficulties with physical and mental health functioning. In the U.S. alone, about 76 million adults have activity limitations.[5] This includes difficulty with or the inability to complete tasks, such as dressing one's self, brushing one's teeth, or opening a jar or medicine bottle. About 35 million U.S. adults have difficulty with physical functioning, the inability to complete activities due to a health problem.[5]

Worldwide, over one billion people live with a disability, with 110 to 190 million people living with significant difficulties in functioning.[47] However, as chronic illness and disability rates have increased over the last century, in recent years, they have stagnated, with some countries even experiencing declines in disability rates; and, for the millions living with disabilities around the world, they have experienced increases in quality of life (QOL). Such progress is not universal, however. Many developing nations have experienced decreases in health and life expectancy. These countries also face increases in disability rates at significantly higher rates than industrialized nations, with children, women, and the elderly from lower income levels especially vulnerable to experiencing disability.

So, what is disability? What health conditions are most likely to result in disability? What groups of people are most likely to live with disability? What does disability look like across the lifespan? This chapter provides an in-depth overview of the etiology of disability from a lifespan perspective, understanding how health during different stages of life can result in disability, and how different groups of people are affected throughout the lifespan.

DEFINING DISABILITY

While disability is a highly examined topic, there is inconsistency in what disability is, with no well-accepted standardized definition. Disability can be highly complex with a variety of bodily functions affected, including: vision, mobility, cognition, learning and memory, communication, hearing, and mental health at different levels of severity.[5] Additionally, two people can be affected by the same condition, but cope and adjust very differently to the illness and/or disability. The environment must also be considered, such as access to treatment, types of treatment, local and national policies, and physical and societal barriers. Finally, the complexity and multiple variables involved create significant issues in the ability to accurately measure disability and, therefore, develop a standardized definition. According to the World Health Organization (WHO):[47]

> *Approaches to measuring (and defining) disability vary across countries, across purpose, and application of data . . . and aspects of disability examined–impairments, limitations, participation restrictions, related health conditions, environmental factors – definitions, question design, reporting sources, data collection methods, and expectations of functioning.*[p. 21]

Furthermore, disability policy can vary significantly to include or exclude certain conditions, making for continued difficulty in truly understanding what disability is. According to Scotch,[42] some disability policies have been developed for specific impairments, such as for people who are blind or have visual impairments or those who are deaf or hard of hearing. Other policy has been broadly defined to include "a nearly infinite variety of impairments and etiologies."[42, p. 385]

Two examples of broad definitions of disability include the Center for Disease Control (CDC) and the American with Disabilities Act (ADA) definitions. According to the CDC:[5]

> *A disability is any condition of the body or mind (impairment) that makes it more difficult for the person with the condition to do certain activities (activity limitation) and interact with the world around them (participation restrictions).*[1]

While the ADA defines disability as:

> *A person who has a physical or mental impairment that substantially limits one or more major life activities, a person who has a history or record of such an impairment, or a person who is perceived by others as having such an impairment.*

Other organizations, such as the Social Security Administration (SSA), have a strict view of disability, with focus on one's ability to work. A person is considered disabled if:

> ➢   the person cannot do the work one did before;

> the SSA decides a person cannot work due to health, even with accommodations; and

> the disability has lasted, or is expected to last, for at least one year or to result in death.

However, none of these explanations provide a full picture of what exactly disability is. These definitions do not include the specific health condition and severity; personal factors, such as the individual appraisal process and coping strategies, attitudes, values, beliefs, emotional regulation, behavior, temperament, and self-image; social factors, including level and type of support; or community/societal attitudes.

These definitions also neglect to include the environment, including physical barriers, social economic status, health insurance, availability and access to care, and service provisions. Such factors can add complex layers to the functioning and needs of the individual. Furthermore, the CDC, ADA, and SSA definitions do not include specific illnesses and impairments. While such exclusion can be helpful for people living with a wide variety of disabilities, they leave much confusion for society to sort out which health conditions and impairments constitute disabilities and how to best serve this population. Moreover, they leave some health conditions and impairments to be decided upon through court precedent as to whether they qualify as a disability, such as post-traumatic stress disorder (PTSD).

Much of health and disability research, medical care, disability policy, organizational structure, and service provision are rooted in the biomedical model, creating further problems in understanding disability. The SSA definition, for example, while providing a narrower view of disability is perhaps too strict, providing a dichotomous view of disability based on the biomedical model. The biomedical model is also built on short-term or acute care and a return to previous health. The biomedical model can especially be found within policies for people in poverty, the elderly, and people with disabilities.[25] Social Security Income (SSI), Social Security Disability Income (SSDI), Medicaid, and Medicare are the defining principles of policy for these populations; however, they do a poor job in addressing long-term health needs. According to Hudson,[25] these programs, while attempting to provide long-term care, are built on an acute care model with little actual focus on long-term care, such as social support, education and rehabilitation. As Hudson stated, policies for certain groups such as the elderly are a "...stepchild in the social policy family in the U.S.," and have historically "...occupied an especially residual place."[p. 61] Disability policy researchers have criticized programs, such as Medicaid, for emphasis on the biomedical model and dichotomous view regarding health and disability. For example, Scotch[42] criticized disability policy's focus in terms of a person's ability to work, and the SSA's strict definition of disability. Monahan and Wolf[29] have criticized policy makers for poor attention to the needs of vulnerable populations, and programming for lack of emphasis on quality of life and over emphasis on institutional care, stating "late-life disability can be said to occupy the margins of social policy."[p. 1]

Such dependence on the biomedical model and lack of care for those with chronic illness can also be found in the poor synchronization between federal programs such as worker's compensation and SSDI and service providers, such as vocation rehabilitation (VR).[42] Programs and policies often work independent of one another, wasting money and resources. The bulk of disability policy is encompassed by health care and income maintenance, hindering more effective and long-term programming like VR. In 1995, economist and disability policy researcher Monroe Berkowitz reported that almost $184 billion was spent on disability programming in the U.S., with over 90% going towards health care ($91 billion) and income maintenance ($78 billion).[42] This left approximately $15 billion, or only about 8% of funding, to go towards rehabilitation and health-related education. The limited emphasis on rehabilitation and health education results in barriers to care including fewer services, providers, high cost of care, long waiting lists, as well as negative societal attitudes including stigma and discrimination.[51] Furthermore, such focus on health care and income maintenance is a reactive measure, only re-emphasizing the biomedical model's lack of focus on quality of life in long-term care. With a reactive system, little funding and service is geared in a proactive (e.g., VR), or even a preventative direction such as health education and promotion, early diagnosis, and treatment.[47] Lacking clear standard definitions of disability, stemming from a focus on the biomedical model of disability, a dichotomous view of ability, and limited policies and services, people with disabilities are left living with poorer health, having less education, realizing fewer employment and other economic opportunities, and experiencing higher rates of poverty than those without disabilities.[51] Such factors create further difficulties, exacerbating the underlying health condition and creating more limited functioning and severity in disability.

The World Health Organization[47] recognized the complexity of disability and has pushed for the move away from the dichotomous view of the biomedical model. The International Classification of Functioning, Disability and Health (ICF), developed by WHO in 2001, is built on the biopsychosocial model of disability. It provides a richer understanding of disability compared to the biomedical model. The goal of ICF is to "assess the health, functioning, activities, and factors in the environment that either help or create barriers for people to fully participate in society."[p. 24] Disability itself is an umbrella term with focus on three dimensions:

> ➢ Impairment in a person's body structure or function, or mental functioning; examples of impairments include loss of a limb, loss of vision, or memory loss.

➤ Activity limitation, such as difficulty seeing, hearing, walking, or problem solving.

➤ Participation restrictions in standard daily activities, such as working, engaging in social and recreational activities, and obtaining health care and preventive services.

The ICF includes the following in the categories of activities and participation:[51]

➤ Learning and applying knowledge;

➤ Managing tasks and demands;

➤ Mobility (moving and maintaining body positions, handling and moving objects, moving around in the environment, moving around using transportation);

➤ Managing self-care tasks;

➤ Managing domestic life;

➤ Establishing and managing interpersonal relationships and interactions;

➤ Engaging in major life areas (education, employment, managing money or finances);

➤ Engaging in community, social, and civic life

There is an understanding in the ICF of the complexity and intertwining of variables such as environment, level and types of support, availability and use of assistive technology, availability and accessibility of services, policy, and attitudes of society towards disability. From this perspective, this chapter will now investigate disability across the lifespan.

DISABILITY ACROSS THE LIFESPAN

Disability can affect anyone at any age, from any economic status, culture, sex, ethnicity, or race. A person can be born with a congenital condition, such as spina bifida, autism, cerebral palsy, type 1 diabetes, muscular dystrophy, learning disabilities, and intellectual disabilities. Disability can also be acquired during adolescence (e.g., an accident or the development of a mental health condition), throughout adulthood (e.g., heart attack, stroke, type 2 diabetes, cancer), or occur late in life (e.g., arthritis or dementia).

Human growth across the lifespan is complex with many variables, creating significant difficulties for researchers to study accurately.[25] Worldwide approximately 93 million children under the age of 14 live with a moderate to severe disability.[45] In the U.S., about 15% of children between the ages of 3 and 17 live with at least one disability. However, these numbers must be kept in perspective as data collection is often inconsistent and unreliable. Whatever the onset of disability–prenatal, infancy, childhood, adulthood–the health condition itself, along with individual, psychological and environmental factors, present unique challenges to be able to effectively study disability. Furthermore, the most significant factor hampering disability lifespan research is stigma. In some countries, people with disabilities, as well as their families, may face ostracism, especially if a child is born with a disability. Because of such stigma, parents of an infant born with a disability may not register the child with the local or national government. This practice prevents children from receiving proper health, education, and social services.[40] This also keeps organizations and researchers from being able to accurately examine disability and the needs of children and families living with disability.

PRENATAL DEVELOPMENT

Genetic and chromosomal etiologies. Genetic and chromosomal disorders are the most significant causes of developmental disabilities. While they are often discussed together, genetic and chromosomal disorders are different. Genes are formed by the protein molecule DNA, and chromosomes are formed by genes. Some developmental disabilities are caused by defects in genetic structure, while other disabilities are caused by defects in chromosomes. Genetic factors, the most common cause, account for about 25% of developmental disabilities. Genetic disorders can be inherited, result from genetic combination errors during fetal development, or be caused by genetic changes due to teratogens.

Some developmental disabilities, such as phenylketonuria (PKU), are caused by single gene disorder. PKU, an inherited condition, is caused by a missing or defective enzyme. Children with PKU are not able to break down a part of an amino acid called phenylalanine. Phenylalanine builds up in the blood and causes multiple health problems, including intellectual disability, seizures, rashes, hyperactivity, and developmental delays. PKU is found more readily in certain populations including Native American and Northern Europeans, affecting about 1 in 10,000 births.

Another single gene disorder, Fragile X syndrome, affects about 1 in 4,000 boys and 1 in 8,000 girls. Fragile X syndrome, the leading inherited cause of intellectual disability, also results in learning disabilities, anxiety, hyperactivity, seizures, and approximately one third of children also have autism.

Other disabilities are due to chromosomal abnormalities. Any chromosome, including the sex chromosomes, can be affected. Chromosomal disorders happen sporadically and are caused by too many or too few chromosomes, or by a change in structure of a chromosome. Trisomy 21, more commonly known as Down syndrome, is an example of a chromosomal disorder. Down syndrome affects all ethnic and racial groups equally, and affects approximately one in every 700 babies born in the U.S., making it the most common genetic and chromosomal condition. Down syndrome is caused by a cell division error, resulting in three copies of chromosome 21. As the fetus develops, the extra chromosome continues to be replicated in every cell of the body. This extra genetic material results in characteristic facial features, congenital heart disease, growth retardation, intellectual disability, and early development of Alzheimer's disease. There is little understanding of the exact cause of Down syndrome. However, research does suggest that it is not inherited, and that parental age, especially maternal age, is a significant factor. A 20-year-old woman has about a 1 in 2,000 probabilities of having a baby born with Down syndrome. As she ages, the chances increase to 1 in 100 by the time a woman is 40. By the time a woman is 49, her chances of having a baby with Down syndrome are 1 in 10.

Some developmental disabilities are not well understood due to the myriad genetics and environment factors involved. For example, spina bifida, a prevalent congenital condition that develops during the first month of fetal development, affects 1 in 1,000 pregnancies.[32] Spina bifida occurs when the development of the spinal cord is interrupted. Any of the systems of the body can be affected, potentially resulting in serious health conditions. Spina bifida can result in irregular brain development, hindering the flow of cerebrospinal fluid, leading to a buildup fluid in the ventricles of the brain, and hydrocephalus. This build up in fluid can result in cognitive impairments, including lowered intelligence, memory, and organization difficulties. As spina bifida affects the nervous system, bowel and bladder control are often affected, as well as the urinary tract (i.e., infections) and kidney functioning. The muscle and skeletal system are often affected in various levels of severity, depending on where on the spinal cord spina bifida occurs. Paralysis of some form is common. People with spina bifida can have dislocated joints and hips, bone defects, and curvature of the spine. People with spina bifida are also at higher risk for other conditions, including higher prevalence for bone fractures and seizures.

The cause of spina bifida is not well understood. It is believed to be caused by an interaction of genetics and environment.[32] There is evidence some medications may cause the condition, as well as deficiencies in certain vitamins and minerals. Women who take folic acid before and during pregnancy have a reduced chance of having an infant born with the condition. As treatment continues to improve, life expectancy continues to increase. The limited research available suggests people with spina bifida live to at least their early adult years. The most common cause for death is not the multiple health problems associated with spina bifida, but functioning of the shunt used to drain spinal fluid from the brain to prevent swelling.

Teratogens. A *teratogen* is an environmental factor or agent a pregnant mother is exposed to that causes or increases the likelihood of a congenital disorder *in utero*. Teratogens cause approximately 7% of congenital disorders in the U.S., and can affect the fetus at any stage of development and lead to a variety of conditions with varying degrees of severity. Teratogens include infection and illnesses in the mothers (e.g., rubella, toxoplasmosis, cytomegalovirus, syphilis, HIV/AIDS, influenza, viruses); alcohol; drugs, including caffeine, tobacco, and prescribed medications; malnutrition and nutritional deficiencies; food additives; and chemical exposure, such as pesticides.[5] Additionally, maternal chemical exposure can result in numerous potential health problems and disabilities in an infant, including intellectual disabilities, hyperactivity, learning disabilities, behavior problems, physical disabilities, and hearing impairments.

Alcohol. Parental behaviors, such as alcohol, tobacco, and drug use, result in conditions that include fetal alcohol syndrome and other intellectual disabilities, hyperactivity, learning disabilities, and low birth weight.[5] Fetal alcohol syndrome, the most common form of intellectual disability, is caused by the mother using alcohol during pregnancy, a condition that is 100% preventable. Fetal Alcohol Spectrum Disorders (FASD) is an umbrella term that includes three conditions: Fetal Alcohol Syndrome (FAS), Partial Fetal Alcohol Syndrome (PFAS), and Neurobehavioral Disorder Associated with Prenatal Alcohol Exposure (ND-PAE). Best estimates indicate about 1 in 50 U.S. children have some form of FASD. Researchers have had a difficult time estimating the prevalence of FASD, and currently there is no FASD comprehensive data set, as FASD assessments are rarely used in larger health assessments.

As FASD is poorly examined, physicians and mental health professionals in turn are not well trained in recognizing signs and symptoms of FASD, with FASD often misdiagnosed as other conditions. FASD symptoms include: growth deficiencies; neurocognitive disorders that affect intelligence, behavior, emotions, attention, learning, and memory, as well as biological drives; and, specifically related to FAS, facial dysmorphia which are specific facial characteristics. These characteristics include: a small head circumference, small and wide set apart eyes, underdeveloped upper lip, poorly developed philtrum, and flattened nose and cheekbones.

Medications. While prescribed medications result in only about 2% of congenital disorders, women should be educated regarding medications they take before and during pregnancy, and be prepared to refrain from taking certain medications unless necessary. This is due to two reasons. One, many medications have subtle or even unknown potential side effects on the developing fetus. Two, of the medications that have been implicated in the development of congenital disorders, some have had significant birth defects. The most famous case regards the sedative and anticonvulsant drug, Thalidomide. Thalidomide was first developed in the 1950s in Europe. Few side effects were found, and with its anti-nausea effect, the drug was soon prescribed to pregnant women to treat morning sickness. During this time, most drug companies around the world did not have to report findings of their drug tests to the government. In the mid-1950s, Thalidomide was quickly promoted and prescribed to thousands of women around the world. In the U.S., however, the FDA was not so quick to allow the drug to be prescribed without appropriate testing. By the end of the decade about 12,000 infants of mothers who took Thalidomide were born with congenital disorders, some very severe, including congenital health disease, malformation of the eyes, and intestine or renal malformation. The most common congenital disorder was pharcomelia, a condition resulting in malformed, or not fully developed, limbs. In the U.S., only 17 infants were affected by this drug. The drug caused other health problems, including intellectual disabilities in some infants, but most infants only experienced physical disabilities. Years later it was realized that Thalidomide also affected the genetic structure of the people with pharcomelia, with 11 of the known 380 children born of people affected by the medication also having congenital limb anomalies.

   Environment. Prematurity and low birth weight both are significant factors affecting health not only during early development, but adulthood.[26,33] Poor nutrition experienced by a pregnant mother also has long-term effects on the fetus. The human genome carries targeted genes that enable a fetus to preserve fat stores, slow down metabolism, and help maintain energy reserves during times of the mother's food scarcity.[33] Malnutrition during fetal development can cause permanent changes in the body, resulting in a cascade of health conditions throughout the lifespan.[37] During childhood, low birth weight leads to more health problems, frequent hospitalizations, lags in language development, and increased likelihood of learning and intellectual disabilities.[26] Low birth weight also leads to adult diseases including: type 2 diabetes, hypertension, heart disease, obesity, kidney disease, and premature mortality. Poverty is also a significant risk factor for disability in children.[37] Children who grow up impoverished are more likely to be malnourished, at higher risk for exposure to disease and environmental chemicals, and less likely to receive adequate health care.

CHILDHOOD DEVELOPMENT
   While some developmental disabilities are diagnosed at birth or soon after, many do not become apparent until early childhood, such as autism spectrum disorder (ASD) and attention-deficit/hyperactivity disorder (ADHD). Other conditions that begin in early childhood may not result in problems until later in life, such as type 1 diabetes, which can cause vision loss, nerve damage, or limb loss later in life. Low birth weight, premature birth, multiple births, older parents, certain medications, and infections during pregnancy are all associated with an increased risk for many developmental disabilities. Many disabling conditions that once resulted in shortened lifespans, today now result in

lengthened life expectancy due to advances in medicine and care. Spina bifida, Down syndrome, cystic fibrosis, and cerebral palsy are all examples of developmental disabilities people can live with through at least young adulthood, if not into adulthood and old age.[31,39]

Injury and violence. Injuries and violence are a leading cause of disability and are the leading cause of death in children in the U.S. and globally.[9] Injuries and violence include road traffic injuries (e.g., motor vehicle, pedestrian, and bicycle), falls, poisoning, fire and burn injuries, drowning, sports injuries, physical abuse, suicide, self-harm, and homicide. Road traffic injuries alone are the main cause of injury and death for children.[9] Children of low-income and in developing nations are most likely to be affected by injuries and violence.[45] Boys are more likely to be injured and experience more severe injuries than girls, and this gap only increases with age. The only category in which girls experience higher rates of injury are fires and burns. Girls are more likely to experience fire injuries in low-income countries or developing nations such as South-East Asia and the Eastern Mediterranean.[47] This is because in such countries girls and women are more likely to cook over and tend open fires. Long-term consequences of burns that result in disability include: chronic pain; sensory problems; neuropathy that includes the sensation of pins and needles, as well as a burning sensation under the skin; psychological health problems; and societal issues, including prejudice and isolation.

Injuries and violence can result in traumatic brain or spinal cord injuries, increased risk for infections and other health problems, physical and intellectual disabilities, and mental health problems including anxiety, depression and post-traumatic stress disorder. Furthermore, disability resulting from childhood injuries can result in further problems, including: educational difficulties, such as poor grades, poor attendance, and inability to attend school; employment difficulties; social difficulties; and behavioral and emotional problems.

Head injuries alone are the most common cause of disability due to injury and violence.[51] Sports-related injuries are an ever-increasing issue, with almost 1.25 million U.S. youth attended to by emergency room departments each year. Head injuries in youth sports are a problem. Unfortunately, due to the culture of sports, over half of youth do not report symptoms of a concussion, or keep playing due to pressure from teammates, coaches, and parents. Often ignored is the fact that symptoms of a concussion can be highly dangerous if left untreated, leading to increased risk for another head injury, longer recovery time, permanent brain damage, or even death.

Illness. Today, millions of children have access to safe water and sanitation, access to better food options, and at least minimal health care that can provide vaccinations and medicine.[6,47] Infectious disease rates have plummeted in many nations, with many diseases (e.g., leprosy, measles, small pox, and hepatitis B) that once plagued countries for generations, disabling and killing millions of people, are now eradicated or reduced to insignificant levels. Measles for example has been reduced by about 90% throughout Africa.[47] However, other illnesses still have devastating effects worldwide. Conditions such as diarrhea, lower respiratory tract infections and HIV are leading causes of death for children worldwide. Environmental toxins including lead and mercury can lead to hyperactivity, learning disabilities, and intellectual disabilities, as well as affect the nervous system

HIV. Of the almost 40 million people living with HIV today, about 3 million are children under the age of 15.[48] While HIV education and prevention has decreased rates globally by almost 60%, many HIV-infected children live in Africa with over 600 children infected every day. Throughout developing and middle-income nations, about 250,000 children were infected in 2013.[47]

Most children are infected through mother-to-child-transmission in which the mother has HIV and transmits the virus to her child during pregnancy, childbirth, or while breastfeeding. Health organizations, such as WHO, work with governments throughout Africa to decrease transmission. If women have access to antiretroviral drugs during early pregnancy and throughout breastfeeding, as well as the infant immediately after birth, this significantly decreases the likelihood the child will develop HIV down to about 5%. However, while today's medicines are highly effective, access to such treatment is not always available, with only about 25% of children having access to HIV medicines.[48] Treatment clinics can be miles from villages, and along with poor infrastructure, transportation, and little income, travel can be nearly impossible. There are also not enough trained people to travel to villages to administer medication or to provide prevention education. Some of the antiretroviral medications must be kept cool, which can be difficult in many low-income and isolated areas. Furthermore, stigma is a significant barrier to care, creating fear and preventing families from seeking treatment.

HIV affects the immune system, and because the immune systems of children are not fully developed, they are unable to fight other infections, becoming sick more easily and more severely than children without HIV. There are many illnesses common among HIV-positive children, including: ear and sinus infections, sepsis, pneumonia, urinary tract infections, intestinal illnesses, skin diseases, meningitis, tuberculosis, diarrhea, and respiratory illnesses. Due to the high risk for infection, HIV-positive infants and young children often do not reach key developmental milestones, resulting in further difficulties. Additionally, half of all HIV-positive children who do not receive adequate treatment die by the age of two, with almost all untreated children dying by age five.

Meningitis and encephalitis. Disease itself causes complications, but conditions such as measles, chicken pox, and pertussis (whooping cough) can also lead to other infections, such as meningitis and encephalitis. Meningitis is inflammation of the membrane that covers the brain and spinal cord, known as the meninges. While meningitis is often caused by viral infections, it can also be caused by bacterial and fungal infections, as well as by parasites. If not treated appropriately, meningitis can result in brain damage leading to various levels of intellectual impairments, learning disabilities, and hearing loss. Children are most susceptible to developing meningitis.

Encephalitis is inflammation of the brain due to viral infections. Like meningitis, encephalitis is more likely to affect children. Encephalitis can result in serious long-term complications such as hearing and vision loss, memory and learning difficulties, and loss of muscle control. While vaccinations have significantly reduced rates of many diseases, they have also reduced rates of meningitis and encephalitis due to viral infections. Worldwide, meningitis and encephalitis usually only occur in small outbreaks. However, in developing nations, especially throughout areas of Africa, there are large outbreaks averaging approximately 500,000 cases per decade.

Asthma. With 7 million children affected, in recent decades, asthma has become the leading childhood chronic illness, and one of the most common causes of disability.[7,44] People with asthma experience inflammation in the airways of the lungs, causing swelling and irritation. This inflammation results in difficulty breathing, tightening of the chest, wheezing, and coughing. The inflammation and resulting symptoms can range from mild to severe. Severe symptoms must receive prompt treatment, as they can result in emergency department visits and even death.

Asthma is a serious health problem and expensive to treat, costing U.S. families over $1000 per child a year, and costing the U.S. over $55 billion annually.[7] While there are many programs available to ensure children receive proper treatment, more must be done. Every year, asthma results in almost 500,000 hospitalizations and 2 million emergency department visits, 9 million doctor visits, as well as nearly 3,500 deaths. Additionally, asthma results in almost 14 million missed days of school per year. Poorly treated asthma hinders a child's ability to keep pace in school, affecting school work and grades, and resulting in increased high school dropout rates.[7,44] Caregivers are also affected, taking time off from work to care for children, losing wages, and decreasing productivity. Urban, low-income, and minority children are most likely to have asthma compared to children from suburban and rural areas, those from middle and higher incomes, and Caucasian children.

Little is known regarding the etiology of asthma. However, allergens, tobacco smoke, obesity, pollution, eczema, and over use of anti-bacterial cleansers and hand sanitizers have all been correlated to the development, as well as trigger, of the illness.[28,44] As etiology is unknown, this makes proper care and management key. Many physicians do a good job educating children on signs of symptoms and identifying triggers, yet few children are taught appropriate asthma management or develop actions plans with their physicians.

Autism. Autism spectrum disorder (ASD) has become a significant concern worldwide. ASD can cause difficulties with the ability to communicate appropriately, interact with others, and form relationships, as well as behavioral and intellectual difficulties.[11] Children with ASD often think, learn, and problem solve differently from their peers, and can have intellectual impairments resulting in academic challenges. ASD now encompasses other disabilities previously diagnosed separately: autistic disorder, pervasive developmental disorder not otherwise specified (PDD-NOS), and Asperger syndrome.[24] These conditions now all fall under the umbrella of ASD. Autism is difficult to diagnose and often not recognized until a child is about three years old. However, many children are not diagnosed until much later.[9] Without early diagnosis, children do not receive early interventions to improve social, communication, and learning skills, and can experience more problems as they grow older.

While the cause of ASD is still unknown, there are multiple risk factors.[11] Researchers agree that much of the development of ASD has to do with genetics, as having one child with ASD is a risk factor for another child to also be diagnosed; ASD also occurs more often in people who have other genetic or chromosomal disorders such as fragile X syndrome. Some teratogens, such as medications, have been connected to the development of ASD. There is some evidence suggesting ASD is more likely to develop during or immediately after birth. Researchers have also found a correlation between older parents and children developing ASD. For many years vaccinations have been implicated in the causation of ASD; however, to date, there is no research that supports this. In fact, *The Lancet*, the journal that published the original study claiming a connection between vaccinations and ASD, has since pulled the study and refuted the author's claims.

There is a significant gender disparity in ASD diagnosis. While the numbers appear to continuously increase, boys outnumber girls in diagnosis by a rate of about 5 to 1.[23] Researchers question why there is such a difference. Some evidence suggests that girls may have genetic protectors.[38] Others have suggested poor reliability of assessments resulting in the over diagnosis of boys.[24] There appear to be differences in symptoms between boys and girls,[38] resulting in girls being under diagnosed[23] or even able to hide their conditions by compensating in other areas.[36] While no real differences in symptoms have been found between infants, toddlers and children, differences have been found during adolescence and adulthood. Women are more likely to have difficulties interacting with others (e.g., having interest in another person's point of view, reading body language, and having empathy) and group interactions and activities. However, girls may be better able to conceal such impairments, so while observed, impairments are not as distinguished. Boys, however, tend to have more repetitive or stereotypic movements (e.g., rocking and spinning) and are more likely to experience sensory irritability, have more restricted interests, and display more social and separation anxiety than girls.

ADOLESCENCE AND YOUNG ADULTHOOD (13 – 24 YEARS)

Aside from the first three years of life, adolescence is the most critical period for mental and physical growth. Adolescent brain development is especially crucial in overall development and health. During adolescence, the brain goes through rapid changes. Gray matter increases throughout the cortex, which is important in neural connectivity and communication between the lobes of the brain for optimal physical, cognitive, and mental functioning. However, this growth occurs at different rates throughout the brain. For example, the limbic system–the center of emotion and memory formation, as well as the center of the reward pathway of the brain–goes through rapid maturation early in adolescence. The pre-frontal cortex, which is the judgement center of the brain and controls emotions and impulses, does not fully mature until early adulthood. Changes and fluctuations in hormones during this period add to what is an already complex developmental process. This whole mixture creates a potentially interesting recipe: a highly intelligent, yet emotionally intense, impulsive teenager.

Adolescent brain development makes this time of life critical and paves the way for later health and behavior. Injury rates skyrocket during adolescence, as do crime rates, alcohol, and drug use. Road traffic injuries, for example, are the leading cause of death and second leading cause of disability for teenagers.[48] Alcohol and drug use often begin during adolescence, peaking in late adolescence and early adulthood. The earlier an adolescent begins using alcohol or drugs, the greater the risk for addiction in later life. Eating habits and exercise behaviors are also important during adolescence and young adulthood, as these behaviors carry on into adulthood and determine later overall health and risk for chronic illness and disability.

Additionally, good mental health is of special concern during adolescence and young adulthood, as many mental health conditions, such as anxiety, depression, bipolar disorder, and schizophrenia, develop during this time of life.[48] Depression, for example, is the leading cause of disability for this age group. Suicide and self-harm are also prominent causes of disability and death for teens and young adults. Therefore, it is vital to focus specifically on mental health, as well as the psychosocial development, of youth and young adults with disabilities.

Mental health. Mental health conditions and suicide are of significant concern during adolescence. Depression is the leading cause of disability among teens and young adults, with suicide the third leading cause of death worldwide and the second leading cause of death in the U.S. for this age group.[48] Many adults with mental health conditions first have symptoms during their teen years. Depressive and anxiety disorders, substance use disorders, bipolar conditions, and schizophrenia spectrum disorders are the most likely mental health conditions to develop during adolescence.

Depression. Depression can vary in severity and be episodic, recurrent, or chronic.[48] Symptoms must be present for at least two weeks, which include sadness, loss of interest in activities, decreased energy, inappropriate guilt, and poor sleep and appetite. While depression is usually an episodic condition, over 20% of cases are chronic, with little or no remission. Furthermore, there is a high recurrence rate, meaning that once a person has depression the first time, he or she has about a 35% chance of having depression again within two years. Over half of all people who have depression once are likely to have a second episode within the next 10 years. Young women are more likely to be affected, with approximately 10% of women compared to 6% of men affected in a 12-month period worldwide.

Depression causes a tremendous burden on society, and is ranked among the leading cause of burden among all disease worldwide.[47] Depression hinders physical health and well-being. It can diminish the ability to participate in daily activities, (e.g., school, relationships, employment, household and personal responsibilities, and leisure activities), besides follow a medical regimen. Regarding adolescent and young adult physical health, depression is correlated with chronic pain including fibromyalgia, chronic headaches and migraines, and gastrointestinal conditions. Depression also affects cognitive functioning such as memory, learning and concentration, and interrupts sleep leading to lethargy during the day. Depression can also exacerbate other illnesses, such as asthma. Depression has been identified as a key risk factor for poor self-image and self-esteem, and health risk behaviors including: alcohol, drug, and tobacco use; eating disorders and obesity; and physical inactivity. Finally, depressive symptoms are often found with other mental health conditions, (e.g., anxiety disorders, bipolar conditions, personality disorders, substance use disorders, and schizophrenia spectrum disorders).

The etiology of depression is complex and not fully understood. Etiology can stem from an environmental factor, such as the loss of a loved one, a break up in a relationship, or by a chronic negative event, such as childhood trauma. From a psychological perspective, depression stems from the negative appraisal of a situation and the dysfunctional thinking that occurs after this negative appraisal process. Over focus on the dysfunctional thoughts results in a downward spiral, causing a person to fall into depression.

Depression can also be caused by an organic factor. Imbalance of stress hormones like cortisol, or neurotransmitters such as serotonin, norepinephrine, dopamine, glutamate, and gamma-aminobutyric acid (GABA) has been implicated in the causation of depression. Etiology can also lie in a mix of environment and organic factors. A person could internalize an event as negative, engaging in dysfunctional thinking that could spiral into depression; the depression can cause stress, resulting in an increase in stress hormones, and offset the neural chemistry in the brain, resulting in an imbalance of neurotransmitters. This perpetuates a cycle, spinning the person further into depression which one may not be able to recover from without psychological and even medical help.

Anxiety disorders. Anxiety disorders are the most prevalent mental health condition in the U.S., affecting almost 10% of the teenage population. Women are twice as likely as men to be diagnosed with anxiety.[4] Minority groups are less likely to be affected by these conditions. Symptoms of anxiety include excessive worry, guilt, feeling agitated or on edge, nervousness, poor sleep, racing heart, tension and muscle aches, and nausea. Anxiety disorders often start during childhood and adolescence and, if not treated adequately, can become debilitating with age. Anxiety is a typical reaction to stress and can be beneficial and adaptive, helping to prepare or rehearse to improve a skill and serving as an alarm in a potentially dangerous situation; it becomes dysfunctional when it is excessive to the point that youth have difficulty coping. Anxiety can interfere with daily activities such as concentration, memory, learning, and test taking, leading to hindrances in academics, job performance, and even relationships. Anxiety disorders include several conditions: generalized anxiety disorder, panic disorder, social anxiety disorder, specific phobia, and separation anxiety disorder. Other disorders such as obsessive-compulsive disorder and post-traumatic stress disorder also have anxiety as a major component of their symptoms, but are no longer classified among anxiety disorders.

The etiology of anxiety disorders includes both psychological and organic factors. Anxiety disorders are often developed in response to an event or a series of events; however, for other people, the triggering event is unknown. Anxiety can also be caused by other illnesses such as asthma and hyperthyroidism during adolescence and young adulthood, as well as other mental health conditions. Abnormal levels of neurotransmitters in the brain can also result in anxiety, as well as disruptions in activity of the limbic system in the brain, especially within the amygdala which is responsible for the regulation of fear and aggression.

Psychosocial development. Adolescents and young adults with congenital or acquired disabilities can experience unique health and social needs that their counterparts do not.[35,39] Teens and young adults with disabilities can require more assistance in developing job skills and gaining employment, developing healthy social and intimate relationships, participating in leisure activities, and managing activities of daily living, such as cleaning, cooking, hygiene, shopping, and balancing a budget. Teens and young adults with disabilities can require assistance in the development of autonomy and independence. These years are important for young adults to spend discovering themselves, developing their personal identity, and becoming independent. However, young adults with disabilities can struggle in this transition from childhood to adulthood. Young adults with disabilities may become stuck in this transition, struggling to leave childhood roles. Young adults with disabilities may be treated as inferior to others, and therefore may require extra support to become autonomous. There also may be added health risks as youth with disabilities age, such as the deterioration of health or further health complications. Therefore, young adults with disabilities require education regarding their conditions and potential health risks.

Young women with disabilities especially require extra support and health education as they transition to adulthood.[35] As women are more likely to experience both physical and mental health conditions, young women with disabilities must learn about how their primary condition can change and about secondary conditions that can occur with age. Health information is critical for young women with disabilities for they are at a higher risk for osteoporosis, obesity, hypertension, and type 2 diabetes, which may occur at an earlier age. More importantly, developing a healthy self-image is critical as women in general, and especially teenagers, struggle with body image, self-esteem, self-efficacy, identity, and sexual identity; this has been found to be more so in women with disabilities.[31] Furthermore, women with disabilities are at a higher risk for abuse compared to able-bodied women. Support in the development of a healthy self-image and participation in health-promoting activities and behaviors can lower risk for the development of secondary health conditions (e.g., depression and anxiety) and enhance self-esteem, self-efficacy, autonomy, assertiveness, and quality of life.

ADULTHOOD (25 – 64 YEARS)

Almost half of the U.S. population lives with a chronic illness with 1 in 4 adults living with multiple chronic conditions. Approximately 20% of the adult population in the U.S. have a disability with a disparate impact on men and women.[5] Men are more likely to have acute health conditions, less likely to live with chronic conditions, and more likely to have severe disability rates.[51] Men are more likely to have better childhood health, better education, and higher social economic status, factors that protect future health and access to health care. However, even though men are more likely to have better access to health care services and fewer functional limitations, they are at risk of dying prematurely and die from acute health conditions.[35,40]

About 25 million American women (19% of the female population) live with some type of disability.[35] Women are more likely to live with chronic illnesses than men, live longer with chronic illness, and live with multiple chronic conditions. Women also are more likely to experience health care disparities, much of this due to attitudinal, informational, environmental, and geographic barriers. Women in general, especially women with disabilities, are more likely to live in poverty and not have adequate health insurance or access to appropriate services including dental care, exercise and nutritional programs, and stress management.[40] Additionally, women with disabilities are more likely to lack support, be single, live in isolation, rely on informal support (i.e., friend, family member, significant other) and not have access to a formal caregiver or personal care assistant to assist with daily activities. Such factors increase the risk for stress, anxiety, depression, co-morbid medical health conditions, and put women at higher risk for abuse.

Arthritis. Arthritis, the most common cause of disability in the world, includes over 100 diseases and rheumatic conditions.[47] It affects 53 million people in the U.S., with about 23 million people experiencing limitations in daily activity.[8] It is predicted that by 2030, arthritis will affect 67 million people, or 25% of the U.S. adult population.

53

Most arthritic conditions include pain, aching and swelling in and around the joints, stiffness throughout the musculoskeletal system, and fatigue. Osteoarthritis (OA) is the most common type of arthritis. Osteoarthritis occurs when the cartilage between joints is inflamed, worn down, and eventually lost over time. Osteoarthritis affects over 27 million people in the U.S. alone, with development usually occurring after age 40, and women more likely to be diagnosed; people under 40 can be affected, usually occurring after an injury. Other forms of arthritis are autoimmune diseases, including rheumatoid arthritis (RA) which occurs when the immune system attacks the lining of the joints, causing a painful swelling and resulting in joint deformity. Other types of arthritis and forms of autoimmune disease include systemic lupus erythematosus (SLE), fibromyalgia, and psoriatic arthritis. Arthritis not only affects the musculoskeletal system, but can affect and damage the heart, lungs, kidneys, liver, and other organs and systems of the body.

Co-morbidity is common in arthritis, with arthritis also exacerbating other conditions.[10] Arthritic symptoms including pain and fatigue. More severe symptoms lead to functional limitations that complicate the self-management of arthritis, as well as of other conditions such as heart disease and diabetes. Arthritis has also been found to affect inpatient and post-hospitalization of other illnesses. When a person does not feel well, is in pain, and exhausted, that person does not want to participate in health-promoting behaviors, including medication treatment, healthy eating, and exercise. Mental health conditions (e.g., depression and anxiety) have also been associated with arthritis. In fact, people, especially women, with arthritis have higher rates of depression compared to those who do not have arthritis.[43] Depression can increase the severity of arthritic symptoms, as well as decrease the use and responsiveness to arthritis treatments, lessen the ability to cope with arthritis, and increase stress, which itself can increase arthritis severity and depressive symptoms. These impacts hamper treatment and decrease quality of life.

Women are disproportionately affected by arthritis. They are twice as likely to develop the condition, representing over 60% of arthritis cases.[35] The CDC predicts this gap will only increase with over 40 million women projected to be living with arthritis by 2030.[10] Women are also more likely to experience limitations in daily activity; over 40% of U.S. women diagnosed with arthritis experience limitations in daily activities and report higher rates of severe joint pain than men.[43] Arthritis also affects racial and ethnic groups differently. For example, African American women with SLE experience a higher rate of premature mortality.[43]

Research differs regarding the discrepancy between the sexes and racial/ethnic groups.[43] There is evidence to suggest arthritis affects women at greater rates due to biological differences between the sexes, as the regulation of the female immune system is different from men. There is also evidence of differences between the sexes in exposure to certain environmental and occupational variables in the etiology of certain arthritic autoimmune diseases.

Other research suggests gender differences lie in social expectations. For example, men in many cultures are expected to be self-sufficient, act as the provider of the family, and not appear weak or show pain;[20,21] work is also a main form of identity to men. As chronic illness represents a threat to a man's ability to work and complete family commitments, men may be less likely to acknowledge the presence or severity of a chronic illness, such arthritis.[21]

Perceived stress, role demands, and role overload can increase arthritis severity and functional limitations, interfere with treatment, and increase interruptions in work. In their study of gender perceptions of balance between work and personal roles and their effect on arthritis, Gignac and colleagues[21] found that for both men and women with arthritis, having a larger work load and more personal demands, such as having children, were associated with work functional limitations. Men were more likely to experience severe symptoms and work-related functional limitations if they had less control over their jobs. Women were more likely to experience severe symptoms if they worked unpredictable hours. While severity of symptoms was greater for both men and women who had children, women were more likely to report severe symptoms compared to men.

Cancer. Cancer is a leading cause of disability and mortality worldwide, with approximately 14 million people affected in 2012 and over 8 million deaths.[8] Over just the next 20 years, cancer rates are expected to increase to over 20 million cases worldwide.[49]

Cancer is another term that accounts for multiple related diseases. It occurs when cells in the human body do not stop dividing, spreading into surrounding tissue. In many cancers, these cells form masses of tissues called tumors. Tumors can start in any part of the body and can break off, spreading to other parts of the body, called *metastasis*. Cancer is caused by a combination of genetic and environmental agents, such as physical carcinogens, like ultraviolet light and radon; chemical carcinogens, such as asbestos, chemicals in tobacco, alcohol, and arsenic; and finally biological carcinogens, including viruses like hepatitis B and C, HPV, and HIV.[49] Behavior is the most significant cause of cancer, such as the use of tobacco, alcohol, poor nutrition, and physical inactivity.[49] Tobacco itself accounts for almost 500,000 deaths in the U.S. and over 5 million deaths worldwide each year, accounting for over 70% of lung cancer deaths worldwide. Tobacco is the most significant risk factor for lung cancer, but also causes other cancers including cancers of the trachea, bronchus, oropharynx, esophagus, larynx, stomach, bladder, kidney, pancreas, and cervix. It has also been connected to colorectal and liver cancer.[8]

The most common types of cancer for men include lung, prostate, colorectal, stomach, and liver.[49] For women, the most common forms of cancers are breast, colorectal, lung, cervix, and stomach. African American men have the highest rates of cancer, followed by Caucasian, Latino, Asian/Pacific Islander, and finally American Indian/Alaska Native men.[8] Caucasian women, on the other hand, are more likely to have cancer, than African American, Latina, Asian/Pacific Islander, and American Indian/Alaska Native women.[8]

Due to advancements in medicine and technology, cancer today has an increasing survival rate, with over 60% of survivors able to return to work after treatment.[30] However, even after successful treatment, people can be left with functional limitations and potential long-term disability. Unfortunately, many post-treatment issues are often not on the radar of physicians or researchers.[2] Persistent postsurgical pain, musculoskeletal pain, sensory disturbances, and other post-treatment conditions can be major problems. For example, breast cancer survival has increased over the last few decades, with a five-year survival rate reaching upwards of 90% throughout North America. Common issues for breast cancer survivors include chronic pain, sensory disturbances, lymphedema, reduced arm function, and medication side effects, all of which hamper physical and psychological functioning, well-being, and quality of life. Sensory disturbances frequently occur around the surgery area and include chemotherapy-induced neuropathy, which can affect the hands and feet. People can feel uncomfortable wearing clothes, holding or manipulating small objects, and experience problems when walking. Cancer survivors also have limitations due to lack of support in the environment and from others, with many left to figure out how to maneuver through the return to work process and accommodations on their own.[30] Lack of support can then lead to stress, anxiety and depression, further hampering physical and mental health, increasing functional limitations, and lowering quality of life. Poor coping skills also exacerbate post-treatment conditions and functional limitations by increasing emotional distress and decreasing a healthy psychological reaction to physical health and stressors.

Diabetes. Nearly 10% of adults over the age of 18 have diabetes.[13] Added to this, it is estimated that almost another 80 million people live with prediabetes, resulting in about one-third of the adult U.S. population being affected.[16] Diabetes develops when the pancreas does not produce enough insulin, or when the body cannot effectively use the insulin it does produce, causing increased levels of glucose in the blood. If diabetes is not properly managed, over time it can result in serious health consequences. In fact, diabetes directly results in 1.5 million deaths annually, and is the seventh leading cause of death in the U.S.[13] Health consequences of diabetes include: cardiovascular disease, such as heart disease and stroke; reduction in blood flow; neuropathy in the feet and foot ulcers, which can lead to lower-extremity amputations; diabetic retinopathy, which can lead to blindness; and kidney failure.[13] Almost half of all people with diabetes die of cardiovascular disease. Diabetes is the also the leading cause of kidney failure and one percent of new cases of blindness worldwide.

Type 1 diabetes, otherwise known as insulin-dependent or childhood-onset diabetes, results from lack of insulin production, occurring when the pancreas is not able to produce enough insulin to direct sugar to the body's cells for energy.

Type 1 diabetes affects about 5% of all people living with diabetes.[13] It can be caused by genetics or a virus, and usually develops during childhood. With proper management, healthy diet, and exercise, people today with type 1 diabetes can live long and healthy lives compared to just a few decades ago.

Type 2 diabetes, which is non-insulin-dependent or adult-onset diabetes, is the most common form of diabetes. It is caused by the ineffective use of insulin. Type 2 diabetes develops when the body develops a resistance to insulin or is not able to develop enough insulin. Risk factors for type 2 diabetes include obesity, physical inactivity, race and ethnicity, and older age.[16] Obesity and physical inactivity have been found to be significant risk factors in the development of diabetes and have directly resulted in the increase of type 2 diabetes not only in adults, but in children as well.[12]

Gestational diabetes, or hyperglycemia, develops during pregnancy. While in most cases gestational diabetes disappears after child birth, it can cause serious health problems for the mother and infant if not treated. Gestational diabetes is more common among African Americans, Latinos, and Native Americans. It is also more likely to occur among women who are obese.[16]

The development and treatment of diabetes is a multifaceted interaction between genetic, social, cultural, and economic factors, which is complicated with disparities in treatment.[16] Worldwide, over 80% of deaths directly due to diabetes happen in low and middle-income countries. Quality of life for those living with diabetes has been found to be affected by current economic status. Mental well-being for those living with diabetes has been found to be affected not only by current economic status but by childhood economic status, as well. The Institute of Medicine reported U.S. minority groups experience significantly different treatment in health care, which has resulted in greater differences in health for these groups compared to Caucasians.

In the U.S., diabetes is more prevalent among ethnic and racial minority groups compared to Caucasians.[13] In fact, African Americans, Latinos, and Native Americans are not only more likely to be affected by diabetes, but "experience a 50-100% higher burden of illness and mortality from diabetes than white Americans."[16,p. 130] African and Latino Americans have an almost 80% higher risk of developing diabetes compared to Caucasians, with almost 20% of African Americans over the age of 20 living with diabetes compared to just 7% of Caucasians. Furthermore, African Americans are 1.5 times more likely to be hospitalized due to diabetes and twice as likely to die from diabetes as Caucasians.

For adult Latino Americans, about 12% live with diabetes and they are 1.5 times more likely to die from diabetes compared to Caucasians. Diabetes has very serious consequences for Native Hawaiians and Pacific Islanders and Native Americans, with over 20% of adults living with diabetes. It is the fifth leading cause of death among these populations, with death rates over 20% higher than the general U.S. population. As for Native Americans, over 16% of the adult population has diabetes, with the death rate from diabetes for this population three times higher than the general U.S. population.

Gender and stress have been found to be risk factors in the management of diabetes with women more likely to experience issues with physical health and diabetic symptoms.[22] Women are more likely to experience a higher body mass index, higher blood pressure, earlier complications of diabetes, and poorer levels of physical activity.[41] Complicating matters, women are also more likely to experience stress due to diabetes; greater concern is for women who have little support, as they can experience more stress and have poorer coping skills than women with diabetes who have more support.[15] Women with positive coping skills are more likely to perceive less stress and perceive more control over their chronic illness and symptoms. With those with poorer coping skills, a lesser perception of control and self-efficacy, and higher rates of depression experience more complications from diabetes.[15]

Much of the disparity in diabetes rates and treatment among various ethnic and racial groups lies among risk factors including: social isolation, low support, less income, and lack of access to nutritional foods.[15,41] Locher and colleagues[27] found that African American women are less likely to have access to nutritional food options and both African American men and women are at risk for lacking a positive support system and being socially isolated. Restrictions in income, transportation options, and even walking options that include both accessible walkways/sidewalks and neighborhood safety are also significant factors in the development and treatment of diabetes. People with diabetes who do not have an adequate support system, or access to healthy foods, community resources, and environments are simply not going to be able to manage their diabetes appropriately.

Heart disease. Heart disease develops when the arteries to the heart narrow and harden and potentially become blocked, hampering blood and oxygen flow to the heart, causing damage and scarring to the muscle. Symptoms are often different between men and women.[41] Men are more likely to experience angina, or chest pain, whereas women are likely to experience shortness of breath, nausea, and fatigue. Other symptoms include pain, numbness, weakness, and even coldness in the arms or legs, and pain in the back, neck, jaw, throat, and abdomen. People can also develop heart disease due to heart arrhythmia, heart defects, weakened heart muscle, and heart infections.

Next to depression, cardiovascular diseases, including heart disease, are the second leading cause of disability in the U.S. Heart disease is also the leading cause of death in the U.S. with over 600,000 deaths annually.[13] Ischemic heart disease is the leading cause of death worldwide with almost 8 million deaths annually, with hypertensive heart disease the 10th leading cause of death. Heart disease is also the leading cause of premature death in the world.

Development of heart disease is a combination of genetic, environment, behavioral, and psychological factors. Having close family members with heart disease increases chances of having heart disease.[34] High cholesterol, high blood pressure, and diabetes represent genetic components, but it can also be caused by behavior, including tobacco and alcohol use and physical inactivity. By themselves, behavioral factors can also cause heart disease. Stress has also been found to be a significant risk factor for heart disease. Heart attacks are more likely to occur after negative events (e.g., divorce or loss of a loved one), natural disasters, or prolonged negative experiences, such as job stress. Additionally, people frequently experience chronic fatigue and depression after a heart attack, causing further difficulties such as increased risk and severity for disability, and increased chances of developing co-morbid conditions; emotional deregulation and chronic depression can lead to heart disease. Gender is also a factor in the development of heart disease, with men at higher risk for developing the chronic illness.[34] This may be in part due to men being more likely to engage in risk taking behaviors. African Americans are also more likely to develop heart disease than Caucasians.[41]

Obesity. In just the last two decades, obesity has become a significant health concern in the U.S. and has become a worldwide epidemic to the point that WHO has called this global issue "globesity."[50] In 1995, 200 million people over the age of 18 worldwide were considered obese, with a body mass index of over 30. In just five short years, by the year 2000, adult obesity climbed to over 300 million. Today, WHO reports that over 500 million adults are obese, with over one and a half billion people overweight. Obesity is not just a serious problem in industrialized nations, but has become a health problem in developing nations as well, with over 115 million people in developing nations considered obese. In the U.S., more than one third of adults are obese, accounting for almost 80 million people.[12]

Consequences of obesity are severe, including the development of other diseases and disability.[14] Obesity increases the risk for diabetes, cardiovascular disease, hypertension, stroke, and sleep apnea, and has been implicated in many forms of cancer. Obesity also puts people at risk for premature death and reduces quality of life.[3] So many other health problems have been related back to the rise in obesity, particularly due to an increased sedentary lifestyle, that obesity and sedentary behavior have now been called "the new smoking." Obesity and its associated causal behaviors have replaced tobacco smoking as the leading cause of chronic illness, disability, and death at a global level.[3]

Obesity has been implicated in loss of productivity in the workplace, with obese employees more likely to call in sick.[12] For the employer, obese employees result in the employer spending more time, energy, and money on replacement workers, training for these people, as well as loss and delay in productivity. Absenteeism in the workplace due to obesity is estimated to cost the U.S. over $8 billion annually. This significant expense creates a huge financial challenge, not only for business, but puts a strain on individual states and the nation, as well. Obesity-related absenteeism leads to higher costs in production and transportation of goods and creates for a less competitive workforce. Furthermore, obesity places a significant toll on the nation regarding health care expenditure.[3] Obesity-related illness costs the U.S. over $210 billion annually, significantly impacting health care and pharmaceutical costs, as obesity-related illness has created a dramatic increase in medication use.

Obesity is not only a consequence of behavior, but complicated by a myriad of additional factors such as genetics, culture, poverty, an environment that provides few opportunities for exercise, increased sedentary lifestyle, food insecurity, over access to poor quality foods, larger portion sizes, inadequate health insurance, limited access to health care, and higher levels of stress for some groups.[12,17] People living in poverty are highly vulnerable to becoming obese and not equipped to appropriately deal with associated health consequences.[19] WHO[50] reports obesity is now more of a problem for people in poverty than famine and starvation, and kills more people than undernutrition does. People in poverty are likely to experience what has been coined *food deserts*, areas of high food insecurity.[19] The USDA[19] estimates that about 25 million people in the U.S. live in areas designated as food deserts, areas in which people live more than one mile from a grocery store in urban areas and more than 10 miles from a grocery store in rural areas. People in these areas, urban or rural, experience limited access to grocery stores, farmers' markets, and generally healthy food options, as well as limited access to adequate and low-cost transportation. If there are farmers' markets accessible, many do not accept food stamps for people to use. In many neighborhoods, if people have access to fruits and vegetables, they are often of poor quality and limited in variety. Instead, people have open access to convenience stores and fast food restaurants that sell mostly cheap, processed foods high in fat, calories, and sugar. Lack of high quality food, as well as limited access to parks for exercise, have been found to be significant factors not just in obesity but the consequences that come with it including heart disease and diabetes.[50] Unfortunately, for millions of people in these areas, they also do not have access to adequate health insurance and health care providers, which only further hampers health and disability.

In the U.S., minority groups are more likely to be obese, with African Americans and Latinos most likely to be affected.[18] African Americans have the highest rate of obesity, affecting almost half of the adult population, with over 40% of adult Latinos affected, compared to about 33% of Caucasians and only 11% of Asian American adults.[12] Among minority men, higher economic status is associated with higher rates of obesity, however, for minority women, poverty is positively correlated with obesity. Creighton and colleagues[18] found that Latino immigrants in the U.S. have healthier lifestyles, including weight, compared to second and third generation Latinos. First generation immigrants are more likely to lead non-sedentary lifestyles, including employment, transportation, homemaking, and active projects; eat smaller portions comprised of healthier foods, including rice, beans, fruit, and vegetables; and are less likely to eat fast food and higher fat foods, such as dairy and processed foods. However, for later generations, they are more likely to eat unhealthy foods, eat more fast food, and partake in a sedentary lifestyle.

THE ELDERLY (65 YEARS AND OLDER)

As medicine, technology, and nutrition have improved in the last 100 years, there has been a significant change in life expectancy and in causes of death. At just the beginning of the last century, communicable diseases (e.g., infections) were the main cause of death. Additionally, for a person with a congenital or acquired disability, life expectancy was usually short, or the person was expected to live a poor health-related quality of life (HRQOL). While at the beginning of the 1900s, life expectancy was only about 50 years, today, people can live well into their seventies and eighties, and more people than ever before are able to live to 100, with many able to enjoy a positive HRQOL as they age.[46] Many people continue to live healthy, active lives as they age and continue to work, volunteer, and help take care of family past the age of retirement. As we continue to age, soon the world will have a larger elderly population than childhood population.

While just a century ago, there were only about 14 million over the age of 80, today over 500 million people worldwide are over the age of 65, and this number is only expected to increase over the next few decades to 1.5 billion by 2050, making up 16% of the Earth's population.[46] Some countries, such as China and India, will of course face more significant increases in life expectancy, but along with this are increases in health and economic burden. Developing nations are expected to see the biggest increase in life expectancy. While it has taken industrial nations 100 years to see increases in life expectancy, WHO[46] estimates that developing nations may see dramatic increases in just one or two generations. However, for these countries, as people live to be older, they also lack resources, policies, and the economic stability to provide adequate care and ensure HRQOL. As WHO[47] states, for many countries, they "may grow old before they grow rich"[p. 5] and place significant burden on the infrastructure of many countries.

With the rise in noncommunicable or chronic illnesses, millions of people are now living many years with illness, disability, and the potential multiple health, social, and economic burdens.[31] Health agencies and researchers have grappled with the question: as we age are we living healthier, happier lives, or is quality of life decreasing? In the U.S., as the baby boomer generation enters their seventies, chronic illness and disability have increased, and some research suggests quality of life has decreased for this population.[31,35] As we age, impairments, activity limitations, and participation restrictions increase, creating the need for reliance on informal and formal support systems. Among the U.S. elderly, over 3% of the population ages 65-74 require assistance with personal care, and about 11% of the elderly population over the age of 75 require personal care assistance.[10]

Mounting evidence suggests that HRQOL can be increased for the elderly through health education during childhood and adolescence, as well as through the elimination of environmental barriers to increased independence and mobility and the development of effective health policies.[29,46] However, many people are faced with inadequate health policies for chronic illness and long-term care, inadequate insurance and access to insurance, and poor health care provision.[31] For example, women have a higher life expectancy than men and are more likely to live with a disability, requiring more health services. However, even elderly women, compared to their younger cohorts, are just as likely to have inadequate health care coverage and limited access to adequate to health services.[35] Such poor care provisions can leave a significant burden on the individual, as well as the family, lowering HRQOL.

For people over 65, the most common disabling conditions include arthritis, heart disease, stroke, diabetes, COPD, dementia, and, recently added to this list, obesity.[31] Arthritis is the most common and longest lasting chronic illness and disabling condition for the elderly, affecting about 40% of people over 65 and, on average for almost 20 years, often becoming more severe as the person ages.[31] Strokes affect almost 30% of people over 65, and diabetes, COPD, and dementia affect about 20% of people over 65. COPD and diabetes both have a long duration, affecting people for about 15 years on average. In the U.S., African American men over 65 are more likely to live longer with diabetes than Caucasians.[46] In fact, the duration of disability for African Americans overall is longer than for other racial groups. Globally, people who have had strokes, have dementia, or are obese experience the highest risk for disability, with women more likely to be affected than men.

Obesity has become a serious problem at a global level, shortening the life span by about 15 years, as well as a high expectancy rate of severe physical disability, including difficulty with physical strength, endurance, mobility, and activities of daily living, with severe disability lasting for about 5 years. Women are more likely to be affected by disability associated with obesity. In general, women spend more than one year longer with each type of disability than men, with about 30% of women over 65 living with a physical disability. Dementia is the only other chronic illness with an even higher risk for severe disability. It also has a significant longevity, lasting upwards of over 20 years; for men, dementia causes the longest period of difficulty.

Dementia. Neuropsychiatric disorders, including dementia, account for almost 7% of the cause of disability for people over 65.[46] Worldwide, almost 50 million people live with dementia with almost 30% of people over the age of 85 living with the disease, affecting over 50% of women over 90.

Dementia is the most devastating of all chronic conditions.[1] It is the sixth leading cause of death in the U.S. There is no known cause, prevention, way to slow it down, or cure. Symptoms of dementia include deterioration in memory, thinking, and behavior with symptoms significantly increasing in severity with age. As the condition worsens, people require assistance with activities in daily living, eventually requiring care 24 hours a day, even with the most basic activities. This care creates a tremendous emotional, social, and financial burden on loved ones, as they are usually the main caregivers. As symptoms become increasingly severe, the burden of care taxes loved ones beyond their capabilities, requiring long-term hospitalization. In the U.S. alone, dementia costs the country over $600 billion a year, with costs associated with informal caregiving at almost $20 billion.[46] In developing nations, where dementia rates have been estimated to be over double that of industrialized nations, the financial burden is much higher.

Dementia is difficult to diagnose, with early symptoms often easy to hide or mistaken simply for typical changes in aging.[1] Additionally, testing for dementia is limited; cognitive tests are sometimes not reliable and formal diagnosis not available until after death during autopsy. With such difficulties in accurate diagnosis, real statistics are hard to develop. However, it is expected that by 2050, dementia is to reach epidemic levels with over 135 million people worldwide living with the chronic illness.

Dementia is another umbrella term comprising several neuropsychiatric disorders that cause physical brain changes.[1] Alzheimer's disease is the most common form of dementia, accounting for upwards of 80% of dementia cases. There is also vascular dementia, dementia with Lewy bodies, dementia due to Parkinson's disease, frontotemporal dementia, dementia due to Creutzfeldt-Jakob disease, dementia due to Huntington's disease, and Korsakoff syndrome.

Alzheimer's disease. Alzheimer's disease is the most common form of dementia. Over 5 million people in the U.S. over the age of 65 have Alzheimer's. Over 3 million of those with Alzheimer's are women.[1] Alzheimer's is progressive, beginning with mild memory loss that often goes ignored. As the condition progresses, people become confused, lose the ability to think and speak effectively, and demonstrate difficulty completing everyday tasks. People eventually lose the ability to communicate and experience severe limitations in completing every day activities, including self-care.

There are theories as to the cause of Alzheimer's disease. It is suspected that protein deposits, called plaques, and protein fibers, called tangles, interfere with neurons, blocking neural communication. Neurons that cannot do their job eventually die, causing permanent damage to the brain. Plaques and tangles appear to begin developing in certain areas of the brain responsible for memory, explaining why people first experience mild memory loss. As neural death spreads, people experience more severe symptoms related to memory, including personality changes and the ability to complete daily activities.

While Alzheimer's can affect people differently, there are three stages people often go through; early, moderate and severe.[1] People during the early stages of Alzheimer's experience problems with word loss, forgetting names, mild difficulty or confusion completing tasks, misplacing items, and difficulty with planning. During the very beginning stages, people often can continue working and living independent lives. As the disease progresses into the moderate stage people require increased care and loss of independence. Moderate symptoms include continued progression of memory loss, word confusion and loss, difficulty with the ability to express thoughts, moodiness, personality changes, and isolation. According to the Alzheimer's Association,[1] specific symptoms of this stage include:

> Forgetfulness of events or about one's own personal history;

> Feeling moody or withdrawn, especially in socially or mentally challenging situations;

> Being unable to recall one's own address or telephone number or the high school or college from which one graduated;

> Confusion about location or what day it is;

> The need for help choosing proper clothing for the season or the occasion;

> Trouble controlling bladder and bowels;

> Changes in sleep patterns, such as sleeping during the day and becoming restless at night;

> An increased risk of wandering and becoming lost;

> Personality and behavioral changes, including suspiciousness and delusions or compulsive, repetitive behavior like hand-wringing or tissue shredding.

As the illness progresses in severity, people require constant 24-hour care. People lose the ability to communicate appropriately, using words and phrases that do not make sense, or taking a long time to process information and form sentences. People can lose muscle control, including the ability to walk, sit up, and even to swallow, resulting in nutritional issues. People eventually lose awareness of their surroundings and the ability to respond to their environment.

SUMMARY

Great strides in the last century have been made to improve global health, yet much more work must be completed. As we continue to create advances in medicine, improve health, and live longer, it is critical that we fully understand what disability is, develop a well-accepted standardized definition, and accurately examine chronic illness and disability. We must also develop policies and services that address long-term health needs, as well as how to manage and decrease disability across the lifespan. There have been major changes in illness over the last century. Today most causes of disability are due to lifestyle choices, as well as the environment, making many types of disability preventable. We must provide highly effective preventive and rehabilitation education and programming. Furthermore, health often depends on the surrounding environment, shaped by culture, politics, economies, and geography. We must remove environmental barriers that prevent access to care, proper nutrition, and exercise.

REFERENCES

[1] Alzheimer's Association. (2015). *Stages of Alzheimer's & symptoms*. Retrieved from http://www.alz.org/alzheimers_disease_stages_of_alzheimers.asp

[2] Andersen, K. G., Christensen, K. B., Kehlet, H., & Bidstup, P. E. (2014). The effect of pain on physical functioning after breast cancer treatment: Development and validation of an assessment tool. *The Clinical Journal of Pain, 1*. doi: http://doi.org/10.1097/AJP.0000000000000156

[3] Apovian, C. (2013). The clinical and economic consequences of obesity. *The American Journal of Managed Care, 19*(11), s219-228. Retrieved from http://psu.summon.serialssolutions.com

[4] Asnaani, A., Richey, J. A., Dimaite, R., Hinton, D. E., & Hofmann, S. G. (2010). A cross-ethnic comparison of lifetime prevalence rates of anxiety disorders. *The Journal of Nervous and Mental Disease, 198*(8), 551-555. doi: http://doi.org/10.1097/NMD.0b013e3181ea169f

[5] Centers for Disease Control and Prevention. (2012). *Disability and health*. Retrieved from http://www.cdc.gov/ncbddd/disabilityandhealth/index.html

[6] Centers for Disease Control and Prevention. (2013). *Leading causes of death*. Retrieved from http://www.cdc.gov/nchs/fastats/leading-causes-of-death.htm

[7] Centers for Disease Control and Prevention. (2015). *Asthma*. Retrieved from http://www.cdc.gov/asthma/default.htm

[8] Centers for Disease Control and Prevention. (2015). *Cancer rates by race/ethnicity and sex*. Retrieved from http://www.cdc.gov/cancer/dcpc/data/race.htm

[9] Centers for Disease Control and Prevention. (2015). *Childhood injury*. Retrieved from http://www.cdc.gov/safechild/images/CDC-childhoodinjury.pdf

[10] Centers for Disease Control and Prevention. (2015). *Data and statistics: Arthritis*. Retrieved from http://www.cdc.gov/arthritis/data_statistics/index.html

[11] Centers for Disease Control and Prevention. (2015). *Data and statistics: Autism spectrum disorder (ASD)*. Retrieved from http://www.cdc.gov/ncbddd/autism/data.html

[12]Centers for Disease Control and Prevention. (2015). *Data & statistics: Obesity.* Retrieved from http://www.cdc.gov/obesity/data/index.html

[13]Centers for Disease Control and Prevention. (2015). *Diabetes.* Retrieved from http://www.cdc.gov/diabetes/home/index.html

[14]Chatterjee, D., & Bandyopadhyay, A. R. (2009). Non-communicable disease and health hazards in Bengali population: A major public health issue in India. *Journal of Human Ecology, 25*(2), 143-146.

[15]Chiu, C. J., & Wray, L. A. (2011). Gender differences in functional limitations in adults living with type 2 diabetes: Biobehavioral and psychosocial mediators. *Annals of Behavioral Medicine, 41*(1), 71-82. doi: http://doi.org/10.1007/s12160-010-9226-0

[16]Chow, E. A., Foster, H., Gonzalez, V., & McIver, L. (2012). The disparate impact of diabetes on racial/ethnic minority populations. *Clinical Diabetes, 30*(3), 130-133. doi: http://doi.org/10.2337/diaclin.30.3.130

[17]Chrysant, S. G., & Chrysant, G. S. (2015). The cardiovascular consequences of excess sitting time. *The Journal of Clinical Hypertension, 17*(7), 528-531. doi: http://doi.org/10.1111/jch.12519

[18]Creighton, M. J., Goldman, N., Pebley, A. R., & Chung, C. Y. (2012). Durational and generational differences in Mexican immigrant obesity: Is acculturation the explanation? *Social Science & Medicine, 75*(2), 300-310. doi: http://doi.org/10.1016/j.socscimed.2012.03.013

[19]Food Research & Action Center. (2015). *Why low-income and food insecure people are vulnerable to overweight and obesity.* Retrieved from http://frac.org/initiatives/hunger-and-obesity/why-are-low-income-and-food-insecure-people-vulnerable-to-obesity/

[20]Gibbs, L. (2007). Identifying work as a barrier to men's access to chronic illness (arthritis) self-management programs. *International Journal of Men's Health, 6*(2), 143-155.

[21]Gignac, M. A. M., Lacaille, D., Beaton, D. E., Backman, C. L., Cao, X., & Badley, E. M. (2013). Striking a balance: Work-health-personal life conflict in women and men with arthritis and its association with work outcomes. *Journal of Occupational Rehabilitation, 24*(3), 573-584. doi: http://doi.org/10.1007/s10926-013-9490-5

[22]Hara, Y., Hisatomi, M., Ito, H., Nakao, M., Tsuboi, K., & Ishihara, Y. (2014). Effects of gender, age, family support, and treatment on perceived stress and coping of patients with type 2 diabetes mellitus. *BioPsychoSocial Medicine, 8.* doi: 10.1186/1751-0759-8-16

[23]Harrop, C., Shire, S., Gulsrud, A., Chang, Y.C., Ishijima, E., Lawton, K., & Kasari, C. (2015). Does gender influence core deficits in ASD? An investigation into social-communication and play of girls and boys with ASD. *Journal of Autism and Developmental Disorders, 45*(3), 766-777.

[24]Harstad, E. B., Fogler, J., Sideridis, G., Weas, S., Mauras, C., & Barbaresi, W. J. (2014). Comparing diagnostic outcomes of autism spectrum disorder using DSM-IV-TR and DSM-5 criteria. *Journal of Autism and Developmental Disorders, 45*(5), 1437-1450. doi: http://doi.org/10.1007/s10803-014-2306-4

[25]Hudson, R. B. (2012). The class promise in the context of American long-term care policy. In D. Wolfe & N. Folbre (Eds.), *Universal coverage of long-term care in the United States: Can we get there from here?* (pp. 61-78). Chicago, IL: University of Chicago Press

[26]Kogan, M. D. (1995). Social causes of low birth weight. *Journal of the Royal Society of Medicine, 88*(11), 611-615.

[27]Locher, J. L., Ritchie, C. S., Roth, D. L., Baker, P. S., Bodner, E. V., & Allman, R. M. (2005). Social isolation, support, and capital and nutritional risk in an older sample: Ethnic and gender differences. *Social Science & Medicine, 60*(4), 747-761. doi: http://doi.org/10.1016/j.socscimed.2004.06.023

[28]Mamun, A. A., Lawlor, D. A., Alati, R., O'Callaghan, M. J., Williams, G. M., & Najman, J. M. (2007). Increasing body mass index from age 5 to 14 years predicts asthma among adolescents: Evidence from a birth cohort study. *International Journal of Obesity, 31*(4), 578-583.

[29]Monahan, D. J., & Wolf, D. A. (2014). The continuum of disability over the lifespan: The convergence of aging with disability and aging into disability. *Disability and Health Journal, 7*(1), S1-S3. doi: http://doi.org/10.1016/j.dhjo.2013.10.002

[30]Morrison, T. L., & Thomas, R. L. (2015). Comparing men's and women's experiences of work after cancer: A photovoice study. *Supportive Care in Cancer, 23*(10), 3015-3023. doi: http://doi.org/10.1007/s00520-015-2670-4

[31]Murtaugh, C. M., Spillman, B. C., & Wang, X. (2011). Lifetime risk and duration of chronic disease and disability. *Journal of Aging and Health, 23*(3), 554-577. doi: http://doi.org/10.1177/0898264310389491

[32]National Institute of Child Health and Human Development. (n.d). *Common myths about spina bifida - management of myelomeningocele study.* Retrieved from http://www.spinabifidamoms.com/english/myths.html

[33]Negrato, C. A., & Gomes, M. B. (2013). Low birth weight: Causes and consequences. *Diabetology & Metabolic Syndrome, 5*(1), 1-8. doi: http://doi.org/10.1186/1758-5996-5-49

[34]Pelletier, R., Ditto, B., & Pilote, L. (2015). A composite measure of gender and its association with risk factors in patients with premature acute coronary syndrome. *Psychosomatic Medicine, 77*(5), 517-526. doi: http://doi.org/10.1097/PSY.0000000000000186

[35]Piotrowski, K., & Snell, L. (2007). Health needs of women with disabilities across the lifespan. *Journal of Obstetric, Gynecologic, & Neonatal Nursing, 36*(1), 79-87. doi: http://doi.org/10.1111/j.1552-6909.2006.00120.x

[36]Postorino, V., Fatta, L. M., Peppo, L. D., Giovagnoli, G., Armando, M., Vicari, S., & Mazzone, L. (2015). Longitudinal comparison between male and female preschool children with autism spectrum disorder. *Journal of Autism and Developmental Disorders, 45*(7), 2046-2055. doi: http://doi.org/10.1007/s10803-015-2366-0

[37]Reyes, L., & Mañalich, R. (2005). Long-term consequences of low birth weight. *Kidney International, 68*(S97), S107-S111. doi: http://doi.org/10.1111/j.1523-1755.2005.09718.x

[38]Rivet, T., & Matson, J. (2011). Gender differences in core symptomatology in autism spectrum disorders across the lifespan. *Journal of Developmental & Physical Disabilities, 23*(5), 399-420. doi: http://doi.org/10.1007/s10882-011-9235-3

[39]Roebroeck, M., Jahnsen, R., Carona, C., Kent, R., & Chamberlain, M. (2009). Adult outcomes and lifespan issues for people with childhood-onset physical disability. *Developmental Medicine and Child Neurology, 51*(8), 670-9. doi: http://doi.org/10.1111/j.1469-8749.2009.0322.x

[40]Rohlfsen, L. S., & Kronenfeld, J. J. (2014). Gender differences in functional health: Latent curve analysis assessing differential exposure. *The Journals of Gerontology Series B: Psychological Sciences and Social Sciences, 69*(4), 590-602. doi: http://doi.org/10.1093/geronb/gbu021

[41]Schwandt, H. M., Coresh, J., & Hindin, M. J. (2010). Marital status, hypertension, coronary heart disease, diabetes, and death among African American women and men: Incidence and prevalence in the atherosclerosis risk in communities (ARIC) study participants. *Journal of Family Issues, 31*(9), 1211-1229.

[42]Scotch, R. (2001). American disability policy in the twentieth century. In P. K. Longmore, & L. Umansky (Eds.), *The new disability history: American perspectives* (pp. 375-392). New York, NY: NYU Press.

[43]Theis, K. A., Helmick, C. G., & Hootman, J. M. (2007). Arthritis burden and impact are greater among U.S. women than men: Intervention opportunities. *Journal of Women's Health. 16*(4), 441-453. doi: http://doi.org/10.1089/jwh.2007.371

[44]Tsung-Chieh, Y., Liang-Shiou O., Kuo-Wei Y., Wen-I L., Li-Chen C., & Jing-Long H. (2011). Associations of age, gender, and BMI with prevalence of allergic diseases in children: PATCH study. *Journal of Asthma, 48*(5), 503-510. doi: http://doi.org/10.3109/02770903.2011.576743

[45]United Nations Children's Fund. (2013). *The State of the world's children 2013: Children with disabilities*. New York, NY: UNICEF. Retrieved from http://www.unicef.org/publications/files/SWCR2013_ENG_Lo_res_24_Apr_2013.pdf

[46]The World Health Organization. (2011). *Global health and aging*. Retrieved from http://www.who.int/ageing/publications/global_health.pdf?ua=1

[47]The World Health Organization. (2011). *World report on disability*. Retrieved from http://www.who.int/disabilities/world_report/2011/report/en/

[48]The World Health Organization. (2014). *WHO calls for stronger focus on adolescent health.* Retrieved from http://www.who.int/mediacentre/news/releases/2014/focus-adolescent-health/en/

[49]The World Health Organization. (2015). *Cancer.* Retrieved from http://www.who.int/mediacentre/factsheets/fs297/en/

[50]The World Health Organization. (2015). *Controlling the global obesity epidemic.* Retrieved from http://www.who.int/nutrition/topics/obesity/en/

[51]The World Health Organization. (2015). *World health statistics 2014.* Retrieved from http://apps.who.int/iris/bitstream/10665/112739/1/WHO_HIS_HSI_14.1_eng.pdf?ua=1

CHAPTER 3

PUBLIC PERCEPTIONS OF DISABILITY

KATHLEEN M. GLYNN

ANDREA PERKINS NERLICH

MICHAEL P. ACCORDINO

Negative attitudes, social exclusion, and mistreatment of people with disabilities have a long and devastating history. From infanticide to euthanasia, the norm and stability of treatment has varied across cultures and civilizations. Globally, social perceptions and treatment of persons with disabilities are neither homogeneous nor static[52] and cultural and religious beliefs undoubtedly influence perceptions about disability.[19] Over time, negative attitudes have changed and mistreatment has generally shifted from overt and severe, to subtle and hidden. Unfortunately, public perceptions of people with disabilities continue to impact their ability to experience full inclusion in modern society, both in the United States and globally.

Culturally-shaped attitudes toward persons with disabilities pose a significant barrier to full participation in society and access to societal resources. Bogdan and Biklen[9] described this process as "handicapism," or the hidden barriers faced by persons with disabilities from society's unequal treatment based on assumed differences or deficiencies. Haller[36] discussed the similar concept of "ableism, wherein dominant beliefs and practices in a society ignore or negatively stereotype people with disabilities. In 1990, the Americans with Disabilities Act (ADA), a landmark piece of disability legislation in the United States, provided civil rights to protect and provide accessibility for persons with disabilities to employment, public accommodations, state and local government services, and communication. The ADA was expected to impact negative societal attitudes by increasing social interaction between people with and without disabilities.[45] The expected positive effect would be the improvement of public attitudes and perceptions, which consequently, would generate favorable public awareness and disability policy. There is no denying the strides made in the ADA era, however, people with disabilities continue to experience barriers to full inclusion in modern society.

The purpose of this chapter is to demonstrate public perceptions of people with disabilities, which ultimately shape attitudes, treatment, public policy, and society's response to these individuals. Historical perceptions of people with disabilities will be overviewed, but predominant attention will be paid to contemporary perceptions and issues currently facing the disability community, including implications for professionals.

HISTORICAL PERCEPTIONS

Throughout history, treatment of people with disabilities has been less than equal to that of other citizens—ranging from unfair to outright inhumane.[44] In Ancient Greece and other cultures, babies with disabilities were cast off mountain tops or abandoned in the woods. Early perceptions regarding the cause of disability were rooted in the belief that mental and physical disabilities were the result of an individual, or the parents of the individual, being responsible for some act deemed displeasing to the gods. People with disabilities were kept as jesters in the Roman Empire courts, experienced acts of infanticide during the Renaissance, and drowned during the Spanish Inquisition. Although lacking proof, disability was a consequence of a sin. Pelka[59] suggested "the most ancient and most consistently applied framing of disability has been in religious or moral terms: the presence of a disability is perceived as a reflection, sometimes good, often bad, on the character of the disabled individual and as a form of divine judgment on that person's family and community."[p.5] In the United States, people with disabilities were hidden away in cellars and attics, placed in overcrowded institutions and asylums, and not permitted access to education in public schools. Much of this treatment was a result of the burden of care falling on the family. Many who did not have the knowledge and resources to provide adequate care were heavily influenced by medical professionals and clergy urging families toward these ostracizing options.

Two major counter movements to the fair treatment of people with disabilities in the 1800s and 1900s were eugenics and Social Darwinism. Eugenics meaning "good in stock" is essentially the belief that crime, poverty, and disability are influenced by heredity.[55] The method for decreasing and ultimately ending such societal problems, therefore, is through the improvement in the quality of the human race by eliminating certain traits, especially by methods of selective breeding and the prohibition of breeding in certain cases (i.e., where a disability is present, or a genetic link is detected). In the mid-1890s, it was legally forbidden in almost half of the of the United States for people with intellectual or emotional disabilities to marry. Social Darwinism, a concept developed in the mid-1800s by Herbert Spencer, is the belief that it is better for society to allow the poor and weak to perish than to sustain their existence and encourage their multiplication through government supported public relief and health programs. This influential idea swept into the United States during the Eugenics Movement (late 1800s through the early 1900s), when society felt civilization would become doomed if persons with disabilities continue to reproduce. It was further believed that healthy and strong individuals were superior and those who were perceived as unhealthy, weak, and "less than" should be subject to the process of natural selection.

During World War II, many people with disabilities felt the notion of eugenics was being augmented by the issue of euthanasia—a merciful way to end a person's suffering and relieve society of the financial burden of caring for disability treatment. From 1939-41, the Nazi T-4 Euthanasia Program was a systematic program designed to eradicate people with physical and intellectual disabilities through mass murder.[22] During this time, propaganda posters were distributed throughout Germany. One poster featured a medical person in a white coat standing behind a person with a physical disability that read, "60,000 Reichsmarks is what this person suffering from hereditary defects costs the People's community during his lifetime. Fellow Germans, that is your money too." With propaganda such as this, it is evident how society could easily adapt a misconception of disabilities.

Misconception is in the eye of the beholder. Disability is at the forefront of public perception because humans are naturally curious and observers are drawn to differences, something Beatrice Wright[79] referred to as *fundamental negative bias*. Like *fundamental attribution error*, in which an observer attributes the source of a person's behavior to one's personality rather than social influences, fundamental negative bias causes observers to focus on a presumed negative quality linked to disability rather than other circumstances.[17] But, where does this negative attribution stem from, beyond the times where sin and wrongdoing were thought to be the culprit for disability?

ORIGINS OF PERCEPTIONS

The degree to which one stigmatizes a person with a disability is correlated to perceived attributes of the condition and context. A 'hierarchy of stigma' has been proposed as to the degree of prejudice society holds in relation to specific disability categories: least toward physical disability, more for cognitive disability, and the greatest for psychiatric disability.[62] Several other disability dimensions also contribute to the stigmatizing views held by members of society: source/responsibility for the condition, aesthetics, concealability, disruptiveness, perilousness, and course.[17] Digesting a philosophy of 'us v. them' may lead society to conclude persons with a disability are not worthy of empathy and fairness.

How persons acquire their disabilities impacts society's response to them. Societal responses toward persons with disabilities are often determined by the perceived responsibility for the disability.[41] Society's response to the underlying acquired disability can promote empathy and motivation to help, and in some cases, to provide economic contributions. Contracting HIV, for example, can be perceived as permissible if an individual was born with the disease or was a survivor of rape; an individual with HIV may be treated with less respect and concern when society equates one's disease to immoral behavior, such as drug use or indiscriminate sexual activity.[59] Similarly, substance use disorders are widely perceived as 'self-inflicted' disabilities based on lack of willpower or a choice. People with substance use disorders will likely be treated with less compassion in a society with such a perspective, rather than by one that views it as a disease. In addition to responsibility for the condition, those perceived as succumbing to their disability, rather than effectively coping, will be met with less empathy.

The extent to which society perceives persons with disabilities as a threat will influence response. People with a disability can mainly be viewed as a threat in two ways, to personal and/or economic safety. Personal safety can be perceived as threatened due to the notions of uncertainly and unpredictability. For example, individuals with posttraumatic stress disorder, schizophrenia, and bipolar disorder are viewed as erratic in their behaviors.[23] Violence, as a threat to personal safety, is often feared; individuals diagnosed with antisocial personality disorders and adolescents with oppositional defiant disorder have the potential to act out in physical violence.[1] Media images tend to confirm these perceptions, especially when linking mental illness or substance use to violent acts.

Disability is also perceived as a threat to economic security. Communities fear a reduction in property values upon the establishment of high-risk rehabilitation centers, such as mental health or substance use treatment facilities. The construction of a corrections facility or half-way house, for example, may require additional safety patrols, and these facilities may be undesirable to those residing within their immediate proximity. From a human resources perspective, employers may avoid hiring a person with a disability because of a perceived threat to productivity or profit. False assumptions by employers about hiring individuals with disabilities include worrying whether the individual will exceed the maximum days off, cause a rise in insurance rates, or require the investment of additional money to meet the person's needs. From a political perspective, disability is an entitlement burden which taxpayers must support.

Some attitudes toward disability, and inevitably society's response to persons with disabilities, are linked to intrapsychic anxiety on the part of the person without a disability—essentially a fear of 'what if' or what may come. Hahn[34] illustrated this in the phenomena of existential and aesthetic anxiety. *Existential anxiety* refers to the threat people with disabilities represent to people without disabilities. It is anxiety created in the general population through the process of identification with a person with a disability (i.e., people who do not have disabilities identify with what it must be like to have a disability). When one sees a person with a disability, a feeling of uneasiness may result because of the frightening possibility of what that person represents and conscious thoughts, such as "I could be just like him in the blink of an eye." *Aesthetic anxiety*, on the other hand, is driven by society's emphasis on physical beauty and perfection. If people with disabilities deviate from the "norm" in terms of appearance or function, then society's reaction is often avoidance, shunning, or discrimination. The reaction is thought to be justified by this ideal.

Perceptions of disability are also gleaned from models of disability prevalent within systems of our society.

MODELS OF DISABILITY

Smart[63] identified four broad categories of disability definitions: clinical, legal, cultural, and personal. Disability definitions are a relevant part of forming stable and concrete ways to measure the accessibility and eligibility of programs. These definitions are so diverse because of the wide range of disabilities and numerous external factors, though there is no universal definition of disability.[63] Altman[2] posited the difficulty in defining disability is due in part to the fact disability is a complicated and multidimensional concept. Disability is often defined through comparisons to socially constructed notions of "normalcy" in each culture.[14] Daudji and colleagues[14] further suggested these frames of reference in which disabilities are perceived can be shaped by multiple mediating factors including, cultural influences, traditional practices, and personal experiences. The following is an overview of historical disability models prevalent in society.

The functional limitations paradigm:Medical model. The medical definition of disability focuses on the physical way the individual is limited in a functioning society. The medical perspective seems to imply or, in some cases, demand that people with disabilities must adapt and adjust to their surroundings, heeding the advice of expert medical professionals. As such, disability within this model emphasizes diagnosis, treatment, and curative focuses. At the same time, there is no corresponding obligation on the part of policy makers to create an environment to accommodate the needs and desires of those with disabilities.[33] The medical definition situates disability as a problem within the individual and fails to acknowledge the wide range of environmental factors that are often the barriers to full participation and inclusion in society.[42]

The functional limitations paradigm:Economic model. Hahn[33] noted that the economic definition of disability was intended to help people with disabilities engage in substantial gainful activity, most notably employment, by examining the necessary job skills needed to perform different forms of employment. Vocational rehabilitation programs utilize the economic definition in treatment plans and in reporting cases closed as successfully employed. The economic definition continues to place focus on the person's limitations and societal adjustments.

The psychosocial paradigm:Sociopolitical model. Much like the Civil Rights Movement of the 1960s, the sociopolitical definition of disability grew out of the movement of people with disabilities demanding change from society. The social model presents disability as a characteristic rather than a medical problem. In this model, the problem is situated outside of the individual with social barriers (such as lack of accessibility and negative societal attitudes) as responsible for inhibiting full participation in society.[18] Rather than requiring a person with a disability to conform, change, or overcome a disability, society now is responsible for change.

   The Psychosocial paradigm:Minority model. The minority group perspective suggests that the major problems confronting citizens with disabilities are essentially like the difficulties of groups encountering discrimination based on physical attributes, such as race or ethnicity, gender, and age. Americans with disabilities not only have one of the highest rates of unemployment and welfare dependency in the country, but have also been subjugated by segregation in education, transportation, housing, and public accommodations. This approach is founded on a sociopolitical definition that views disability as the product of the interaction between individuals and the environment. The minority-group paradigm is supported by three major postulates:

> ➤ aversive attitudes are the main source of the barriers encountered by persons with disabilities;

> ➤ most aspects of the environment are shaped or molded by public policy; and

> ➤ public policy is, therefore, a reflection of widespread social attitudes.[35]

The minority group model more accurately addresses the aversive attitudes faced by people with disabilities.

SHIFTING TOWARD THE PRESENT DAY

   The more contemporary psychosocial paradigm prevents disability from being seen solely as bodily impairment and moral failing without consideration of social and environmental variables. This model has facilitated a significant change in the way disability has been viewed by society, as well as how people with disabilities can shed light on the social and environmental barriers that inhibit rehabilitation. Consequently, disability becomes an aspect of diversity, like race, ethnicity, sexual orientation, religion, etc. Most importantly, sources of prejudice, stereotypes, and stigma are brought to light.[18]

   In terms of history, one of the eras where people with disabilities were seen in a positive light was during World War II. During this time, not only did people with disabilities demonstrate they could contribute to society by working in factories to produce supplies for the war effort, but in fact, a small group of people with developmental disabilities took part in active combat and were promoted to higher ranks.[49] Even though this group of veterans was institutionalized after the war, these events were a major turning point in attitudes toward disability and created a historical precedent that could be repeated if society's values and attitudes foster it. As we turn now to look at perceptions of disability in the present day, Gallagher and colleagues[27] highlight the societal response to people with disabilities:

> *We humans, particularly those in affluent cultures, seem to abjure inconvenience—and nothing seems to conjure up the dread of inconvenience more than a person who needs more time in comparison with others, whose daily life seems more cumbersome than some of us think it should be, or requires resources other people covet as their own. Freedom, individualism, and independence dominate our cultural ethos to the extent that those who cannot 'keep up' or who 'burden' others are almost unquestioningly seen to be problematic both to themselves and to others. It is not necessarily so. The social model of disability would have us reconsider these cultural values, and perhaps even enjoin us to value the reminder that the most important things in life are not at all about convenience or independence.[p.1134]*

PRESENT DAY PERCEPTIONS

Societal perceptions toward individuals with disabilities are influenced by comparisons made to those without disability. Individuals tend to recognize able-bodiedness as the frame of reference against which to measure ability.[10] This represents a social valuation of ability, where there is greater criticism of those who need assistance or accommodation. Those who do not attain the standard, or at least try to overcome the disability or to reach for the standard, are linked with dependency. This viewpoint reflects *ableism*, prejudicial attitudes and discriminatory behaviors toward persons with disabilities. Society may inadvertently, or perhaps apathetically, discriminate against people with disabilities by not incorporating more universal design in the structure and function of services, transportation, architecture, communication systems, and other public spaces. There is a danger in ableist societies, given the fluid and ubiquitous nature of disability. Pelka[59] reflected on this notion:

> *People with disabilities belong to what is sometimes called "an open minority"—meaning anyone can at any time become disabled, no matter what his or her community of origin…There are, however, also advantages to being "an open minority," which disability activists have put to good use. For one thing, the experience of disability is so*

common (even if generally unacknowledged) that most every extended American family has at least one or more members with a significant disability. This reality cuts across all the other divides of American society.[pp.25-26]

Combating discrimination and the structures of an ableist society have been the foundation for the Disability Rights Movement. Although lobbying and political activism by specific disability groups was occurring early in the 20th century, a broader coalescing of people with disabilities around issues common to the whole disability community began in earnest in the 1970s. Nationwide protests to force the implementation of Section 504 of the Rehabilitation Act of 1973, the Independent Living Movement, and the rise of disability studies as an academic field of inquiry all emerged in this time.[37] Disability rights became a civil rights fight, moving from a place of charity to a position of equality, acknowledging there is no pity or tragedy in the experience of disability. The work of the Disability Rights Movement has brought about mainstreaming in classrooms, civil rights protections for people with disability, advances in technology and Internet access to improve communication and collaboration, and a new ethos of political activism for people with disabilities. On a global level, the United Nations adopted the Convention on the Rights of Persons with Disabilities in 2006, championing the enjoyment of human rights and fundamental freedoms by persons with disabilities.[69] This has led to a contemporary model of disability that defines how a person can have membership in both the general and disability community.

CONTEMPORARY MODEL OF DISABILITY

Important social changes, spearheaded by the increasing influence of the Disability Rights Movement, have promoted a growing search for an alternative to the functional limitations paradigm that has traditionally dominated research and practice. Wright's[78] seminal work was a major contributor to this philosophical shift that is still prevalent today. Wright extended a list of value-laden beliefs and principles about disability, to lend to a constructive view of life with a disability—to be used to guide professional and personal behavior. Among these are a person's fundamental need for respect and encouragement, the impact of the environment and society on the experience of disability, recognition of each person's uniqueness, and the need for a coordinated societal response (i.e., professionals, activist, support groups, citizens) to strive for a better way of life for people with disabilities.

Historical models of disability have received criticism for failing to advance the social and economic position of people with disabilities. Per the functional limitations paradigm, disability resides exclusively with the individual and emphasis is centered on a clinical assessment of a person's remaining skills and abilities. This model fails to focus on problems external to the individual, such as the individual's social and work environment. Opponents of the minority model posit that this model prevents or otherwise makes people with disabilities opposed to getting the necessary help to cope with their conditions, such as special education, because it is viewed as stigmatizing and promoting segregation.[27] As a result, the minority model may create unnecessary obstacles to independence and promote dependency. Others have confronted the efforts to remove labels on people with disabilities as just another form of labeling.[3] What is clear is that there is a major disagreement over how to characterize a "lived" disability experience acceptable to the individual, treatment provider, and advocate. Furthermore, there is a lack of empirical research and evidence to confirm or support the minority model;[48] consequently, much of the evidence that does exist is anecdotal.

New models have emerged that embrace or affirm the collective and personal identities of members of disability culture and these affirmation models replace those that view disability as a tragedy or aberration.[66] Darling[13] put forth the *Typology of Disability Orientations*, recognizing that each person's disability orientation is influenced by identity (pride and shame), model (social and medical), and role (activism and passivity). This model embraces that not all people with disabilities will share the same perspective on the experience, or engage with the Disability Rights community. Darling asserted a new model had to encompass both the normalization model, premised on most people in society having the same goals (i.e., people with disabilities want a lifestyle like those without disability), and the affirmation model, where the disability experience. is valued. The orientation one holds is impacted by differential access to opportunities.

Through an extensive literature review, Darling[13] presented seven orientations varied in the approaches one has access and accepts the norms/goals of the cultural majority and the approaches one has access and accepts the norms/goals of the disability subculture. These orientations exemplify all permutations of a person's desire for affiliation and one's access to participating in that culture/subculture. Individuals can change orientations over their lifetime, given the accumulation knowledge, strengthening of identity, or acquisition or loss of resources. The following describes the typology of the seven orientations (CM refers to norms of the cultural majority; DS refers to the norms of the disability subculture; + indicates has access/accepts; - indicates does not have access or does not accept; +/- indicates may or may not have access):

➤ *Typicality* (CM: + access/acceptance; DS: +/- access and - acceptance): individuals who adopt this orientation accept the norms of larger society, accompanied by resources that allow them to be participants in the culture. Individuals may look to "pass" as those without a disability and are open to medical and technological intervention, although will reject stigmatizing devices (i.e., white cane). One may consider himself to be a person who "happens to have" a disability. Most social interactions are with those who do not have a disability and may reject the societal stigma of disability. While there is not necessarily shame in one's disability identity, there is also no evidence of pride.

➤ *Personal activism* (CM: - access and + acceptance; DS: + access and - acceptance): individuals who adopt this orientation accept the norms of larger society, but do not have access to participate in it. They may become involved in the disability subculture to achieve the *Typicality* orientation. Individuals may engage in disability activism, but only to gain greater access to larger society; once their efforts are successful, they will again strive toward typicality. Their advocacy efforts are not necessarily aligned with the larger disability community, but focused more to regain personal control.

➤ *Affirmative activism* (CM: +/- access and - acceptance; DS: + access/acceptance): individuals who adopt this orientation identify with the disability community to achieve personal goals, but not as a temporary identity status like with *Personal Activism*. Although they seek to gain greater access in society at large, they still view disability as their primary positive identity.

➤ *Situational identification* (CM: + access/acceptance; DS: + access/acceptance): individuals who adopt this orientation can be viewed as "chameleons", able to maintain multiple identities and employ them when most appropriate given the situation. Because this person has both access to and acceptance of both the majority culture and disability subculture, one may choose typicality in interactions with those without disability, but reject this orientation while participating in the disability community. These individuals might not gain as much acceptance with those in the disability community who do not accept larger society.

➤ *Resignation* (CM: - access and + acceptance; DS: - access/acceptance): individuals who adopt this orientation desire *Typicality*, but do not have access to larger society, nor do they have access to or knowledge of disability subculture because of isolation. Those in rural areas, without access to technology, or those living in poverty may encompass this orientation.

> *Apathy* (CM: +/- access and - acceptance; DS: +/- access and - acceptance): individuals who adopt this orientation, theoretically, are apathetic or uninformed regarding the norms of either the majority culture or the disability subculture. Those with significant disabilities, like a severe mental health condition or intellectual disability, may not be able to interpret the stigma or 'differentness' they experience.

> *Isolated affirmative activism* (CM: - access/acceptance; DS: - access and + acceptance): individuals who adopt this orientation may not have access to the disability subculture, but arrive at an affirmative orientation to disability on their own. Given the strength of the Disability Rights Movement, this is not a likely orientation, although those individuals would join in collective activism upon learning of its existence.

This conceptualization of disability describes internal processes to the person, but also incorporates how one expresses a personal identity in interactions. As identity does not occur in isolation, there are many external forces (e.g., controversial medical choices, political agendas, enduring perceptions toward disability). The following will overview contemporary issues impacting perceptions of people with disability to bring the continuing challenges of people with disabilities to the forefront and continue the thoughtful debate on how to advocate for greater equality and inclusion.

CONTEMPORARY TOPICS IN DISABILITY PERCEPTIONS

Memes, media, and inspiration porn. Given the widespread audience reached through mass media, messages conveyed through various outlets play a significant role in shaping public perceptions. Historically, individuals with disabilities were either ignored in mass media or portrayed negatively (e.g. objects of pity, villainous characters). Research on disability portrayals in recent years has revealed several common themes in news media, social media, and Hollywood movies: pathetic, powerless objects of pity; tragic but brave; "supercrip" phenomenon (where someone has a disability, but also some other superpower or skill); overcoming the odds to become heroes or champions; struggle and then accomplishment; inspiration; exceptional accomplishment for everyday activities; and disability as a fate worse than death.[35] These narratives perpetuate stereotypes surrounding disability by reinforcing perceptions on people without disabilities and feeding into the insidious ableist narrative.

More recently a trend in media representation of disability has been towards "inspiration porn." Believed to be coined by the late disability activist Stella Young, the term is used to describe things such as news stories, social media memes, and advertisements that depict a person with a disability often doing something completely ordinary (e.g., walking, running, drawing a picture) or displaying the person showing some type of physical prowess (e.g., lifting a heavy barbell) then captioning it with phrases like "your excuse is invalid" or "before you quit, try."[31] Young[80] explained she deliberately used the term "porn" because the images objectify people with disabilities for the inspiration and motivation of people without disabilities, but essentially do nothing to promote equality or empower individuals with disabilities. One can easily turn on the nightly news or scroll through a social media feed and undoubtedly there will be an inspirational news story or meme related to disability. While on its surface some may interpret this type of representation in media as a step forward; with deeper analysis and hearing perspectives of individuals with disabilities, the messages of these inspirational stories can be harmful as they perpetuate the myth that individuals with disabilities are inspiring for completing ordinary tasks or simply getting out of bed each day. Davis and Thibedeau Boyd[15] suggested two simple ways to easily determine if a particular piece of media falls into this inspiration porn category by asking, "would this story, picture, meme, etc. have the same relevance or meaning if the highlighted individual did not have a disability?" and "Who is the target audience? Is it intended for everyone, including people with disabilities, or is it meant to appeal predominantly to able-bodied people?"

As the use of social media rapidly increases, it has become a primary method of sharing cultural and political views and information, reaching vast numbers of the public. One example of this type of sharing is using memes, an image with a caption circulated through social media platforms; users and their connections can "like" or "share" the image, resulting in a huge number of public spectators viewing these memes in newsfeeds each day, incorporating the content into their thinking. Hadley[32] identified three salient disability meme themes: the charity case meme; the inspiration meme; and the cheat meme. The inspiration meme is exactly what Stella Young described as "inspiration porn" whereas the charity meme is an image of a person with a disability with a caption that pushes the person viewing it to take pity on or help these "poor sufferers" lead better lives. The third theme, the cheat meme, refers to those images of people with disabilities that are captioned with comments suggesting that they are being lazy to get benefits (suggesting if a person can walk, talk, or work they are not truly a person with a disability) and therefore not deserving of things like a wheelchair or accessible parking space.

The type of memes described above essentially do nothing for the disability community in terms of promoting equality, empowerment, or changing negative public perceptions. As such, many in the disability rights community have begun to produce "counter memes," intended to refute the stereotypes being perpetuated and share experiences with other people with disabilities who "get it" (e.g., a picture of a typical white man driving a car captioned with "I love someone with normalcy, share if you love someone with normalcy".[32] Further, the *Stop Making It Weird* campaign (#stopmakingitweird) is a campaign to combat the "weirdness" (often the attitudes, actions and beliefs of people without disabilities have towards people with disabilities) that results in behaviors that make people with disabilities uncomfortable (e.g., clapping only for a person with a disability who presents among a group of able-bodied individuals).[15] Further, many people with disabilities are speaking out against able-bodied television and film actors playing the roles of people with disabilities, roles that are often portrayed inaccurately or overexaggerated by the able-bodied actors. On a positive note, Mellifont,[51] utilizing critical content analysis of news coverage of the inaugural New York City Disability Pride Parade, found several progressive themes the disability community can find encouraging. These themes include calls for social improvements in the treatment of people with disabilities, social inclusion, and solidarity among the disability community. Such pride events and support from those outside the disability community have the potential to bring disability perceptions closer in line with other social justice movements.

DEBATE QUESTIONS

Do "counter" memes, such as those being put out by the disability rights community, have the power to influence perceptions of disability? Why or why not? How might social media be used to combat some of the negative attitudes and stereotypes surrounding disability?

Discuss media portrayals of disability you have seen in recent times, movies, news, and social media. Do you believe these representations are empowering? Damaging? What kind of messages do they send about disability?

How can people with disabilities be represented in the media without falling into the inspiration porn trap? If you enjoy these types of inspirational stories, discuss what you enjoy about them and if you think a person with a disability would enjoy them in the same way.

Being PC: Language and self-representation. Language has the power to influence public perceptions as it shapes our thoughts and behaviors. The words used to define and delineate groups of people are critical as they have significant implications on how individuals within a group, or a cultural group, are perceived. As society evolves and progresses, language also changes, and it can often seem daunting to keep up with what is "politically correct" or preferred in each time or context. Moreover, what is considered politically correct or "PC" may not be what is considered most respectful or empowering to individual members of a culture or group.

Language surrounding disability is no exception and it continues to evolve. Words play a significant role in shaping social perspectives about people with disabilities. Research suggests that disability language can have a direct impact on the self-identity of a person with a disability.[76] This is not surprising given that pejorative terms, such as "feeble minded," "moron," "idiot," "imbecile," and more recently "retard." have been used to refer to individuals with disabilities and, though outdated and offensive, are still often used to describe people, things, or ideas in a negative manner.[75] As noted above, language used in media also has a significant impact on public perceptions. Language used in movie scripts often reflect stereotypes and stigma and are made without concern about the implications of the portrayal of the lives of people with disabilities.[75]

Strides have been made not only to improve the language people use to refer to people with disabilities, but also understanding the impact words have on their self-worth. On a social level, the "R-Word Campaign: Spread the Word to End the Word" has brought attention to the problematic use of the "R" word. On a legislative level, the passage of Rosa's Law signed into law by President Obama in 2010, replaced the term "mentally retarded" with intellectual disability.[63] These actions are important steps forward in recognizing the impact of pejorative language and enacting changes that have gained significant public attention.

Several organizations and agencies have endeavored to establish specific guidelines for the most appropriate and sensitive ways to refer to people with disabilities. Perhaps most notable is The American Psychological Association (APA) endorsing *person-first language* where the person is always put before the disability (e.g., person with autism).[18] The rationale behind person-first language is to reduce stigma, stereotyping, and prejudice towards people with disabilities. Person-first language also suggests avoiding terms like "suffering" and "victim," which perpetuate the assumption that life with disability or illness is always terrible. Does someone with cerebral palsy suffer? Maybe there is suffering in some aspects (as we all experience on some level), but, perhaps in other areas, his or her life is wonderful. Person-first language separates the person from their disability highlighting that above all, people are people first.

While the rationale for using person-first language may seem logical and progressive, there has been opposition from members of the disability community. In response to person-first language, there is a growing movement among the disability rights community, disability culture, and in the field of disability studies to promote the use of *identity-first language* where disability becomes the focus (e.g., disabled people or autistic).[18] The reason identity-first language is so important to individuals with disabilities is that they can claim this piece of their identity with pride, similar to other cultural groups. Proponents of identity-first language argue that the "politically correct" person-first language promotes the perception that disability should be separated from the person and therefore implies that disability is bad or shameful. Examples of proponents of identity-first language are individuals who identify as "autistic" or are part of Deaf culture, who consider themselves a linguistic minority using American Sign Language, viewing deafness as a dimension of diversity to be celebrated, versus a deficit. The National Federation for the Blind has rejected person-first language as they believe that blindness is nothing to be ashamed of and by separating it from the person insinuates that it is undesirable or troublesome.[75]

When we consider these two linguistic approaches, the differences can be better understood in the context of the previously discussed models of disability. Person-first language was born out of the social model whereas identity-first language out of the minority group model. Preference in language will likely depend on which model one operates from and how one views their individual disability (and overall) identity. While the debate about language continues to evolve and in time we may see a new camp of preferred language, the more important piece to remember is the underlying attitudes and messages spread through the language we use. Professionals who understand that language has the power to influence perceptions and attitudes will be more cognizant of the words they use. Further, counselors and professionals working with individuals with disabilities should get to know each individual and his or her preference.

DEBATE QUESTIONS

> *Discuss the pros and cons of using person-first language and identity-first language as a counseling professional. What are some potential consequences of subscribing to one or the other?*

> ➤ *Thinking about language and attitudes, discuss the influence language has in shaping attitudes and how attitudes shape language. Is one more powerful than the other?*

> ➤ *Discuss who you believe has the strongest influence on the language we use. Family? Friends? Media?*

Harm reduction. Public opinion surrounding those who engage in intravenous drug use has been historically poor. Fears related to intravenous drug use include disease transmission, littering of dangerous needles, and overdose. Much of the overall perception comes from deep-seated negative views toward drug use, seen by many as a moral failing or one in which a user lacks self-control.[5] Public perceptions impact on public policy and the overall milieu around drug culture, making it difficult for those with substance use disorders to seek services or reduce the harm associated with the drug use. In contrast, countries with a greater tolerance and more pragmatic view around harm reduction, like the Netherlands, provide testing services and education about safer drug use, resulting in less misuse of the substances.[70]

Harm reduction is a principle that acknowledges the reality that drug use often continues despite treatment efforts. On the path to treating a substance use disorder and stopping substance misuse, the intermediary goal is to reduce the negative consequences of drug use, such as opioid overdose and the spread of disease.[7] Two forms of harm reduction, needle exchange programs (NEPs) and take-home naloxone, have been met with resistance. Negative perceptions of these interventions are commonly based on the concern these programs condone, or even promote, illegal drug use, and do nothing to re-integrate people who use drugs back into society.[60] However, changing perceptions about these programs involves acknowledging substance use and its related issues (e.g., poverty, disease, crime) requires a more practical solution beyond mere drug enforcement and control.

Needle exchange programs have been a controversial public health strategy, as this intervention seemed antithetical to the "war on drugs," and would perhaps cause a rise in drug use by removing obstacles.[74] However, research has demonstrated a reduced rate of HIV transmission without increasing drug usage in areas with NEPs. This information was not enough to stem negative opinions of NEPs because of their link to drug use and drug control efforts. National public policy was slow to come on board with support for needle exchange, but with a situation such as this, a national issue is not a local problem, until it is. Local support for needle exchange has come through viewing NEPs and syringe access interventions as a health policy, not a drug control policy, to reduce the stigma around the intervention and contain health care costs.[71] For example, in March of 2015, then-Governor Mike Pence of Indiana declared a public health emergency because of an outbreak of 185 new cases of HIV in the southeastern part of the state.[74] Despite his moral opposition, he called for the opening and funding of temporary NEPs so intravenous drug users could dispose of used syringes and obtain sterile ones. National law was passed by Congress in December of 2015 to fund NEPs in response to rapidly rising rates of injection drug use across the country, although the costs of the syringes themselves are not covered in the bill, only the funding of the programs.

Take-home naloxone, an opioid antagonist, is approved for administration by nonmedically trained people who may witness opioid overdose. The purpose of naloxone is to counteract the effects of acute opioid overdose until medical attention can be sought. Naloxone itself does not have a psychoactive effect and presents no potential for abuse.[7] Worldwide, an average of 48% of those who consume opioids have experienced a nonfatal overdose, with 90% having witnessed an overdose.[24] The United States is currently faced with an opioid epidemic that resulted in 63,600 overdose deaths in 2016 alone.[39] Communities with trained naloxone responders have seen a decrease in opioid fatalities through overdose reversals. Critics of naloxone interventions argue that individuals who use opioids will rely on naloxone to rescue them, and it is futile to save them because they will continue to use.[5] Those who potentially could administer naloxone, like other co-users or medical professionals, are wary of doing so and calling emergency services for fear of arrest or malpractice. However, many states have now extended "good Samaritan" provisions to protect these individuals.[24]

Public opinion surrounding naloxone has not been as positive as that for NEPs, as preventing disease prevents a high cost to society, whereas reducing drug-related death does not produce a clear economic benefit.[7] Messaging around support of these harm reduction techniques must create a personal connection to the public to increase support for them. Bachhuber and colleagues[5] found that coupling factual information on naloxone with the sympathetic narrative of a person who lost a loved one to overdose led to significantly higher support for naloxone policies and its use. The strategy of humanizing those who use substances and basing the message around human rights should lessen the gap between "us" and "them."[60]

DEBATE QUESTIONS

Do harm reduction interventions condone drug use? Even if data suggests they do not increase drug use, does it not "send the wrong message?"

Discuss how you would shape advocacy efforts and messages around support for harm reduction interventions. Consider how you would reach your most staunch opponents.

Bioethics and genetic testing. As noted earlier, the U.S. has a significant history of practicing eugenics, becoming a leader in the movement in the early 1900s, where practices such as separating "undesirables" from the general populations in state institutions, as well as sterilizing individuals with disabilities without their consent to "clean the gene pool" were all too common.[75] While these early practices may seem unthinkable today, current bioethical issues such as genetic counseling, prenatal testing, and the aborting of fetuses deemed "impaired" are generally considered eugenic.[65] *Genetic counseling* is a process used to evaluate and understand an individual or family's chances of inheriting a genetic medical condition wherein a genetic counselor meets with individuals and families to discuss genetic "risks" of developing a disability. *Prenatal testing* provides information about the health of a fetus before it is born. Nowadays, pregnant women are routinely given several options for prenatal tests, including those that are noninvasive, and tests are increasingly more specific in their ability to detect genetic conditions. *Disability-selective abortion* is the choice to terminate a pregnancy due to the detection of a genetic anomaly (i.e., after learning the results of a prenatal test).[54]

Widespread public recognition of bioethical issues arose during and after World War II where the now well-known abuses of vulnerable populations occurred.[4] Today, many people without disabilities continue to view disability from the medical model and therefore perceive bioethical dilemmas much differently than those in the disability community who view them from the sociopolitical or minority group models.[63] As such, there is a divide between bioethics and disability rights when it comes to issues such as assisted suicide, infanticide, prenatal testing, and disability-selective abortion. Turner[68] discussed bioethical issues in the context of dominant social narratives throughout history that are based on the widespread notion that living with disability is undesirable, underscoring how these narratives have essentially shaped and fostered the development of the technologies we have today to detect and prevent genetic anomaly.

Currently, some nations (e.g., the Netherlands) practice euthanasia by starving, dehydrating, denying lifesaving surgeries, or administering lethal injections to babies with disabilities.[63] Domestically, Princeton professor Peter Singer, a philosopher who has written about bioethical issues, is an outspoken advocate for abortion and euthanasia of babies identified with certain types of disabilities, as well as for death for anyone (of any age) who has a severe disability.[63] Singer is a strong believer that life with a disability is equated with suffering and misery, therefore not worth living. Even when personally confronted by Harriet McBryde Johnson, a lawyer with a disability who refuted Singer's views, his perception that her life was pitiful remained unchanged.[29] Although Singer's views may appear more provocative and overt than the average person without a disability, his perceptions echo a widespread public assumption about living a life with a disability.

Although there is controversy and struggle between Disability Rights activists and scholars and those in traditional bioethics, one area of intersectionality lies with autonomy, with both camps proponents of the individual's right to make one's own choices.[4] However, those in the disability rights community look beyond the simple right to autonomy to critically examine how widespread negative perceptions about life with disability are at the root of these bioethical issues, and in turn view ending life due to the presence of disability as legal discrimination. Standard bioethics tends to generalize that life disrupted by disability or illness is hopelessly tragic, while ignoring how rehabilitation, adaptation, and changes in life pursuits can enhance quality of life. Additionally, bioethics also fails to recognize the extent to which people with disabilities experience disadvantages due to the barriers located within society.[4] Garland-Thompson[28] argued that disability is inherent to the human condition, a dimension of diversity to be valued, and that bioethical questions about preventing life with disability are rooted in eugenic logic. Rather than focusing on why disability should be eliminated, Garland-Thompson raised the bioethical question of why we might want to *conserve*, rather than *eliminate*, disability in our world with counter eugenic arguments; this shifts thinking of disability as a *deficit* to a *benefit* and a contribution to society. These benefits and contributions include educating others about their experiences through the rich narratives and perspectives of people with disabilities, in the unique position of living in a society that was not necessarily designed for them.

Steinbach and colleagues[64] examined public perceptions of disability in connection with noninvasive prenatal genetic screening (NIPS), interventions widely available for screening for Down Syndrome along with an expanding list of other genetic conditions. In this study, participants supported the availability of these tests regardless of their attitude towards disability. Although some participants did not link disability to their support of NIPS, a majority of those who did presented disability as something that is exclusively burdensome: a hardship on the individual, their family, and on society. Potential harmful implications of individual genetic testing have been raised, such as the misuse of individual genetic information easily leading to group stigmatization, particularly for individuals in vulnerable groups if genetic information is used to reinforce prejudice.[20]

Given the widespread bias about life with disability in our society, there is a need for education for genetic professionals and obstetric providers about what life with disability is really like to fully provide their patients and clients with true informed consent.[58] All too often families are not given information about resources, supports, or even narratives from families whose lives have been enriched by their family member with a disability.

DEBATE QUESTIONS

Prenatal testing is routinely offered to pregnant women as part of their prenatal care. What type of information should be given to mothers and partners before and after these tests?

Autonomy is one area where bioethics and disability rights overlap. Discuss how the argument of autonomy, in bioethical debates and implications for people with disabilities, is used as a rationale for practices discussed in this section.

Do you believe genetic testing has the potential to eliminate or greatly reduce the population of individuals who live with genetic conditions in our society? If so, how might this loss impact society as a whole?

Violence and mental health. Stigma and perceptions related to mental health conditions lead individuals to avoid and discriminate against those living with the conditions. Stigma results in individuals withdrawing socially, experiencing shame in the diagnosis, avoiding treatment, and experiencing myriad negative outcomes,[57] in addition to negative perceptions a person attributes to oneself once a mental health condition manifests.[11] Lifetime prevalence for having any mental condition is 58.7% using retrospective studies, indicating that over half of people will meet the criteria for a mental condition in their lifetime.[47] Such high prevalence makes it difficult to sustain negative impressions regarding mental health conditions, given the likelihood of eventually having a condition or loving someone who does.

An overarching concern regarding those living with mental health conditions is that of dangerousness, either through violence toward others or perceived criminality. For example, in a survey about public attitudes toward disability, most respondents recognized schizophrenia as a mental health condition (85%) and that individuals living with the condition could lead independent lives through ongoing care (79%); however, nearly two-thirds of respondents felt that violent behavior (60%) was a given symptom.[53] The attributable risk of mental health conditions and violence equates only to an average of 5% across several nations.[1] Most individuals with schizophrenia are not prone to violence and typically withdraw from most social interactions; those who are violent, often experience their condition co-morbid to substance use or psychosis. Substance use disorder and prior violence tend to be better predictors of violence than the presence of a psychiatric diagnosis alone.[1]

The public relies on media and news to provide crucial information about the state of affairs in the country and the world. However, the news media, and those featured, can quickly influence perceptions of mental health conditions through a few mere sound bites. For example, media consistently portray the perpetrators of mass shootings to be Caucasian and have a mental health condition. In a comprehensive review of 152 cases of mass murder in the United States, Taylor[67] found mental health reasons to be the motivation for committing the offenses in only 29.6% of the cases. Perpetrators were disproportionately male and less than half of them were Caucasian. Most mass shootings were motivated by a triggering event (e.g., relationship issue, financial crisis). Even if the person experienced mental health concerns, that was not the reason for the attack; rather, the triggering event was the proverbial "straw that broke the camel's back." However, rather than searching for the reason or motivation behind a mass shooting, media personnel often seek out evidence of mental health conditions to explain the event, falling prey to a confirmatory bias and desire to sensationalize.[1]

Agenda-setting theory is the lens through which to understand the impact of media on public perceptions toward mental health and violence. According to this theory, "salience of messages in the media transfers to the public. Said another way, people spend more time thinking about the ideas that are prominent in the news."[77, p.645] Therefore, when the media increase their coverage of incidences finding a connection between mental health and a mass shooting, the public naturally creates a perception about the link between psychological conditions and violence, increasing negative attitudes toward this group. The public's belief about this association is unfounded, as research continues to provide evidence of low incidences of violence by people with mental health conditions, though the negative stigma toward people with psychiatric disabilities directly relates to the known fact that these individuals are more likely to be victims of violence rather than the perpetrators.[77]

Improper emphasis on mental health conditions as the root of violence, in most cases, results in a politicizing of the issue and subsequent unwarranted policies. In 2015, during an interview related to a mass shooting in Oregon, then front-running Republican candidate Donald Trump stated on *Meet the Press* that "it's not a gun problem, it's a mental illness problem," continuing his campaign message that mass shootings and gun violence are more related to broken mental health systems than proof of the need for tighter gun control laws.[72] In response to a mass shooting at a Texas church in 2017, President Trump again intimated the tragedy was not a gun issue, but "a mental health problem at the highest level."[73] Ahonen and colleagues[1] found, through literature review and interviews with international mental health research experts, the link between violence (especially gun violence) and mental health conditions is weak, even weaker when substance use is considered. In addition, the research has shown that conduct disorder and antisocial personality disorder are the only two conditions that are more common precursors to violence.

Remedies to misperceptions about the violence risk of people with psychiatric disabilities begin with understanding the universal nature of mental health conditions. Emphasizing their high prevalence can begin to lessen the stigma surrounding the conditions and demystify the risk,[47] though a medical approach to these messages has proven to be less than successful.[43] Developing anti-stigma campaigns that promote public awareness and knowledge, providing better treatment for those living with mental health conditions, promoting evidence-based practices, and investing in research are all ways to stem the tide of stigma.[53] One such effort is Mental Health First Aid, which trains professionals, peers, caregivers, and citizens to recognize and respond to the signs of mental distress.[16] With suicide the 10th leading cause of death in this country, intervention is critical. For professionals, there is heightened need for better screening for the risk of violence, as this is proven to be a stronger predictor of future violence. There is less accuracy when employing strict clinical judgment for this assessment, but most screening instruments are not validated on psychiatric populations.[1] Improved, validated assessment measures will assist in the crusade toward preventative care.

DEBATE QUESTIONS

➢ *Given the proliferation of negative, inaccurate portrayals of individuals with psychiatric disability and their link to violence, how do mental health advocates combat and address this phenomenon?*

➢ *What is the responsibility of people with power to accurately portray the risk of people with mental health conditions and correct negative perceptions? Is it irresponsible of government leaders to not fact check their assumptions and mislead the public for political gain?*

Sexuality and parenting with a disability. Despite being a fundamental aspect of human existence, sexuality is not typically discussed in conversations around disability, rendering it taboo, deviant, or nonexistent.[26] In most circumstances, people with disabilities are regarded as asexual beings; if a sexual existence is acknowledged, it is assumed one is heterosexual. Human rights for people with disabilities have come to the forefront, however, the forbidden nature of sexuality has relegated sexual rights for people with disabilities to a secondary rights issue.[21] While unemployment and discrimination in public services do have an impact that permeates a person's life, sexuality must also be a basic necessity for those who value it. Public perceptions must change for these barriers to be overcome.

Stigma around sexuality varies depending upon the nature of the disability. Those with physical disabilities, such as spinal cord injury, are assumed to not be able to engage in sexual activity. Those with 'hidden' disabilities, like psychiatric disabilities or neurological conditions, are likely to not have trouble in the function of sexual performance, but research shows that others are less likely to feel comfortable in romantic or sexual relationships with them.[21] Adults with developmental disabilities are typically prevented from romantic and sexual relationships/expression because of perceived risk and vulnerability;[26] oftentimes, even innocent hand holding is discouraged. Individuals with developmental disabilities have little sexual knowledge and education, especially related to contraception, sexual health, and legal sexual rights (e.g., marriage, abortion, right to consent). Some feel that individuals with developmental disabilities do not have the cognitive ability to consent to sex, necessitating a caregiver to provide consent, while others consider surrogate consent a denial of sexual rights.[61] In defending the practice of sterilization, some have even offered that individuals would experience greater freedom and independence if the risk of pregnancy were removed, though most view sterilization without consent as a form of violence or inhumane treatment.[6]

The potential outcome of sexuality, pregnancy and parenting with a disability challenges longstanding societal assumptions. Throughout history, people with disabilities have endured forced sterilization or loss of parental rights, given assumptions of perpetuating disability genes or unfit parenting, assumptions that are wholly unfounded. For example, mothers with disabilities including Deaf mothers experience higher rates of state government intervention, even though these parents are no more likely to engage in neglect or maltreatment.[25] Each year, over 44,000 American women with severe mobility disabilities report being pregnant. Iezzoni and colleagues[42] investigated the public responses to these women during their pregnancy and subsequent motherhood. Many women reported that onlookers were curious, intrusively curious, or hostile regarding their circumstance. Some openly questioned how the pregnancy occurred, as though it was different than typical conception. Others gave "dirty looks" or made comments about bringing a child with disabilities into the world, though most women did not have a genetic disability that could be passed on to their child. Some acted oblivious to the mothers, refusing to acknowledge their pregnancy, as if it was not possible. Some reported that onlookers made comments related to their competency as a mother, with one stating a health care provider reported her to social services, despite no evidence of negligence. Overall, mothers with disabilities stated they could not imagine nondisabled women being subjected to similar public reactions and queries, although many had grown accustomed to these encounters, combating them with humor, irony, and sarcasm.

Improved perceptions regarding disability and sexuality are driven by education and knowledge. Factors related to greater staff acceptance of sexual behavior by those with intellectual disabilities included younger caregiver age, less religiosity, and more education and training. Lack of sex education training on the part of staff perpetuates negative perceptions toward client sexuality because they are unprepared to handle situations in an appropriate way and provide effective counseling and intervention.[61] Better staff training is the first line of action to provide better sex and sexuality education to consumers with disabilities. People also generally do not have access to sex-positive messages regarding disability. Exposure to positive sexual images of people with disabilities, including documentary films, reality-based television programming, and better portrayals in movies, would improve impressions of individuals with disabilities and normalize sexuality.

DEBATE QUESTIONS

> *In a time of such sexual liberation and dialogue, what about disability and sexuality keeps individuals with disabilities from being included in this movement? What can be done to change this impression?*

> *After a long history of "being my brother's keeper," how can we change impressions of sexuality for individuals with developmental disabilities, so they can explore and express it in safe and meaningful ways?*

Dying with dignity and end-of-life decisions. In the U.S., ongoing debates surround end-of-life decisions for people with disabilities who are considered terminally ill, including euthanasia, assisted suicide (also referred to as "aid in dying" or "death with dignity"), and futile care (i.e., involuntarily withholding life-sustaining treatment). Currently, six U.S. states permit physician-assisted suicide wherein a physician prescribes a lethal dose of drugs to an individual who wishes to end his or her life. Several states, such as New Mexico, Montana, California, and Texas, have introduced legislation to legalize some form of euthanasia. In an ableist society where many barriers exist, and negative attitudes remain, it is plausible that the general public might conclude that living with a disability would be painful and unbearable. A primary reason many support legalization of assisted suicide is to eliminate intractable pain and suffering. However, in Oregon, the first state to legalize assisted suicide, pain was rarely one of the reasons people requested the intervention. Rather, it was psychosocial factors such as loss of autonomy, decrease of engagement in activities, loss of dignity, and feelings of being a burden that were reported by Oregon physicians as reasons for issuing lethal prescriptions.[12] In Oregon, physicians (presumably operating from the medical model) are the gatekeepers to who can end their life. In such a system, people without disabilities who ask for death are provided suicide prevention services, and people who have disabilities receive lethal prescriptions. This kind of double standard underscores the pervasive societal view that life with disability is not worth living.

Several high-profile bioethical end-of-life cases, such as those surrounding Dr. Jack Kevorkian, Terry Shiavo and more recently, Brittany Maynard, have been brought to the attention of the public through mainstream media, which has sparked national debate on these end-of-life issues. Haller[36] pointed out the salient "better off dead than disabled" attitude prevalent in society is reflected in news media surrounding the assisted suicide debate with little discussion of alternatives aimed at improving quality of life, such as independent living options, treatment for clinical depression, or better pain management and palliative care. Krahn[46] further suggested that such laws allowing the right to die based on functional dependence are discriminatory and devalue the many lives of people with disabilities who experience functional limitations.

Disability rights groups such as "Not Dead Yet" actively oppose such legislation and suggest such laws set up a double standard wherein some people get suicide prevention and others get suicide assistance simply based on the health status of the individual, arguing this is discrimination under the ADA.[12,63] Unfortunately, the narratives of groups like Not Dead Yet are not often highlighted in the mainstream media and therefore do not often reach a large portion of the general public. Rather, groups such as Autonomy, Inc. and Compassion and Choices have dominated the narrative,[12] and have subsequently had a central role in introducing laws in many states that would legalize aid in dying, continuing the myth that life with disability is not worth living and potentially threaten the lives of people with disabilities.

Given the devaluation of people with disabilities through the "fate worse than death" perception and the push towards cost savings in managed care bureaucracies,[30] individuals living with disabilities may fear that at some point, their lives may be terminated against their will. This fear is based not on the belief that society will overtly target people due to their disabilities per se, as was done during the Nazi Regime, but that society will offer euthanasia as an option to save a loved one with a serious disability from financial burden, remove family members from stressful care giver roles, and provide an option to cease being a financial burden on the state. Given that in Oregon there is no formal monitoring or control once a lethal prescription has been written, there are additional fears for individuals with disabilities who may be in situations where they are coerced into taking, or given, lethal dose against their will.

DEBATE QUESTIONS

> *If you were working with an individual who expressed their desire to seek out assisted suicide, given your understanding of the disability rights view on this issue, how would you respond? Which ethical principles are at play in such a scenario?*

> *Discuss ways the widespread "fate worse than death" perception many people without disabilities hold could be diminished.*

Harassment and Bullying. Anecdotally, many consider experiences of mild bullying a rite of passage, akin to 'boys will be boys' and 'that's just part of growing up.' However, harassment, bullying, and peer aggression can lead to negative emotional, physical, and academic consequences for the victims.[38,50] What may be viewed as 'harmless fun' perpetrated by youth, is in fact a violation of students' civil rights under federal antidiscrimination law. Bullying, in general terms, is characterized by:

> intent to harm;

> repeated occurrence of aggression, or the potential to repeat; and

> an imbalance of power, although the exact perception of bullying may vary across cultures and contexts.[56]

Bullying and harassment can be physical, verbal, or, more recently, cyber-based aggressive actions or indirect exclusion. Prevalence of bullying and harassment peaks in middle school, with a tapering off in the high school years;[8] although, there may be greater prevalence of online victimization in the high school environment with greater access to unsupervised technology.

Disability harassment is defined as "the unwelcome bothering, tormenting, troubling, ridiculing or coercing of another person related to the disability of that person and is composed of verbal behavior or gestures distinguished from physical violence or force."[40, p.3] Bullying and victimization would elevate the action to include physical aggression. Students with disabilities report three types of bullying, in the real and virtual worlds:

> marginalization (e.g., patronizing, ignoring, speaking slowly),

> denigration (e.g., mocking, goading into breaking a rule), and

> intimidation (e.g., threatening, tripping, hitting).[56]

Victimization of students with disabilities can have compound lifetime impact for this group, as poorer outcomes in relation to the general population already exist in the areas of high school completion, postsecondary degree attainment, and employment.

In a study of the retrospective middle and high school bullying experiences of college students with disabilities, McNicholas and colleagues[50] found two-thirds of their participants reported being subjected to peer victimization *sometimes, frequently,* or *constantly,* compared to national averages for middle and high school students in a range of 20-26%. Research also finds teachers and adult staff are more likely to verbally, relationally, or physically bully students with disabilities, as opposed to typical students, contributing to a school culture where these actions are socially acceptable.[38] Negative consequences related to disability harassment in the transition years include decreased attendance, not attempting gainful employment, and/or dropping out of the workforce if harassment is experienced on a future job.[40] Those with disabilities impacting socialization skills, like intellectual disabilities and autism spectrum disorders, are more vulnerable to victimization because they have a limited social network for peer support, cannot articulate their need for help well, and lack conversational skills to diffuse difficult encounters.[8] Those with more visible disabilities also experience higher rates of victimization.

Students who have supportive relationships with peers, family, and staff experience less peer victimization. Family and peer support have a stronger impact, given the closeness of relationships from an ecological perspective.[50] Peer acceptance, however, is paramount at this developmental stage for youth and could serve as a more significant buffer and resource against bullying. Parental support and advocacy does play a part in role modeling confidence and self-advocacy within the student. Students with disabilities who are taught effective coping skills for addressing harassment, such as problem solving, self-advocacy, distancing, and telling an adult, fare better in the face of victimization.[38]

Environments that do not address social inequities of students with disabilities perpetrate the dominant cultural message that stigmatizing and targeting these students is permissible.[38] School and workplace cultures that tolerate general incivility and harassment of others based on diversity characteristics are more likely to foster disability harassment.[40] School policies that clearly delineate rules and consequences for peer victimization lead to positive school climate, an atmosphere of trust and respect, and lower incidence of bullying.[50] Derogatory language aimed at students with disabilities is viewed as a form of bullying; campaigns for person-first language and movements like "Spread the Word" are in line with anti-bullying curricula seeking to create positive learning environments.[75] Better training for staff, teachers, and counselors on recognizing the signs of bullying, increasing awareness of its prevalence, and intervening in effective ways are suggested as a better defense within the school setting.[56]

DEBATE QUESTIONS

What interventions and policies should be instituted to create positive, anti-bullying school climates? Could a standard model be used, or should each school address the issue at the local level?

While bullying is never permissible, acts perpetrated by adults appear to be a far worse offense than those enacted by peers. How should teachers and staff who engage in bullying be disciplined and corrected?

IMPLICATIONS FOR COUNSELING

Counselors are poised to combat negative perceptions toward people with disabilities on an individual level with the consumers served, as well as on a community or society-level through professional behavior and advocacy efforts. Modeling appropriate attitudes and behavior will serve to normalize perceptions toward disability and hopefully open others to being more inclusive in their relationships and personal interactions.

➢ Counselors working with people with disabilities should operate from an asset-based approach.[17] Assist the person in focusing on the tangible and intangible factors that are strengths and sources of pride for the person. This can be personality attributes (e.g., humor, courage), achievements (e.g., degrees, awards), and skills/talents (e.g., sports, writing) that can be highlighted as a person is adjusting to one's disability. These positive points can be used as the foundation for socialization, relationship building, and community involvement.

➤ People with disabilities are more likely targets of bullying and harassment than people without disabilities. This can impact on a person's self-esteem, confidence, and perceptions of safety. Routine screening and assessment of bullying should be conducted with new and continuing clients to determine the impact of previous experiences, address the feelings associated with this, and assist individuals to develop skills to combat against future experiences.[39] New disability-specific screening measures should be developed, as 60% of students indicated victimization was directly related to their disability.[50]

➤ It is acknowledged language plays a central role in the development of perceptions. Counselors should remain cognizant of the evolving nature of language and are encouraged to get to know the preferred terminology of the individuals with whom they work.[18] Taking a lead from the APA, counselors should err on the side of person-first language to be respectful, but mirror the language preferences of clients who ascribe to identity-first language. In all cases, it is appropriate to ask what terminology is preferred, given that self-expressions may differ.

➤ Counselors should be aware of the portrayals of people with disabilities in the media, especially social media. Messaging around disability events and disability rights should be strengths-based and not rely on memes and slogans meant to engender pity, charity, or use inspiration inappropriately. Advocate for better media portrayals and educate others; the use of "counter" memes is one way to combat stereotypes and challenge others to think critically about using people with disabilities to make themselves motivated or inspired.[32]

➤ Counselors should engage in professional discussions regarding bioethical issues, raising questions with health care providers about the assumptions made regarding life with disability. Encourage consumers to self-advocate and share their narratives to challenge these perspectives. Use the sociopolitical and minority models, disability pride, and Garland-Thompson's[28] notion of "conserving" disability to offer alternative platforms to the medical model to frame these arguments.

REFERENCES

[1]Ahonen, L., Loeber, R., & Brent, D. A. (2017). The association between serious mental health problems and violence: Some common assumptions and misconceptions. *Trauma, Violence, & Abuse.* Advance online publication. doi: 10.1177/1524838017726423

[2]Altman, B. M. (2001). Disability definitions, models, classification schemes, and applications. In G. L. Albrecht, K. D. Seelman, & M. Bury, *Handbook of disability studies* (pp. 97-122). Thousand Oaks, CA: Sage Publications.

[3]Anastasiou, D., & Kauffman, J. K. (2011). A social constructionist approach to disability: Implications for special education. *Exceptional Children, 77*(3), 367–384.

[4]Asch, A. (2001). Disability, bioethics, and human rights. In G. L. Albrecht, K. D. Seelman, & M. Bury, *Handbook of disability studies* (pp. 297-326). Thousand Oaks, CA: Sage Publications.

[5]Bachhuber, M. A., McGinty, E. E., Kennedy-Hendricks, A., Niederdeppe, J., & Barry, C. L. (2015). Messaging to increase public support for naloxone distribution policies in the United States: Results from a randomized survey experiment. *PLOS One.* doi: 10.1371/journl.pone.0130050.

[6]Barton-Hanson, R. (2015). Sterilization of men with intellectual disabilities: Whose best interest anyway? *Medical Law International, 15*, 49-73.

[7]Bazazi, A. R., Zaller, N. D., Fu, J. J., & Rich, J. D. (2010). Preventing opiate overdose deaths: Examining objections to take-home naloxone. *Journal of Health Care Poor Underserved, 21*, 1108-1113.

[8]Blake, J. J., Lund, E. M., Zhou, Q., Kwok, O., & Benz, M. R. (2015). National prevalence rates of bully victimization among students with disabilities in the United States. *School Psychology Quarterly, 27*, 210-222.

[9]Bogdan, R., & Biklen, D. (1977). Handicapism. *Social Policy, 5*(5), 14-19.

[10]Brittain, I., & Beacom, A. (2016). Leveraging the London 2012 Paralympic Games: What legacy for disabled people? *Journal of Sport and Social Issues, 40*, 499-521.

[11]Centers for Disease Control and Prevention, Substance Abuse and Mental Health Services Administration, National Association of County Behavioral Health & Developmental Disability Directors, National Institute of Mental Health, & The Carter Center Mental Health Program. (2012). *Attitudes toward mental illness: Results from the behavioral risk factor surveillance system.* Atlanta, GA: Centers for Disease Control and Prevention.

[12]Coleman, D. (2010). Assisted suicide laws create discriminatory double standard for who gets suicide prevention and who gets suicide assistance: Not Dead Yet Responds to Autonomy, Inc. *Disability and Health Journal, 3*, 39-50.

[13]Darling, R. B. (2013). *Disability and identity: Negotiating self in a changing society.* Boulder, CO: Lynne Rienner Publishers.

[14]Daudji, A., Eby, S., Foo, T., Ladak, F., Sinclair, C., Landry, M. D., & Gibson, B. E. (2011). Perceptions of disability among south Asian immigrant mothers of children with disabilities in Canada: Implications for rehabilitation service delivery. *Disability and Rehabilitation, 33*(6), 511-521.

[15]Davis, C. J, & Thibedeau Boyd, J. M. (2017). Stop making it weird: Why I'm not clapping. *Journal of Vocational Rehabilitation, 46,* 321-325.

[16]Drexler, P. (2016, January 8). Why do we fear mental illness? [Blog post]. Retrieved from https://www.psychologytoday.com/blog/our-gender-ourselves/201601/why-do-we-fear-mental-illness

[17]Dunn, D. S. (2016). Teaching about psychosocial aspects of disability: Emphasizing person-environment relations. *Teaching of Psychology, 43,* 255-262.

[18]Dunn, D. S., & Andrews, E. E. (2015). Person-first *and* identity-first language: Developing psychologists' cultural competence using disability language. *American Psychologist, 70,* 255-264.

[19]Edwardraj, S., Mumtaj, K., Prasad, J. H., Kuruvilla, A., & Jacob, K. S. (2010). Perceptions about intellectual disability: A qualitative study from Vellore, South India. *Journal of Intellectual Disability Research, 54*(8), 736-748.

[20]Eltis, K. (2007). Genetic determinism and discrimination: A call to re-orient prevailing human rights discourse to better comport with the public implications of individual genetic testing. *Journal of Law, Medicine & Ethics, 35,* 282-294.

[21]Esmail, S., Darry, K., Walter, A., & Knupp, H. (2010). Attitudes and perceptions towards disability and sexuality. *Disability and Rehabilitation, 32,* 1148-1155.

[22]Evans, R. J. (2005). *The Third Reich in power: 1933–1939*. London: Allen Lane.

[23]Falvo, D. &. Holland, B. (2018). *Medical and psychosocial aspects of chronic illness and disability* (6th ed.). Burlington, MA: Jones & Bartlett.

[24]Farrugia, A., Fraser, S., & Dwyer, R. (2017). Assembling the social and political dimensions of take-home naloxone. *Contemporary Drug Problems, 44*, 163-175.

[25]Frederick, A. (2017). Risky mothers and the normalcy project: Women with disabilities negotiate scientific motherhood. *Gender & Society, 31*, 74-95.

[26]Friedman, C., & Owen, A. L. (2017). Sexual health in the community: Services to people with intellectual and developmental disabilities. *Disability and Health Journal, 10*, 387-393.

[27]Gallagher, D. J., Connor, D. J., & Ferri, B. A. (2014). Beyond the far too incessant schism: Special education and the social model of disability. *International Journal of Inclusive Education, 18*(11), 1120-1142.

[28]Garland-Thompson, R. (2012). The case for conserving disability. *Bioethical Inquiry, 9, 339-355.*

[29]Garland-Thomson, R. (2015). A habitable world: Harriet McBryde Johnson's "Case for My Life." *Hypatia, 30(1)*, 300-306.

[30]Golden, M., & Zoanni, T. (2010). Killing us softly: The dangers of legalizing assisted suicide. *Disability and Health Journal, 3*, 16-30.

[31]Grue, J. (2016). The problem with inspiration porn: A tentative definition and a provisional critique. *Disability & Society, 31*, 838-849.

[32]Hadley, B. (2016). Cheats, charity cases and inspirations: Disrupting the circulation of disability-based memes online. *Disability & Society, 31*, 676-692.

[33]Hahn, H. (1985). Towards a politics of disability: Definitions, disciplines and policies. *The Social Science Journal, 22*(4), 87-105.

[34]Hahn, H. (1988). The politics of physical differentness: Disability and discrimination. *Journal of Social Issues, 44*, 39-47.

[35]Hahn, H. (1991). Alternative views of empowerment: Social services and civil rights. *Journal of Rehabilitation, 57*(4), 17-19.

[36]Haller, B. A. (2010). *Representing disability in an ableist world: Essays on mass media.* Louisville, KY: The Avocado Press.

[37]Hartley, M. T. (2012). The disability rights community. In D. R. Maki & V. M. Tarvydas (Eds.), *The professional practice of rehabilitation counseling* (pp. 147-164). New York, NY: Springer.

[38]Hartley, M. T., Bauman, S., Nixon, C. L., & Davis, S. (2015). Comparative study of bullying victimization among students in general and special education. *Exceptional Children, 81*, 176-193.

[39]Hedegaard, H., Warner, M., & Miniño, A. M. (2017). *Drug overdose deaths in the United States, 1999–2016. NCHS Data Brief, no 294.* Hyattsville, MD: National Center for Health Statistics.

[40]Holzbauer, J. J. (2004). Disability harassment of students in transition from school to work: Implications for rehabilitation counseling. *Journal of Rehabilitation, 35*(4), 3-7.

[41]Huskin, P. R., Reiser-Robbins, C., & Kwon, S. (2017). Attitudes of undergraduate students toward persons with disabilities: Exploring effects of contact experience on social distance across ten disability types. *Rehabilitation Counseling Bulletin.* Advanced online publication. doi: 10.1177/0034355217727600

[42]Iezzoni, L. I., Wint, A. J., Smeltzer, S. C., & Ecker, J. L. (2015). "How did that happen?" Public responses to women with mobility disability during pregnancy. *Disability and Health Journal, 8,* 380-387.

[43]Ilic, M., Reinecke, J., Bohner, G., Röttgers, H., Beblo, T., Driessen, M...Corrigan, P. W. (2011). Protecting self-esteem from stigma: A test of different strategies for coping with the stigma of mental illness. *International Journal of Social Psychiatry, 58,* 246-257.

[44]Karten, T. J. (2015). *Embracing disabilities in the classroom: Strategies to maximize students' assets.* New York, NY: Skyhorse Publishing.

[45]Kilbury, R. F., Benshoff, J. J., & Rubin, S. E. (1992). The interaction of legislation, public attitudes, and access to opportunities for persons with disabilities. *Journal of Rehabilitation, 58*(4), 6-9.

[46]Krahn, G. L. (2010). Reflections on the debate on disability and aid in dying. *Disability and Health Journal, 3,* 51-55.

[47]Lawson, N. D. (2016). Public perception of the lifetime morbid risk of mental disorders in the United States and associations with public stigma. *SpringerPlus, 5:1342.* doi: 10.1186/s40064-016-2974-y

[48]Loja, E., Costa, M. E., Hughes, B., & Menezes, I. (2013). Disability, embodiment and ableism: Stories of resistance. *Disability & Society, 28*(2), 190-203.

[49]Marshak, L. E., Dandeneau, C. J., Prezant, F. P., & L'Amoreaux, N. A. (2010). *The school counselor's guide to helping students with disabilities: Grades K–12.* San Francisco, CA: Jossey-Bass.

[50]McNicholas, C. I., Orpinas, P., & Raczynski, K. (2017). Victimized for being different: Young adults with disabilities and peer victimization in middle and high school. *Journal of Interpersonal Violence.* Advance online publication. doi: 10/1177/0886260517710485

[51]Mellifont, D. (2017). Hold your traditional discourses! A study exploring newspaper and web news reporting of New York's inaugural disability pride parade. *Asia Pacific Media Educator, 27,* 138-153.

[52]Munyi, C. W. (2012). Past and present perceptions towards disability: A historical perspective. *Disability Studies Quarterly, 32*(2).

[53]The National Alliance on Mental Illness. (2008). *Schizophrenia: Public attitudes, personal needs.* Arlington, VA: Author. Retrieved from https://www.nami.org/getattachment/About-NAMI/Publications/Surveys/SchizeExecSummary.pdf

[54]National Institute of Health. (2013, March 29). *Genetic testing: How it is used for healthcare.* Retrieved from https://report.nih.gov/NIHfactsheets/ViewFactSheet.aspx?csid=43

[55]O'Brien, G. V. (2011). Eugenics, genetics, and the minority group model of disabilities: Implications for social work advocacy. *Social Work, 56*(4), 347-354.

[56]Pampel, F. (n.d.). *Bullying and disability: An overview of the research literature.* Denver, CO: OMNI Institute. Retrieved from http://coddc.org/Documents/Bullying%20and%20Disability%20-%20An%20Overview%20of%20the%20Research%20Literature.pdf

[57]Parcesepe, A. M., & Cabassa, L. J. (2013). Public stigma of mental illness in the United States: A systematic literature review. *Administration & Policy in Mental Health, 40,* 384-399.

[58]Parens, E., & Asch, A. (2003). Disability rights critique of prenatal genetic testing: reflections and recommendations. *Mental Retardation and Development Disabilities Research Review, 9,* 40-47.

[59]Pelka, F. (2012). *What we have done: An oral history of the Disability Rights Movement.* Amherst, MA: University of Massachusetts Press.

[60]Rapid Response Service. (2012, December). *Rapid response: Public perception of harm reduction interventions.* Toronto, ON: Ontario HIV Treatment Network.

[61]Saxe, A., & Flanagan, T. (2014). Factors that impact support workers' perceptions of the sexuality of adults with developmental disabilities: A quantitative analysis. *Sexuality and Disability, 32,* 45-63.

[62]Smart, J. (2012). *Disability across the developmental life span for the rehabilitation counselor.* New York, NY: Springer Publishing.

[63]Smart, J. (2016). *Disability, society, and the individual* (3rd ed.). Austin, TX: Pro-Ed.

[64]Steinbach, R. J., Allyse, M., Michie, M., Liu, E. Y., & Cho, M. K. (2017). "This lifetime commitment": Public conceptions of disability and noninvasive prenatal genetic screening. *American Journal of Medical Genetics A, 170A,* 363-374.

[65]Stone, D. (2002). *Breeding superman: Nietzsche, race and eugenics in Edwardian and interwar Britain.* Liverpool: Liverpool University Press.

[66]Swain, J., & French, S. (2000). Towards an affirmation model of disability. *Disability & Society, 15*(4), 569-582.

[67]Taylor, M. A. (2016). A comprehensive study of mass murder precipitants and motivations of offenders. *International Journal of Offender Therapy and Comparative Criminology.* Advanced online publication. doi: 10/1177/0306624X16646805

[68]Turner, A. (2016). Changing the debate: A twentieth-century history of people with disabilities, their families, and genetic counseling. *Oregon Historical Quarterly, 117*(2), 117-134.

[69]United Nations. (2016). *10th anniversary of the adoption of Convention on the Rights of Persons with Disabilities (CRPD).* Retrieved from https://www.un.org/development/desa/disabilities/convention-on-the-rights-of-persons-with-disabilities/the-10th-anniversary-of-the-adoption-of-convention-on-the-rights-of-persons-with-disabilities-crpd-crpd-10.html

[70]Van Schipstal, I., Mishra, S., Berning, M., & Murray, H. (2016). Harm reduction from below: On sharing and caring in drug use. *Contemporary Drug Problems, 43*, 199-215.

[71]Vernick, J. S., Burris, S., & Strathdee, S. A. (2003). Public opinion about syringe exchange programmes in the USA: An analysis of national surveys. *International Journal of Drug Policy, 14*, 431-435.

[72]Vitali, A. (2015, October). *Trump: Mental illness, not guns, to blame for America's mass shooting problem.* Retrieved from https://www.nbcnews.com/meet-the-press/trump-mental-illness-not-guns-blame-america-s-mass-shooting-n437901

[73]Vitali, A. (2017, November). *Trump says gun control would've made 'no difference' in Texas church shooting.* Retrieved from https://www.nbcnews.com/storyline/texas-church-shooting/trump-says-gun-control-would-ve-made-no-difference-texas-n818236

[74]Weinmeyer, R. (2016). Needle exchange programs' status in US politics. *American Medical Association Journal of Ethics, 18*, 252-257.

[75]West, E. A., Perner, D. E., Laz, L., Mursick, N. L., & Gartin, B. C. (2015). People-first and competence-oriented language. *International Journal of Whole Schooling, 11*(2), 16-28.

[76]Wheeler, S. (n.d.) *Language and disability identity.* Retrieved from http://sandrawheeler.com/Language_Disability.pdf

[77]Wilson, L. C., Ballman, A. D., & Buczek, T. J. (2016). News content about mass shootings and attitudes toward mental illness. *Journalism & Mass Communication Quarterly, 93*, 644-658.

[78]Wright, B. A. (1983). *Physical disability: A psychosocial approach* (2nd ed.). New York: Harper & Row

[79]Wright, B. A. (1988). Attitudes and the fundamental negative bias. In H. E. Yuker (Ed.), *Attitudes toward persons with disabilities* (pp 3-21). New York, NY: Springer.

[80]Young, S. (2014). *I'm not your inspiration, thank you very much*. Ted Talk. Retrieved from https://www.ted.com/talks/stella_young_i_m_not_your_inspiration_thank_ you_very_much

CHAPTER 4

DISABILITY IDENTITY

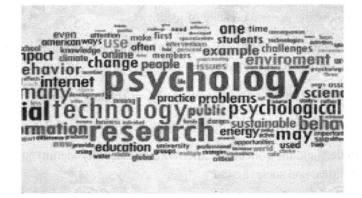

ANDREA PERKINS NERLICH

Mankind has struggled since its origins to understanding what constitutes the "self." Each person has a strong and consistent desire to understand who he or she is, both as an individual and in the context of multiple group memberships. This is the crux of what comprises identity. In many ways, the discovery of self satisfies the ultimate existential question—*who am I?* Certainly, one discovers self within the context of personal exploration of one's interior life, and in relation to the presentation of self to others. The self is both influenced by, and influences, the multiple environments inhabited by the person. Because of this reciprocal relationship, the self is ever-changing; it can develop in a positive trajectory or regress during periods of one's lifetime. The simultaneous positive and negative features of self are constant in their communication and struggle for control. The dimensions of a person's self are expressed through one's personality, behavior, interests, and role performance. They are also shaped by the cultural and ecological context of the person, including disability. To this end, this chapter will:

➢ explore the general concept of identity;

➢ contextualize identity development within the multiple roles and environments inhabited by a person over time;

➢ recognize the role disability may play in shaping identity;

➢ explore theories of disability identity development; and

➢ understand the collective experience of disability identity and its role in political and social action.

UNDERSTANDING IDENTITY

The term self has been described in various ways throughout the field of psychology. Baumeister[2] was perhaps most succinct in describing self: "Your self is the totality of you, including your body, your sense of identity, your reputation (how others know you), and so on. It encompasses both the physical self and the self that is constructed out of meaning."[p. 247] Correlates of self include: identity, who one is; self-esteem, the evaluative component of self; and self-concept, ideas about oneself. Identity is a sense of self defined by a unique set of personal characteristics, affiliations, and social roles. Identity is predicated on a person becoming a distinct individual, consolidating attributes and traits that become consistent over time. Through this process of individuation, the person comes to an awareness that he or she is separate and distinct from others.

Given this definition, we understand people derive understanding and meaning in unique ways. Symbolic interactionism provides a frame of reference to understand how individuals interact with one another to represent their worlds (contexts), through the creation of dialect, ideas, and images (symbols);[41] the symbols created shape the behaviors of individual. Blumer,[3] who initially coined the term, outlined the premises for symbolic interactionism:

> ➤ a person acts toward things based on the meanings one holds for those things;

> ➤ the meaning of such things is derived from social interactions one has with others; and

> ➤ meanings are managed in, and modified through, an interpretive process one uses when engaging in social interactions.

This perspective suggests that a person's self-concept is derived from "definitions he or she has received from interacting in society. The looking-glass reflects the appraisals received from others."[10, p. 33] Therefore, the construction of self is dynamic with the environment around a person.

As multiple components of self-concept, a person may possess several identities, but the most salient identity at any given time will be influenced by one's current situation. People use mindsets, or *personal identities,* composed of the traits, characteristics, values, and ways of being to guide perceptions, behavior, and interactions.[7] Identity exists within a person's mind, but only becomes apparent when a person plays a role.[10] Fulfillment of relationship functions in a person's social ecology relate to *role identities.* The content for inclusion in one's identity, from identity categories (e.g., gender, class, ethnicity) to role identities (e.g., parent, sibling, child), is dependent upon the cultural world one inhabits.[1] *Social identities* refer to a person's acknowledgement of being part of a group and his or her feelings about group membership. Finally, the self is shaped by the contexts and situations surrounding a person, and therefore shapes a person's behavior in those contexts.[34] A person is not merely reactive to social cues, but rather moderates responses based on who they are "in the moment." A person may choose to present as having different identities at any point in time, depending on the circumstance, level of acceptance of a person's identity, or perceived danger or benefit to expressing that identity,[10] resulting in a *situational identity*.

Carter[7] codified the elusive nature of identity to comprise cognitive, social, and behavioral notions, acknowledging the impact of development and contexts on its formation. First, self and identity are each viewed as a *mental construct,* since they are represented in the memory of the person: organizing learned social norms and expectations, evaluations of others, and self-judgments into one's self-concept. Second, distal and proximal social contexts, such as early schooling, parenting practices, and current career and social expectations, create the parameters within which a person exercises his or her identities. Micro-level influences like day-to-day personal interactions, as well as the macro-level influences of society and culture, provide messages and feedback to further refine one's self-concept. The confluence of these factors results in identity as a *social product*. Lastly, identity is manifest through the actions of a person. At times, context could lead a person to select an identity and behavior that will be readily endorsed by those around them to find acceptance in a regarded social group. These behavioral outcomes represent self and identity as a *force in action*. How a person wants to be perceived in any moment will influence the behaviors and actions one demonstrates.

Identities can be focused on the past—what used to be true of one; the present—what is true of one now; or the future—the person one expects or wishes to become, the person one feels obligated to try to become, or the person one fears one may become. Identities are orienting. They provide a meaning-making lens and focus one's attention on some, but not other, features of the immediate context.[34]

Personality psychologists tend to view self and identity as a stable feature of a person, formed through development and becoming a relatively permanent trait by adulthood; conversely, social psychologists focus on the situational influences of self and identity, recognizing the malleability of these as a state, given a person's current circumstances.[9] From a dynamic perspective, however, self is conceptualized as "stable *and* variable, consistent *and* inconsistent, rational *and* irrational, planful *and* automatic, agentic *and* routinized."[32, p. 27] "To the extent that the self is a tool for meaning making, maintaining sense of worth, and regulating behavior, then an effective self should be sensitive to new information and so be malleable and variant across change in features of the external (time, situation) and internal (motivation) environment."[7, p. 81] The process of identity development will now be explored.

IDENTITY DEVELOPMENT AND CONTEXT

Self is a product of both cognitive and social construction.[26] It is influenced by cognitive development, educational exposure, sociocultural context, parenting/family influences, and media socialization and exposure. As a child's cognitive processes develop, so too do their self-representations, including self-awareness, self-appraisals, and global self-esteem. In the social realm, children interact with others to receive external appraisals, make comparisons, and internalize expectations. Interactions in early life between child and parent, as well as extended family, serve as the template for understanding how identity is developed. As their world expands, interactions with peers and other adults, as well as the wider sociocultural and political context, continue this development. The goal is congruence between one's internal self-image and the self one projects to the world.[21]

To begin the process of crafting one's identity, an individual can engage in reflective actions or "sponge" reactions. In reflective actions, a person views the world around oneself like viewing one's reflection in a mirror—as an observation. The person evaluates what is viewed against his or her current view of self, determining the degree to which what is seen "fits" with one's developing sense of self. This can be understood through the analogy of trying on different clothing in a store. A person settles on "outfits," or aspects of one's persona, that feel good or complement the self. This process of finding the proper fit will be lifelong, however, as it is far from accurate at times and may need to be updated as the person experiences new contexts.

The sponge reaction is a process of internalization that may be approximately synonymous with the one described above, but with one significant difference. Here the individual is viewed as a seemingly passive object that merely assimilates behaviors and thinking paradigms, placing them in his or her behavior repertoire without an evaluative process. To further the above analogy, this would be more like having a personal shopper or parent who chooses the outfits, rather than a person having input into the selection and appropriateness for oneself.

Investigation of the roles and contexts of identity development generally has Erickson[14,15,16] as its starting point. His eight stages of psychosocial development may well be the benchmark from which other views are evaluated. While identity development is often associated with adolescent development, it is not solely confined to this period of the life cycle. Multiple tasks throughout the eight stages of life both enhance identity development and point to the fact that it is a continual process. Gender roles, sexual interests, accomplishment of educational and vocational tasks, and relationship formation are all components of how one develops an identity, from an interpersonal and intrapersonal perspective, across the lifespan.

The period of adolescence, however, has long been associated with the development of self or identity. Multiple theorists, including Freud, Erikson, Marcia, Piaget, and Kohlberg, have postulated adolescence as crucial to the development of identity. Hutchinson[27] indicated that, in Erikson's developmental stage of *identity versus role confusion*, the major task is "to find one's place in the world through self-certainty versus apathy, role experimentation versus negative identity, and anticipation of achievement versus work paralysis."[p. 234] When examining this definition, one sees an underlying process of *action*; self-certainty, role experimentation, and anticipation of achievement are equated with activity. While some of this "work" takes place in the adolescent's mind, identity development is ultimately an action. A person needs to live in the world, try on different roles, and constantly evaluate them for their effectiveness, while determining how these roles fit with one's ever-evolving sense of self. Many times, the process is essentially one of trial and error but, at its foundation, it is both a learning and growth process. Separation and individuation are the key goals of identity development at this stage, but they form the basis for the self that will engage in relationships in adulthood.[21]

Addressing Erikson's notion of identity crisis, Marcia[29,30] posited the adolescent stage consists neither of identity resolution nor identity confusion, but rather the degree to which one has explored and committed to an identity in a variety of life domains, such as vocation, religion, relational choices, gender roles, and politics. Marcia's theory of identity achievement argues that two distinct parts form an adolescent's identity: crisis (i.e., a time when one's values and choices are being reevaluated) and commitment. He defined a crisis as a time of upheaval where old values or choices are being reexamined. The end outcome of a crisis leads to a commitment made to a certain role or value. The process moves the adolescent through a series of identity statuses: identity diffusion, identity foreclosure, identity moratorium, and identity achievement. Identity achievement is the desired end where the individual explores various roles and subsequently makes a commitment to a course of action.

Identity formation is a process that continues across one's life, coming to the foreground as social contexts shift, as in assuming a new life role or moving into a new career.[36] Contemporary research acknowledges that much of the work of identity achievement occurs in emerging adulthood, rather than adolescence. One's first identity is not necessarily enduring, as a person may reorganize and reinvent his or her identity to be adaptable to changes across the lifespan.[37] Gleaned from these processes of identity development is the understanding of self as a social phenomenon, where interactions with others and ideologies spur a person into a reflective process of fit. From the symbolic interactionist perspective, there is no sense of self at birth, but it develops as a function of social interactions.[7] Self-construction is rooted to and dependent upon interpersonal processes within the social realm, with both significant individuals and social groups.[32] We begin to recognize the perspectives and evaluations of others about us. Eventually, we can integrate the perspectives of others and use it to take perspective of ourselves, as a social standard.

Regardless of perspective and theory, three factors in identity development are prominent. First, identity is a lifelong, developmental process. Second, identity is formed as the result of internal processes and the influence of other individuals and environments. Third, there is no correct, proper, or perfect identity; everyone is constantly involved in the process of becoming who one is, always engaged in the process of becoming a person. From this general view of identity, the discussion will now focus on a specific identity, its development, and the influence of personal and interpersonal contexts—disability identity.

UNDERSTANDING DISABILITY IDENTITY

Disability is a universal component of the human condition. Human artifacts provide evidence of disability as a characteristic of the human condition throughout recorded history. Disability spans across race/ethnicity, gender, sexual orientation, age, religion, and socio-economic groups. Like height, weight, sex, and eye color, disability is ultimately just one of many variations in human existence. Disability has been used historically to demonstrate difference (rather than a dimension of diversity), with a generally negative connotation to this difference. Yet, given the universality of disability, this approach is illogical. With estimates in the United States at between 50 and 60 million for individuals with disabilities—approximately 20 percent of the population—it is difficult to understand this negative connotation when both the incidence and prevalence rate is at such a level.

Like the concept of self, disability is amorphous and difficult to define. There is no absolute consensus regarding the operational components of a disability definition. There have been numerous attempts to define disability within the context of various life spheres: vocation, legal system, activities of daily living, recreation and leisure, function, medical and/or psychiatric diagnosis, and accessibility. The purpose of this approach is to approximate a definition to serve as the foundation for service eligibility, legislation, benefits, and treatment approaches. For example, in the legal realm, the Americans with Disabilities Act (ADA) attempted to create a definition that was encompassing of the dynamic nature of disability, but ended up leaving too much for the court systems to interpret, and perhaps not uniformly. Stein[39] documented a definition of who has a disability according to the United States Supreme Court in response to a case involving the ADA: "According to the Court, to fit under ADA, an individual has to be neither too little disabled nor too greatly disabled; has to be credentialed as disabled if an employer perceived of her as disabled, but only if the employer admits that it did so; and always needs to be able to perform essential job functions while at the same time (absent accommodations) be functionally impaired from conducting not only the job at issue, but a range of other jobs as well."[p. 909] The Court unintentionally obfuscates the matter by being both obscure and narrowly focused.

The modern, practical definition of disability used in the counseling professions is guided by the International Classification of Functioning (ICF) model posited by the World Health Organization (WHO).[42] The ICF is a classification of health and health-related domains, considering personal and environmental factors that impact on the disability experience of the person. These domains "help us to describe changes in body function and structure, what a person with a health condition can do in a standard environment (their level of capacity), as well as what they actually do in their usual environment (their level of performance). These domains are classified from body, individual, and societal perspectives by means of two lists: a list of body functions and structure, and a list of domains of activity and participation. In ICF, the term *functioning* refers to all body functions, activities and participation, while *disability* is similarly an umbrella term for impairments, activity limitations and participation restrictions."[p.2] Consistent with this model, disability is theorized to be experienced along a continuum, throughout a person's life, where no person is ever absolutely free from or consumed by a disability. The condition is experienced in different ways depending upon the person and context at any given point in time.

A working definition for who has a disability is postulated in the following: a person has a disability if s/he consider her/himself to be a person with a disability. There are two limitations to this definition, however. First, the premise upon which the definition is based assumes disability is a primary component of a person's individual identity. While a person may experience a health condition, as referenced above, one may not base prominent features of identity on this characteristic. Second, in many instances, people with disabilities are often not in control of how they are viewed by others; even if disability is not considered a prominent feature of identity for the individual, others may make it such.

Understanding these limitations, Smart[37] described the difference among disability, the "disabled role", and the self-identity of a person with a disability, as these terms are often considered synonymous. Disability is related to functional loss and limitations, as well as the demands and day-to-day management of the disability. Conversely, the disabled role is the rules and limitations imposed on a person with a disability by society. These include unspoken requirements such as ignoring discrimination, managing the effects of the disability to make others more comfortable, and not being demanding (e.g., with requests for accommodations). Those who refuse to conform to this role, she argues, are often "considered to be denying the disability or to be an angry, bitter, tormented individual."[p. 218] The issue, however, does not lie within the person, rather it is with how society views him or her. Finally, self-identity that includes one's disability is integral to many people with disabilities. The disability is an inextricable part of the self; many cannot contemplate life without their condition. Hahn and Belt[25] explored disability identity through the lens of disability activists, inquiring about desire for a cure to one's disability, a view that would align with the medical model of disability. Those who rejected a desire for a cure had a stronger positive affirmation of personal disability identity.

Within the disability rights and activism communities, as well as now permeating into general culture, disability identity is viewed as a positive source of pride. This view is a strong departure from the early conceptualizations of disability identity. In his work *Stigma: Notes on a Spoiled Identity*, sociologist Erving Goffman[22] coined the term "spoiled identity" to refer to an identity that causes a person to experience stigma through possessing an attribute discredited by society. This separates people into two groups: those viewed as "normal" and those who are not. Those living with an identity society has labeled as less worthy may begin to internalize this notion. In the plenary session for the Society for Disability Studies conference in 2013, panelist and disability studies scholar Rosemarie Garland-Thomson, noted the impact of Goffman's work on her disability self-identity:

Stigma made me disabled. The effect of experience of reading
Stigma is to identify with the invitational "we" that is a convention of
Goffman's rhetorical narrative style. By coolly noting what he calls the
"pivotal fact" that "The stigmatized individual tends to hold the same
beliefs about identity that we do; Goffman issues a rhetorical invitation
to what race theorist W.E.B. Dubois described in 1903 as "double
consciousness," the experiential paradox between one's felt and
ascribed identities. Simply put, one's felt identity is how one
experiences oneself as an embodied, perceiving, conscious subject at
the center of one's own world. One's ascribed identity is the subject
position other people project upon one or understand one to occupy.
Reading the rough, gaudy prose of "abominations of the body";
"shameful differentness"; "atrocity tales"; "spoiled identities," and
"contagious moral blemish[es]"; functions as an unnervingly poetic
hailing to the stigmatizing social rituals of disability identity. Form
and content merge, then, in the rhetorical experience of entering the
perverse taxonomy of "normals" and the "stigmatized".[6]

Countering the catastrophic view of disability, Swain and French[40]
developed the affirmative model of disability to present a non-tragic
interpretation of disability that encompasses positive social identities, both
individual and collective. This model challenges the presumption of disability
as misfortune or abnormality, freeing individuals to determine their own
lifestyles, culture, and identity. In contemporary conceptualizations, disability
identity relates to "possessing favorable or beneficial self-beliefs regarding
one's own disability as well as having positive ties to other members of the
disability community."[12, p. 95] harnessing this more optimistic view. The
following will overview conceptualizations of the development of disability
identity.

DISABILITY IDENTITY MODELS

A person's self-concept is comprised of multiple identities based on
statuses such as culture, gender, disability, and religion, although some of these
identities may be more salient to the person depending upon the situation. A
person may possess any of these statuses, but not develop identity around them.
However, a person may not be in control of the identities ascribed to them, or
the salience of said identities, as is often the case with disability identity. The
salience of one's identity may be elevated when a personal interaction or

societal condition calls it to a person's attention through stigma and discrimination.[10] In describing the awkwardness of social barriers people with disabilities must endure, Garland-Thompson[19] noted: "Confused responses to racial or gender categories can provoke the question 'What are you?' Whereas disability interrogations are 'What's wrong with you?'"[p. SR1] People with disabilities recognize disability as a part of identity, but like others, define themselves by multiple functions and roles.[37] The question could be asked then, how does one develop a disability identity?

Gill[21] presented a model of disability identity development as a departure from the medical model and its assumption that a person needs to overcome a disability to fit in to society. The model was in response to the dilemma she perceived, as a person with a disability, about how to balance the struggle of self-identity as a person with a disability against fitting into dominant society and identifying with the disability community. She described this process as a person traveling "a liberating arc away from society and back, moving from a desire for social integration, through a distancing from mainstream society to focus on both group affiliation and personal integration, to a renewed effort to relate to society from a position of greater self-definition."[p. 45] Her model presented a progression of identity development based on four types of integration, although not everyone will achieve all levels:

➢ *Coming to feel we belong*: The task of this level is to fit into society. Whether a person is born with or acquires a disability, the person asserts the right to equal status and access. The inability to fit in is blamed more on restrictive environments, attitudes, and roles rather than on the person's limitations.

➢ *Coming home*: The task of this level is integrating with the disability community. Some individuals with disabilities avoid contact with this community because they perceive it perpetuates segregation, or their own internalized stigma and stereotypes lead them to devalue these relationships; some cannot participate in the community due to isolation. Despite these obstacles, many people with disabilities see value in relating with others who have 'been there.' Shared experience allows people to develop a culture and acceptance.

➢ *Coming together*: The task of this level is internal integration of similarity and difference, affirming the disability experience as positive and important in one's identity. A person with a disability

117

must reconcile there are aspects of the self, resulting from impairment, that cause limitation and aspects that are not impacted. The societal expectation is to appreciate and value one's positive attributes, and ignore the 'bad.' Obviously, this standard would result in identity conflict if a person was unable to integrate the valued and ignored parts of the self. In rejecting this societal values imposition, a person can reclaim and embrace limitations as part of an integrated self to appreciate how one fits into the dominant and disability culture through understanding one's sameness and differentness.

➢ *Coming out*: The task of this level is integrating the internal self with one's external presentation—how one appears to others. The integration of the "private knowledge of self and the ideal image we wish to present to others is one of the final thresholds to positive disability identity."[p. 45] This indicates a pride one has in the self, as well as with the disability community, and a willingness to impact relationships with mainstream society by publicly affirming this identity. Through the 'coming out' process, a person with a disability can express a more authentic self to relate to those with and without disabilities.

As a psychologist specializing in disability issues, Gibson[20] established the Disability Identity Development Model to assist practitioners working with individuals with life-long disabilities. The purpose of this three-stage model was to provide context to practitioners to understand the possible perceptions and struggles of their clients with disabilities, appreciating the fluid nature of disability identity development; clients can span stages or revert to previous ones depending on the circumstance. Over the course of the stages, the person with a disability moves from a state of *Passive Awareness* of disability, where there is little acknowledgement, control of, or association with disability or members of the disability community. The second stage, *Realization*, heralds the beginning of awareness of one's disability, an internal struggle with making meaning of the experience, expressions of anger and self-hate, and preoccupation with appearance, the perceptions of others, and projecting oneself as "superman/woman." The final stage, *Acceptance*, signals a shift from 'being different' to embracing one's disability in a positive light and integrating more fully into the world; this includes making positive self-appraisals, incorporating others with disability into one's life, and engaging in advocacy and activism.

In exploring the personal narratives of individuals with disabilities, Dunn and Burcaw[13] found that disability identity, like other salient identities, can be mobilized or inactive given situational circumstances. They found individuals with disabilities came to understand themselves and their relationship to others by engaging in community with peers who share a common experience. They extracted the following common themes in relation to disability identity formation:

> *Communal attachment:* the desire to affiliate with others with disabilities.

> *Affirmation of disability:* internal thoughts and feelings that those with disabilities should be included in society, with the same rights and responsibilities as other citizens.

> *Self-worth:* valuing oneself with a disability, as equal to those without one.

> *Pride:* being proud of one's identity as a person with a disability, while recognizing this is a devalued quality by others.

> *Discrimination:* awareness that people with disabilities, including oneself, can be targets of prejudiced behavior in daily life.

> *Personal meaning:* finding significance, making sense, and identifying benefits with having a disability.

Most recently, Forber-Pratt and Zape[18] investigated the development of disability identity in ADA-generation individuals with disabilities through qualitative interviews with those who lived most of their life since the legislation's passage. Narratives explicated the four distinct statuses of their Model of Social & Psychosocial Disability Identity Development:

> *Acceptance status:* whether a congenital or acquired disability, a person comes to terms with having a disability through a range of emotions and accepts it. Close friends and family are also accepting of the disability.

> *Relationship status:* a person begins to build a network of people with disabilities, typically with similar disabilities. This includes

an initiation and socialization to the disability community through conversation and observations to form connections. Affiliation with the disability community is not done to the exclusion of relationships with people without disabilities.

> *Adoption status:* a person assumes the core values of the disability community and culture. This serves as a catalyst for the person to determine the degree to which he or she will incorporate this shared culture into one's own self-identity. Critical to this status is understanding the nuance of how presenting one's disability identity will be an asset or a threat in various circumstances. Individuals grow more knowledgeable about laws, policies, and 'unwritten rules' of being a person with a disability.

> *Engagement status:* a person becomes a role model for others in the disability community, paying it forward to those in other statuses. This status relates to identity synthesis, in that a person embraces the self and immerses oneself in the disability community.

CONTEXTUAL FACTORS IMPACTING ON DISABILITY IDENTITY

Hahn[23] postulated that disability identity is primarily the result of the confluence between individuals and their environments. To borrow from statistical terminology, the development of one's (disability) identity is the result of a "goodness of fit." For example, if the environment contains all the resources an individual requires to complete necessary tasks, then there is a goodness of fit between the individual and the environment. Any individual, whether possessing a disability or not, requires that interaction as a minimum to achieve necessary functioning. Personal and contextual characteristics can influence this dynamic and have variable impact on the strength of disability identity.

Disability identity has been found to be more salient for those with an affirmative activism orientation toward disability, those who have been discriminated against, those with a more visible disability, and those who do not have competing minority identities (e.g., gender, race).[10] Disability severity is a strong predictor of disability identification; those whose disability is more severe will likely experience greater stigma and environmental barriers, making disability a more salient characteristic to one's identity.[5] Age was found to negatively impact the expression of disability identity through activism, as those who were older were less likely to espouse a sociopolitical model of disability.[11] Time with disability and age at onset impacted on the strength of disability identity, as the longer a person possessed a non-disability identity, the more difficult it was for the new identity to form.[12] Disability identity can also be viewed as a fluid state based on the nature of a person's disability; those with conditions that vacillate in intensity or degenerate may cause a person to question the positive valence of one's identity.[18] From an outcome perspective, those who do not have a strong disability identity may experience lower self-esteem,[8] greater psychological distress,[4] and less personal and group advocacy activity.[33]

Despite contextual differences among individuals, theories of disability identity development present several consistencies about the process. First, a person with a disability comes to understand the disability experience from an individual perspective, accepting it as a positive quality with personal meaning. Second, disability identity is formulated through a socialization process, mostly with other people with disabilities, but also through the acceptance of others in the person's intimate circle. Individuals formulate a disability identity by mirroring and modeling others within the community.[17] Third, individuals strengthen their personal disability identity through participation in the disability community, as well as reciprocating to others who are formulating their own identity. Finally, despite being an initiated member of the disability community, a person must continue to exist within society at large, which may not be as accepting or allow full expression of one's positive disability identity. This last point calls for a response from people with disabilities to assist in defining and shaping a more inclusive society through community action and activism. A more cohesive collective disability identity is necessary to affect this change.

COLLECTIVE DISABILITY IDENTITY

Before the turn of the new millennium, Gill[21] delineated the struggles impacting the collective identity of people with disabilities through exploring narratives with them and their allies over the prior twenty years: inaccessible environments and transportation systems impeding community organizing; poverty limiting resources; categorization by medical and social service systems that creates divide within the disability community; and societal values that continue to stigmatize and devalue the disability experience. Two decades later, these struggles persist. In a retrospective of disability issues at the 25th anniversary of the ADA, Massey[31] noted similar concerns, with a contemporary tone: stigma, lack of workforce diversity, lack of accurate representation of people with disabilities in media/culture, technology and Internet inaccessibility, and the need to normalize the disability experience in society.

Societal change comes from active, concerned citizens. As noted earlier, higher levels of stigma spurs individuals to greater identification with disability and the disability community.[5] From affiliation with the disability community, individuals are motivated to better the status of the group by counteracting stigma and its effects. Those who strongly identify as a member of the group are more likely to perceive discrimination, but also delegitimize it; greater identification with the disability community means individuals attribute negative outcomes to the social system, rather than disability limitations.[33] Challenging the status quo and working to change it through group advocacy is the foundation of a collective disability consciousness.

The origins of collective disability identity can be traced back to the work of Hahn[24] who proposed the minority group model of disability. Like other social conceptualizations of disability, the origin of disability is located not within the individual, but rather in the intersection of the individual and the environment; returning to "goodness of fit," disability results when a person is unable to perform a task because of a barrier (e.g., resources, access, attitudes). The assumptions for the minority group model included:

> ➤ that the source of major problems confronting people can be attributed primarily to social attitudes;

> ➤ that almost every facet of the environment has been shaped or molded by public policy; and

> ➤ that, at least in a democratic society, policies are a reflection of pervasive attitudes and values."[p. 4]

Since public policy plays a defining role in shaping the social and physical environment, activism to create more inclusive politics is necessary to remedy inequality and confront discrimination. The creation of an identity to support these actions is required.

The concept of "identity work" refers to the range of activities in which individuals engage to create identities, individual or collective, to give meaning to themselves and others. With respect to participation in political or social activism, Snow and McAdams[37] stated an individual must go through an identity work process to embrace the role of movement supporter that melds the personal and collective identity, including: identity amplification, identity consolidation, identity extension, and identity transformation. Identity amplification "involves the embellishment and strengthening of an existing identity that is congruent with a movement's collective identity but not sufficiently salient to ensure participation and activism."[p. 49] This requires a move of one's political or movement identity to a position of greater salience, akin to moving from the sidelines to a position of action. In identity consolidation, the person adopts an identity that combines two prior identities previously seen as incompatible because they are associated with different traditions. Here a person engages in a process of investing oneself in new roles, responsibilities, and contexts, and evaluating one's current experience to construct a coherent identity. Identity extension involves expanding the pervasiveness of one's personal identity to be congruent with the movement, making personal and movement identities indistinguishable and merged, rather than compartmentalized. Finally, while the first three identity construction processes are linked to past or current identity, identity transformation results in a dramatic change so that one's identity is reconstructed to allow a new identity to emerge, an active change agent for the movement in the future.

Four types of interactions provide the sources of information and experience that inform identity work: narratives, texts, rituals, and confrontations with opponents.[28] Through participation in a community movement, members share their stories or personal narratives that reveal aspects of self-concept salient to them, and the cause. The messages transmitted speak to awareness, action, commitment, and vigilance. Texts are shared stories, like the narratives, but in written form that can be transmitted more widely to coalesce the group's message and meaning. Rituals are symbolic acts, signs, and gestures that portray the values and unity of the group. Examples include holding rallies and parades, displaying hand gestures/symbolic body language, and singing/playing anthems. Confrontations and interactions with opponents or outsiders usually result when a member of a group is engaged in activism. Opposition may cause a person to strengthen a political/movement identity as one is reaffirmed in energy and purpose for the cause. From these interactions, a person can move toward a collective or political disability identity.

Putnam[35] proposed the conceptual framework of political disability identity, which can be used to understand collective identity development toward disability activism. She identified six domains to structure this framework, summarized below:

➢ *Self-worth:* the building block to an external political identity is for a person to inherently value oneself, considering internal and external influences that may impinge on this positive assessment. This includes knowledge of one's capabilities, belief that one can contribute, and a consciousness regarding how individuals with disabilities are undervalued in society.

➢ *Pride:* primary to the development of pride is taking ownership of one's disability identity and viewing disability as a universal condition, rather than a difference to be hidden. In this domain, individuals recognize disability is not intrinsically negative, but can be limiting in certain contexts and environments. One's disability identity grants membership in the disability community.

➢ *Discrimination:* the catalyst for disability rights is knowledge that people with disability are routinely discriminated against by other members of society. However, much discrimination is based on negative stereotypes rather than personal experience/knowledge of disability. Because of discrimination, people with disabilities are treated differently, many times negatively, and denied access and opportunities to social and economic resources.

➢ *Common cause:* despite variations in needs based on impairment and functional limitation, people with disabilities experience common issues and concerns around which they can rally political action. Common experiences include lack of access to health care, social and economic participation, and social community integration. Common cause translates into political action when members believe they can change/modify these experiences, see the root of these issues as similar, and trust that developing a common political agenda is the way to rectify the inequalities.

➢ *Policy alternatives:* public policy is the medium through which funding, service eligibility, and program administration is defined; it also colors and constructs attitudes about and acceptance of people with disabilities as a social norm. Public policies that would enhance political engagement of people with disabilities must be predicated on the beliefs that disability is not a characteristic of the individual, contributors to disability can be identified/addressed, and opportunities to reduce or eliminate disability can be created.

> ➢ *Engagement in political action:* through political action comes greater social inclusion and reduced marginalization. Individuals with disabilities engage in political action to shape societal experiences for all in the disability community. There is strength in numbers and the disability community can be a powerful political constituency group, although a political minority group. Political engagement is necessary to affect policy change.

Putnam recognized, however, that all people who espouse a disability identity, and even become involved with the disability community, do not necessarily go on to engage in disability politics, though likely all perceive a political influence in the problems they face. There is a fear that identity politics could be limiting in scope because it is focused too narrowly on a single identity.[11] And, as mentioned previously, a single disability identity can be elusive.

Darling[11] stated that "by promoting a collective identity, social movements can shape the personal identities of their members, as well as those nonmembers who become aware of the movement's message."[p. 73] However, Garland-Thompson[19] noted that pride movements for people with disabilities have not gained as much traction and prominence in the consciousness of the American people. She attributed this to people with disabilities not having a clear collective notion of what it means to have a disability. Movements based on sex, race, sexual orientation, and gender identity have a stronger ideal as to who should belong. As noted in Chapter 1, perceived differences among disability groups slow momentum for collective identity and action. And, as previously mentioned in this chapter, lack of a clear definition of disability, variability in disability identity, and societal barriers that prevent mobilization of the disability community all present obstacles to collective political action. Research shows, however, that participation in the disability community and disability rights movement results in numerous positive benefits, including higher self-esteem, better mental health, and less isolation.

It would appear from discussion here that the status of the disability and disability rights community has not changed in the past three decades—the same barriers prevail, efforts to assume collective disability pride continue to be disjointed, and disability continues to be a devalued characteristic. Yet, in that time, American society has seen responses such as passage of the Olmstead Act, the first ever Disability Pride parade, Gallaudet University student protests for a president from the Deaf culture, and the rise of the "Spread the Word to End the Word" campaign. Individuals with disabilities have new mediums for engaging in the disability rights community; the challenge will be teaching younger generations to not take for granted the progress made before their birth, nor let the oldest generations continue to be mired in the outdated medical model and "spoiled identity" paradigms. These generational differences can create further barriers to the activism of all people with disability.[11] To continue forward progress, those striving for collective disability identity can be heartened by the words of Darling:[10]

> *...stigma has not disappeared; rather, it continues to be a potent force in the shaping of identity among many, or even most, individuals with disabilities in modern society. Even identities like disability pride, which reject stigma, appear to have developed as a direct response to it. The major change in disability identity over the past fifty years appears to be one of increasing diversity. Although in the past most people with disabilities seem to have seen themselves through the lens of stigma, today people have more identity options that, we can hope, will continue to increase in the future.*[p. 155]

IMPLICATIONS FOR COUNSELING

➤ Although a person with a disability might be coming to a counselor for services, it should not be assumed his or her disability is the presenting problem. The disability will likely have impact on the person's life and can be explored within the context of the presenting problem; however, to make it the salient issue or, worse, ignore it entirely for fear of offending, is detrimental to developing rapport with the person, respecting that person's expression of disability identity, and achieving optimal outcomes.[20]

➤ Tracking where a person is in the trajectory of the development of his or her disability identity is important for service efficacy. Individuals may be more or less willing to identify as having a disability, exhibit variability in how favorably they view their impairment, and have limited interactions with others with disabilities. Interventions should be tailored to meet the person where he or she is developmentally; if a person is not accepting of his or her disability, encouraging a meeting with a large group of people with disabilities could stunt progress and damage rapport.[17]

Attention should be paid to both the internal and external processes involved in disability identity development.

➤ One method for understanding a person's identity development is through encouraging him or her to share narratives. Allowing an individual to "tell one's story," in depth, will reveal pertinent identity themes: acceptance, stigma, self-worth, activism, communal attachment. This will provide the foundation for continuing his or her development.[13]

➤ Professionals can encourage participation in the disability community to further disability identity, moving toward a collective disability identity. Interventions and opportunities can be developed around the four types of interactions (i.e., narratives, texts, rituals, confrontations) to build a greater sense of affiliation and connection to the disability community.

REFERENCES

[1]Adams, G. (2012). Context in person, person in context: A cultural psychology approach to social-personality psychology. In K. Deaux & M. Snyder (Eds.), *The Oxford handbook of personality and social psychology* (pp. 182-208). New York, NY: Oxford University Press.

[2]Baumeister, R. F. (2005). Self-concept, self-esteem, and identity. In V. Derlega, B. Winstead, & W. Jones (Eds.), *Personality: Contemporary theory and research* (3rd ed., pp. 246-280). San Francisco, CA: Wadsworth.

[3]Blumer, H. (1969). *Symbolic interactionism: Perspective and method.* Berkeley, CA: University of California Press.

[4]Bogart, K. R. (2015). Disability identity predicts lower anxiety and depression in multiple sclerosis. *Rehabilitation Psychology, 60,* 105-109.

[5]Bogart, K. R., Rottenstein, A., Lund, E. M., & Bouchard, L. (2017). Who self-identifies as disabled? An examination of impairment and contextual predictors. *Rehabilitation Psychology.* Advance online publication. http://dx.doi.org/10/1037/rep0000132

[6]Brune, J. A., & Garland-Thompson, R. (2014). Forum introduction: Reflections on the fiftieth anniversary of Erving Goffman's Stigma.

Disability Studies Quarterly, 34(1). Retrieved from http://dsq-sds.org/article/view/4014/3539

[7]Carter, C. S. (2012). Self-awareness. In M. R. Leary & J. P. Tangney (Eds.), *Handbook of self and identity* (2nd ed., pp. 50-68). New York, NY: Guilford Press.

[8]Chalk, H. M. (2016). Disability self-categorization in emerging adults: Relationship with self-esteem, perceived esteem, mindfulness, and markers of adulthood. *Emerging Adulthood, 4*, 200-206.

[9]Crocker, J., & Canevello, A. (2012). Self and identity: Dynamics of persons and their situations. In K. Deaux & M. Snyder (Eds.), *The Oxford handbook of personality and social psychology* (pp. 263-286). New York, NY: Oxford University Press.

[10]Darling, R. B. (2013). *Disability and identity: Negotiating self in a changing society.* Boulder, CO: Lynne Rienner Publishers.

[11]Darling, R. B., & Heckert, D. A. (2010). Orientations toward disability: Differences over the lifecourse. *International Journal of Disability, Development and Education, 57*(2), 131-143.

[12]Dunn, D. S. (2015). *The social psychology of disability.* New York, NY: Oxford University Press.

[13]Dunn, D. S., & Burcaw, S. (2013). Disability identity: Exploring narrative accounts of disability. *Rehabilitation Psychology, 58*, 148-157.

[14]Erikson, E. H. (1968). *Identity: Youth and crisis.* New York: W. W. Norton.

[15]Erikson, E. H. (1974). *Dimensions of a new identity: The 1973 Jefferson lectures in the humanities.* New York: W. W. Norton.

[16]Erikson, E. H. (1980). *Identity and the life cycle.* New York: W. W. Norton.

[17]Forber-Pratt, A. J., Lyew, D. A., Mueller, C., & Samples, L. B. (2017). Disability identity development: A systematic review of the literature. *Rehabilitation Psychology, 62*, 198-207.

[18]Forber-Pratt, A. J., & Zape, M. P. (2017). Disability identity development model: Voices from the ADA-generation. *Disability and Health Journal, 10*, 350-355.

[19]Garland-Thompson, R. (2016, August 21). Becoming disabled. *New York Times,* SR1.

[20]Gibson, J. (2006) Disability and clinical competency: An introduction. *The California Psychologist, 39*, 6-10.

[21]Gill, C. J. (1997). Four types of integration in disability identity development. *Journal of Vocational Rehabilitation, 9*, 39-46.

[22]Goffman, E. (1963). *Stigma: Notes on spoiled identity.* New York, NY: Simon & Schuster.

[23]Hahn, H. (1985). Toward a politics of disability: Definitions, disciplines, and policies. *The Social Science Journal, 22*, 89-105.

[24]Hahn, H. (1994). The minority group model of disability: Implications for medical sociology. *Research in the Sociology of Health Care, 11*, 3-24.

[25]Hahn, H. D., & Belt, T. L. (2004). Disability identity and attitudes toward cure in a sample of disability activists. *Journal of Health and Social Behavior, 45*, 453-464.

[26]Harter, S. (2012). Emerging self-processes during childhood and adolescence. In M. R. Leary & J. P. Tangney (Eds.), *Handbook of self and identity* (2nd ed., pp. 680-715). New York, NY: Guilford Press.

[27]Hutchinson, E. D. (2008). *Dimensions of human behavior: The changing life course* (3rd ed.). Los Angeles: Sage.

[28]Kiecolt, K. J. (2000). Self-change in social movements. In S. Stryker, T. J. Owens, & R. W. White (Eds.), *Self, identity, and social movements* (pp. 110-131). Minneapolis, MN: University of Minnesota Press.

[29]Marcia, J. E. (1966). Development and validation of ego-identity status. *Journal of Personality and Social Psychology, 3*, 551-558.

[30]Marcia, J. E. (1980). Identity in adolescence. In J. Adelson (Ed.), *Handbook of adolescent psychology* (p. 159-187). New York: Wiley.

[31]Massey, W. (2015, July 24). *The ADA at 25: What's next for disability rights?* Retrieved from http://www.cnn.com/2015/07/24/living/ada-25-anniversary-disability-rights-feat/index.html

[32]Morf, C. C., & Mischel, W. (2012). The self as a psycho-social dynamic processing system: Toward a converging science of selfhood. In M. R. Leary & J. P. Tangney (Eds.), *Handbook of self and identity* (2nd ed., pp. 21-49). New York, NY: Guilford Press.

[33]Nario-Redmond, M. R., & Oleson, K. C. (2016). Disability group identification and disability-rights advocacy: Contingencies among emerging and other adults. *Emerging Adulthood, 4*, 207-218.

[34]Oyserman, D., Elmore, K., & Smith, G. (2012). Self, self-concept, and identity. In M. R. Leary & J. P. Tangney (Eds.), *Handbook of self and identity* (2nd ed., pp. 69-104). New York, NY: Guilford Press.

[35]Putnam, M. (2005). Conceptualizing disability: Developing A framework for political disability identity. *Journal Of Disability Policy Studies, 16*, 188-198.

[36]Ryan, R. M., & Deci, E. L. (2012). Multiple identities within a single self: A self-determination theory perspective on internalization within contexts and cultures. In M. R. Leary & J. P. Tangney (Eds.), *Handbook of self and identity* (2nd ed., pp. 225-246). New York, NY: Guilford Press.

[37]Smart, J. (2012). *Disability across the developmental life span for the rehabilitation counselor.* New York, NY: Springer Publishing.

[38]Snow, D. A., & McAdam, D. (2000). Identity work processes in the context of social movements: Clarifying the identity/movement nexus. In S. Stryker, T. J. Owens, & R. W. White (Eds.), *Self, identity, and social movements* (pp. 41-67). Minneapolis, MN: University of Minnesota Press.

[39]Stein, M. A. (2003). Forward: Disability and identity. *William and Mary Law Review, 44,* 907-920.

[40]Swain, J., & French, S. (2000). Towards an affirmation model of disability. *Disability & Society, 15*(4), 569-582.

[41]West, R. L., & Turner, L. H. (2017). *Introducing communication theory: Analysis and application* (6th ed.). New York, NY: McGraw-Hill Education.

[42]World Health Organization. (2002). *Towards a common language for functioning, disability and health: ICF.* Geneva: WHO

Heartfelt acknowledgement goes to Dr. Joseph Stano, the author of this chapter in the first edition.

CHAPTER 5

SELF-CONCEPT AND SELF-ESTEEM

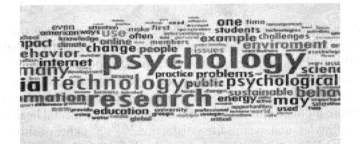

ANDREA PERKINS NERLICH

JAMIE MITUS

Although the terms are used interchangeably in the literature and common vernacular, the constructs of self-concept and self-esteem are not synonymous. Miller[54] identified the components of self-concept as the physical self (body image), functional self (role performance), personal self (morality), and self-esteem (self-worth). Self-esteem, therefore, is conceived as the affective and socially-evaluative component of self-concept. Miyahara and Piek highlighted a clear delineation between the two notions:

> *Distinction has recently been made between self-concept and self-esteem. The former, also termed self-estimation, self-identity, self-image, self-perception, self-consciousness, self-imagery and self-awareness is considered to describe how aware an individual is of their limitations, attributes, or personal characteristics, and involves no comparison with others. Self-esteem, on the other hand, is a value judgment where the individual determines the value of his or her own unique attributes and limitations. It is also termed self-acceptance, self-respect, self-regard, self-worth, self-evaluation, and self-feeling.*[55, p. 220]

Positive self-concept is considered both a desirable goal in its own right and a means of facilitating subsequent achievements, as an intermediate variable that will lead to other positive outcomes.[76] Forming a positive self-concept may affect one's overall social and psychological well-being. Individuals with positive self-concepts seem to experience higher levels of self-esteem, more intimate interpersonal relationships, better mental health, healthier lifestyles, and overall life satisfaction.[5,6,10,66,84] Other positive outcomes noted in the research include one's ability to effectively manage negative threats to the self and employ strategies that strengthen self-concept.[35] As stated by Waterman, "... a clear sense of personal identity constitutes an aspect of optimal psychological functioning."[84,p. 50]

Although important to a person's general well-being, developing an understanding of the self from a positive perspective can prove challenging for some people given personal and social circumstances that may hamper this type of growth. This challenge, at times, may be observed among individuals with disabilities, where various personal and social barriers preclude them from opportunities that foster the formation of a positive self-concept. According to Watson,[85] individuals with disabilities may experience a loss of self that leads to a process whereby they attempt to negotiate their lives in an effort to achieve the "norm." Some individuals with disabilities may experience disruptions to their self-concept as a result of an acquired disability;[2,9,30,32,66] while others, such as those with congenital disabilities, may feel an inferior sense of self due to low societal and familial expectations.[23,60,70] While some individuals with disabilities form a healthy self-concept, others may struggle to find comfort in their personal identities.[77,85] Evidence of this struggle is supported in some studies that indicate greater negative self-perception among those with versus those without disabilities and more so in certain groups with disabilities, such as those with acquired versus congenital disabilities.[5,6,29,67]

A variety of factors may account for the formation of a positive or negative self-concept among individuals with disabilities. Such factors, as highlighted by Vash,[82] may include characteristics of the individual (e.g., personality traits, social roles) and characteristics of the disability (e.g., type of disability, level of function affected by the disability). More importantly, however, is the social context (e.g., family support, friends, work environment, community accessibility, cultural context) and its interactive effect in shaping one's self-concept. These interactions, frequently coated with social stigma, stereotypes, and oppression, may lead to an internalization of the existing stereotypes about disability and deter the individual from forming a positive self-concept.[60,69]

The objective of this chapter is to discuss self-concept and self-esteem in general and in relation to people with disabilities, accounting for the factors that play a significant role in the development of self-concept and the outcomes that can transpire based on whether a positive or negative self-concept is constructed. Drawing from the literature in social psychology, sociology, and rehabilitation counseling, this chapter is organized into four sections:

- ➢ an overview of self-concept, highlighting theoretical models and the self-evaluation process leading to self-concept formation;

- ➢ an overview of self-esteem and the factors impacting its development and maintenance;

- ➢ a detailed look at research related to disability and its impact on self-concept and self-esteem;

- ➢ implications and interventions for use in counseling.

OVERVIEW OF SELF-CONCEPT

Rehabilitation professionals are expected to provide services that promote the psychosocial well-being of consumers. To do this effectively, it is important for professionals to develop an in-depth understanding of consumers as individuals in relation to their environment. This requires becoming intimately familiar with the consumer's own sense of self and the way in which the self-concept influences affect, motivation, and behavior in the world. Exploring self-concept with a consumer not only heightens the counselor's capability to intervene in a positive way, but it may also elevate consumers' self-awareness in ways that facilitate their capacity to accomplish goals.[52,62] This, in turn, may lead to positive outcomes, such as self-efficacy, self-confidence, and self-esteem, as self-concept is an indicator of a person's psychosocial adjustment and general well-being.[24,52]

To address self-concept with consumers, rehabilitation professionals must first understand the definition of self-concept and the way in which it develops to protect, preserve, and enhance the person. We will now turn to a discussion about self-concept with respect to each of these areas.

THE UNIVERSAL VERSUS MULTIDIMENSIONAL SELF

Generally speaking, there have been two schools of thought about the definition of self-concept. From a historical stance, self-concept is seen as a universal or unidimensional construct in which the self is considered to be global, singular, and stable overtime.[35,50,51] Markus and Kitayama[50] explained further that the universal self involves people's ability to develop awareness that they are physically distinct as human beings from others relative to both space and time. People have a sense of "I" in the context of the environment[50] and recognition of their own physical and spiritual presence.[66] Making this distinction allows people to determine who they are as singular entities relative to others.

More recently, researchers have argued in favor of a multidimensional self-concept, in contrast to the unidimensional self.[72] In the words of Kling, "...the self is conceived of as a multifaceted construct that is composed of a variety of unique self aspects, such as the self as a student, the self as an athlete, or the self as an introvert."[41, p. 981] Developmentally, the multidimensional self evolves into a relatively complex construct by adolescence, at which time it is possible to show contradictory sides of oneself under different circumstances. Furthermore, variation in affect towards each dimension of the self may occur with some dimensions viewed more positively over others.[20,78] Marcus and Wurf[51] asserted that advances in research to link self-concept to motivation and behavior have been blocked by the limited scope of the universal self. Some researchers argue that the mixed findings associated with the development of self-concept relate directly to the use of global versus multidimensional measures of self-concept.[43] The global definition fails to account for the array of motivations and behaviors that can be observed within multiple facets of one person's life.[52]

MODELS OF THE MULTIDIMENSIONAL SELF

People have the potential to hold beliefs about many facets of themselves, which feed into their self-concept.[80] As illustrated in Figure 1, some facets may include physical appearance (e.g., brown hair, green eyes, etc.); traits, competencies, and values (e.g., introverted, artistic, hardworking, etc.); role assignments (e.g., husband, mother, student, worker, etc.), and life experiences.[3,47,77] With the advent of the multidimensional self, several models have emerged in an effort to explain its complexity.[36,52,80] A few of these models will be presented as a way to illustrate how people come to understand who they are as a person.

FIGURE 1

FACETS OF SELF CONCEPT

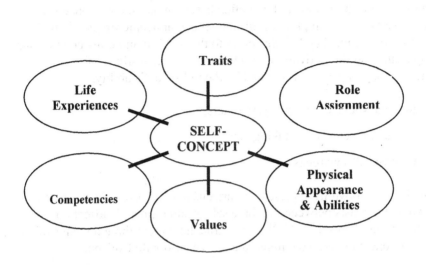

Self-concept, presented in a model by Leonard and colleagues,[47] involves three general attributes of self-perception including traits, competencies, and values. Self-concept in relation to these three areas is affected by the level and strength of a person's perception about them. According to the authors, level refers to the extent to which the person believes she/he possesses the attribute. This may be reflected in the following two statements, "I am good in science" versus "I am bad in science." In this example, level is determined by the operative words "good" and "bad" to distinguish the extent to which the person perceives his/her competency specific to science. Strength, on the other hand, describes the degree to which the person firmly believes in the level of a given attribute. Using the example above, the person may vary in the extent to which she/he believes in being good in science. The person may say, "I strongly see myself as being good in science" versus "I guess I see myself as being good in science." Here strength of self-perception is determined by the key words "strongly" and "guess." Leonard and colleagues stated that when someone is firmly anchored in his/her perceptions about the level of a particular attribute, it is usually a result of receiving clear and consistent feedback about that specific attribute. Feedback may come from multiple sources (e.g., friends, family, coworkers) and occur in many settings (e.g., work, school, home), but consistency is necessary in order for a strong self-perception to form.

In another model described by Higgins,[36] self-concept is exemplified in three domains (a) the actual self, (b) the ideal self, and (c) the ought self. The actual self is represented by the attributes an individual or someone else believes are presently characteristic of that person. The ideal self, in contrast, is a representation of attributes the person or someone else desires for him or her, and is often seen in the form of hopes, dreams, and/or aspirations. In terms of the ought self, this is how a person or someone else believes the person should be in terms of possessing certain attributes. This is the part of the self that feels a sense of duty or obligation, and it is often based on moral conscience versus personal desires. An assumption of this model is that people frequently make comparisons of the ideal and ought selves to the real self and draw conclusions that may shape certain motivations and behaviors in their life.[3,36] These comparisons may in part be stimulated by the individual's ability:

- ➤ to make social comparisons to others,

- ➤ to assume perspective taking, and

- ➤ to have self-awareness.[20]

The conclusions drawn from these comparisons may be driven by the extent of discrepancy that exists between the three selves and ultimately affect how people feel about themselves.[3,36,51] To illustrate how these three domains of the self relate to one another, we will use a case scenario with Colleen.

CASE STUDY
COLLEEN

Colleen is a 24-year-old female who acquired a traumatic brain injury three years ago following a motorcycle accident. Prior to the injury, Colleen was on track to graduate in four years, having just begun her senior year. Like her older siblings, she was expected to graduate by the time she was 22. Personally, she would have been fine if she needed an extra year or two to finish, but family pressures led her to proceed more quickly. After the injury, Colleen spent a significant amount of time in rehabilitation and is ready to return to school on a part-time basis. She now thinks she will be able to graduate by the time she is 27. Colleen aspired to become a high school math teacher ever since she can remember, but the nature of her injury affected her mathematical ability and, as a result, she has shifted majors to become a physical education teacher instead.

Colleen's ideal self in this scenario is her vision of being a high school math teacher and someone who is mathematically skilled. This, however, conflicts with her real self who presently is someone with less mathematical ability and a student working towards becoming a physical education teacher. In terms of the ought self, Colleen envisioned herself as a 22-year-old college graduate versus her real self which is a 24-year-old college student. This standard appears to have been set by her family and is one she felt the need to achieve. Ideally, Colleen would have been fine graduating a little later, but felt pressure to abide by the family rule. Given the scenario, Colleen is likely to perceive some discrepancies between the three self-domains in that she fell short of achieving her ideal and ought self. This may elicit certain emotional or behavioral responses due to the discrepancies. When the real self does not match up to the ideal or ought selves, a person may experience a host of negative emotions including sadness, depression, or disappointment.[3,36] In terms of Colleen, she may experience these feelings because of her shortcomings in graduating on time and becoming a math teacher. Consequently, she will need to realign her ideal and ought selves to relieve some of these feelings. Colleen may even feel some resentment towards her family for placing an expectation upon her to which she felt obligated, but subsequently was not able to achieve.

As portrayed in Figure 2, another related model sketches the self-concept as being temporal in nature specific to the past, present, and future selves.[51] The premise of the model is that people hold certain beliefs about themselves specific to a variety of attributes (e.g., traits, physical appearance, role assignments), which may or may not differ across the three time periods. Self-perceptions of the past and the future are often used on an evaluative basis to acquire insight about the present self. For example, in a study by Ellis-Hill and Horn,[26] individuals who had a stroke rated their present self more poorly than their past self, prior to the stroke. Yet, among the control group, no difference occurred between their perceptions of the past and present selves. It is likely the comparisons between the two temporal selves, in combination with the onset of the stroke, contributed to the lower rating observed of the present self among those in the stroke group. People tend to reflect on past memories as a way to determine which aspects of the self they wish to maintain or recapture in the present versus which parts of the self they wish to leave behind. When compared to the future self, individuals will evaluate where they are in the present in relation to various positive and negative self-concepts of the future. This, in turn, motivates the person towards pursuing certain goals to achieve the positive selves and avoid situations that may lead towards negative selves.[71]

FIGURE 2

TEMPORAL SELVES

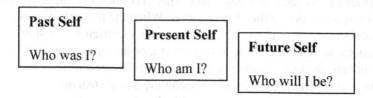

The three temporal selves are considered to be fluid in that people at any point and time can shift and slide between them. In some instances, however, there are individuals who may situate their current self more readily in any one of the temporal selves versus remaining active in the present. According to Charmaz,[12] some individuals who experience transition in their lives, as in the case of chronic or traumatic disability, may be more inclined to do this. Focusing exclusively on the past or future self while in the present may be observed in those who frequently reminisce about the past or routinely discuss plans for the future while resisting acknowledgment of the present self. Individuals may do this as a way to protect, enhance, or preserve their self-concept in response to the transition that has occurred. To demonstrate how the past, present, and future selves operate in relation to one another, we turn to the case of Patrick.

CASE STUDY
PATRICK

Patrick, a 49-year-old male, worked for 27 years as a firefighter. He was diagnosed with degenerative disk disease after falling off a scaffold while putting out a fire and herniating lumbar disks in his lower back. Furthermore, he sustained a fracture in his left foot that has led to the onset of arthritis. Patrick has undergone four back surgeries and two additional surgeries to address the fracture in his foot. He underwent extensive physical therapy but is now limited to light duty activity. The unpredictable nature of the back pain and steady progression of the arthritis have, in part, led to Patrick's early retirement from the fire department. Shortly after the injury, Patrick was treated differently by the captain in the firehouse and his "brothers." He believes that in some respects he was pushed out with little consideration as to how the company could bring him back. Prior to the accident, Patrick was on the cusp of being promoted to lieutenant. He was very close to many of the guys in the firehouse and was known to be the "older brother" figure. Prior to the accident,

Patrick saw himself as extremely assertive and as someone who had no issue with going after things he wanted. He saw himself as being very goal-driven. Now Patrick avoids setting goals or making plans and instead takes things as they come. He is less ambitious about going after things and rarely spends time socially with the "brothers." According to his family, many conversations with Patrick center on the "old days" and the firehouse, instead of his current or future plans. Patrick acknowledges his family's concerns, but feels his best days are behind him now, leaving no desire to look ahead.

Based on the scenario of Patrick, it appears he is primarily situated within his past self, as opposed to his present or future selves. Patrick's disability, although stable at present, will continue to progress because of the arthritis and disk degeneration, creating ambiguity about his future. According to Charmaz,[12] some individuals who live with uncertain conditions may slide into the past self as a means to find stability within their self-concept. For Patrick, this appears to be the case as noted by the fact that many of his conversations focus on the past. Patrick may recognize a discrepancy between his current and past selves in that he is less driven now than he used to be. Shifting to the past may allow him to manage the discrepancy in a way that stabilizes the uncertainty with which he presently lives.

We will now alter Patrick's scenario as a way to illustrate how his self-concept might be situated more in the present and future, as opposed to the past.

CASE STUDY
PATRICK

Despite the back and foot injuries, Patrick has maintained his assertive and ambitious personality to forge ahead. Despite losing his promotional opportunity to become a lieutenant, Patrick elected to maintain his professional identity by redirecting his career towards becoming a fire inspector. Shortly after retiring as a firefighter, Patrick used his connections to become employed by an "old brother" Keith, who after retirement started a fire inspection business. Patrick has now been with the company five years and was approached by Keith about taking over the business. Patrick says he has a vision for the business to expand beyond inspection into safety and hazard prevention. He is also interested in building a community-friendly reputation for the business that includes educational programming to local elementary and secondary schools about safety and hazard prevention. Unlike most programs, however, he is especially interested, because of his own disability, in tailoring a portion of the safety program towards the specific needs of people with disabilities. According to Patrick's family, he has really come a long way from six years ago. They hardly ever hear him talk about the "old days" anymore.

In contrast to the previous scenario, Patrick's sense of self seems to be situated mostly in the present and the future. This is evident in that he rarely talks about the past anymore. He also has a vision for the future and seems driven to expand the fire inspection business in a positive direction. Keith's trust in handing over the business suggests some level of satisfaction in how Patrick performs on the job, which to some extent requires a focus in the present. It is also evident that, despite the loss he incurred from his injury, he reconstructed his self-concept to incorporate his disability in an optimistic way. His desire to provide safety prevention programming specifically for individuals with disabilities stands as evidence for this, as well as his possible adoption of a new identity, that of an advocate. Patrick's shift towards focusing on the advocate self may further serve as a measure to preserve his self-concept both in the present and future despite any negative residual effects he encounters from his injuries.

THE FORMATION OF SELF-CONCEPT

There are many factors that influence the formation of self-concept. The person needs to have a fundamental self-awareness in order to engage in an evaluative process that leads to self-understanding. Self-awareness involves being attuned to one's own feelings, thoughts, and behaviors to monitor and regulate whether one is preserving and/or enhancing one's self-concept.[3] Since the multidimensional self is believed to be fluid across time and context,[3,69] maintaining self-awareness throughout life is necessary for the person to continuously engage in an evaluative process.

During the self-evaluation process, people may use several criteria to appraise themselves. During the appraisal process, they determine which information to integrate into, versus discard from, their belief system to shape their self-concept. We will describe four types of criteria commonly used by people as part of this evaluative process.

The first evaluative criterion that affects the formation of self-concept is inference and introspection. In this process, people evaluate their physiological, cognitive, emotional, and motivational reactions within a given situation. Conclusions are then drawn from these situations, in relation to the reactions, in an effort to better understand the self.[20,38,51] Let us look at a case scenario with Dennis as an example.

CASE STUDY
DENNIS

Dennis is a 24-year-old male who has a mild form of cerebral palsy. He recently met with a rehabilitation counselor to work on his vocational goals. Aside from working, he is hoping to live independently. During a conversation with his parents, Dennis expresses his wish for more independence. His counselor showed him some transitional housing options as a step towards achieving this goal. His parents, however, object to the idea and insist that he continue living at home. Dennis becomes very upset with his parents during the conversation. Later on, he finds himself thinking about why he reacted so strongly towards his parents. After reflecting on it for a while, he realizes that his anger was in response to the fact that he ideally sees himself becoming an independent adult living on his own, and yet, his parents do not share in this perception of him. Dennis realizes that his parents' resistance caused him to doubt his own capability to become a more independent person, which in turn made him angry. Through this realization, Dennis acknowledges just how important it is to his self-concept to become as independent as possible.

In the foregoing case scenario, it is evident that Dennis reflects on his self-concept in response to the dispute he had with his parents. Initially left to question himself, he appears to evaluate his ability to live independently in contrast to his parents' perspective. In so doing, Dennis likely accounts for multiple facets of the self to conclude that he is someone who has the physical capability, intellect, emotional maturity, and motivation to live independently. The opposing view of his parents likely led to Dennis' intensified connection to identify as an independent person.

A second means of evaluating the self, as mentioned earlier, involves making comparisons between the *past*, *present*, and *future* selves and the *real*, *ideal*, and *ought* selves.[36,51] In other words, people compare and contrast various facets of the self to their *present* or *real* selves as a way to determine who they are. Through this evaluative process, people may identify self-facets that have been present throughout their lives, while concurrently identifying those facets that have changed over time. We will look at the case of Susan as an example.

CASE STUDY
SUSAN

Susan is a 45-year-old woman who has been deaf since birth. When thinking about the past and the present, Susan realizes she has always identified heavily with the Deaf community. In coming to this conclusion about herself, Susan compares her earlier years to her current life. As a child, she attended a school that was specifically for children who are deaf. During her college years, she attended Gallaudet University. Most of her friends, past and present, are other individuals who are deaf, although she has a few friends from work who hear. Susan has, for years, participated in social and volunteer events that center on the Deaf community. Her past and present selves appear to be relatively similar and stable over time. Susan's self-concept as a person within the Deaf community is strong as a result of this stability and the extent to which her life activities have focused around others who are deaf.

Comparisons between the selves also allow people to evaluate what kind of a person they are currently (i.e., real self) in relation to who they would like to be (i.e., ideal self) or feel they should be (i.e., ought self). This point can best be portrayed in a study by Taleporos and McCabe[77] about body perception of individuals with disabilities. According to one participant, "I'll catch a glimpse of myself in a store mirror and I'll think, oh my god, why can't my legs look like they're doing what they're told to and not be sticking out or spasming ... Why can't they just sit properly."[p. 301] This participant clearly expresses a desire for a physical self (i.e., ideal self) that is quite different from the way in which her physical self currently exists (i.e., real self).

An *I* method of evaluation occurs through a process of social comparison where one looks to others to determine one's self-concept.[18,51] In this situation, the criteria of comparison are externally directed towards other people instead of internally towards the individual. The way in which people evaluate themselves may vary based on the specific attribute in a given context. For example, people with paraplegia may perceive their physical selves as athletic when playing basketball with other individuals who have spinal cord injuries. Yet, this perspective may shift when playing basketball with individuals who do not have a spinal cord injury. The individual will utilize both situations to make an overall decision about who they are as an athlete.

Finally, the *I* criterion used by people to evaluate their self-concept is feedback from other individuals. In this situation, feedback may come in the form of verbal or written appraisal, as well as the behavioral actions of others. The content of the feedback is generally task- or socially-oriented.[47] Once feedback has been given, people take the information and decide on its level of importance to their self-concept. If deemed important, they may incorporate the feedback into their self-concept. If unimportant, the feedback will, most likely, be discredited.[47,51]

Aside from the evaluation process, the formation of self-concept is also influenced by the degree of importance and centrality a person assigns to a specific attribute of the self. According to Epstein, "the self-concept includes only those characteristics of the individual that he is aware of and over which he believes he exercises control."[27, p. 406] In other words, while one is likely to rate oneself on a number of self attributes, only those aspects seen as important to the self are likely to be salient to the person, with other aspects of the self falling to the background. A person may believe, for example, she is a great friend, a good athlete, and a poor math student. However, when asked to describe herself, the first thing mentioned is being a good friend because of the importance placed on this aspect of the self. Only on occasion might she mention being a poor math student, because this aspect of the self is considered unimportant and is less salient to her.

Now that we have defined self-concept and provided a brief summary on how it develops within a person, we will turn to a general discussion about self-esteem.

OVERVIEW OF SELF-ESTEEM

Self-esteem can be best defined as an evaluative component of self-concept, by which a person judges his or her own worth.[54] It represents a person's global level of self-acceptance and self-respect.[1] Self-esteem is viewed as a fundamental human motive, a drive for self-maintenance; it is enhanced through reflected appraisals, self-perceptions, and social comparisons.[83] Along similar lines, Coppersmith[14] delineated the theoretical bases for self-esteem:

> *significance*: acceptance and attention from valued others;

> *competence*: successful performance on valued tasks;

> *virtue*: adherence to moral and ethical standards; and

> *power*: the ability to exert control over one's life and others.

Consistent with the universal vs. multidimensional self framework, self-esteem should be conceived as both a global and domain-specific construct. Additionally, much like other personality aspects, it can be viewed as a global trait (i.e., an overall view of oneself) or a global state (i.e., how oneself is viewed at a particular point in time).[46] With self-esteem defined as the affective domain of self-concept, it is advanced that there is an aspect of self-esteem linked with each of the facets of self-concept (refer to Figure 1). Once a belief has developed about a particular self-attribute, people are likely to rate how they feel about that particular self-facet. The assignment of this feeling equates to self-esteem. The relationship between self-concept facets and overall self-esteem varies with the importance the individual allocates to that specific facet of self-concept, a concept known as the individual importance hypothesis.[1] The relationship between competence in a given domain and a person's perception of the importance of that domain is a major determinant of self-esteem in that area. The value people assign to a given life domain, or its centrality, determines the satisfaction they will derive from it,[4] as well as the magnitude of impact success and failure will have on their esteem.

While self-esteem has been defined as a global construct, it may not be "global" or universal when viewed through a culture-, age- or gender-specific lens. It has been demonstrated that a higher correlation exists between self-esteem and life satisfaction for societies that value individualism rather than collectivism, demonstrating a variation in the importance of self-esteem across cultures.[75] As a person ages, the importance of domain-specific self-concept facets will change in their salience, causing a shift in the importance of facets to a person's overall self-esteem; in other words, over time and developmental periods, what a person chooses to value (e.g., popularity, beauty, achievement, parental role) will evolve, and subsequently impact the self-esteem he or she attaches to that facet.[1] Physical function and participation also weigh greatly into the self-esteem and self-perceptions of those who are aging.[19] Gender stereotypes and role expectations, in general or by culture, may also color the importance attributed to specific life domains, resulting in gender differences in domain-specific self-esteem, like for the ability to provide for a family or rear and raise children. There may also exist gender differences as to where self-esteem is derived, with females drawing more shame from how others view them in contrast to how males view themselves in relation to others.[25]

Disability can influence the maintenance and further development of self-esteem,[53] insofar as it prevents a person from participating in and/or demonstrating competence in valued life domains. The distance between the "perceived" (actual) and the "ideal" self determines whether a person experiences high or low self-esteem.[47] When the person's "perceived" self is lower than the "ideal" self on a valued attribute, say from a functional limitation, the person is likely to experience lower self-esteem. Miller[54] identified the following mechanisms that decrease self-esteem in the face of chronic illness and disability:

> ➢ cognitive distortions (e.g., inaccurate perceptions of situation, negative self-talk);

> ➢ social isolation;

> ➢ self-denial and doubt;

> ➢ fixation on role incompetence; and

> ➢ self-care incompetence.

Strategies to enhance self-esteem should target the assessment and abatement of these mechanisms in order to empower individuals to pursue goals of the desired self. Self-esteem has been identified as a significant force in motivating consumers to work toward lifestyle and rehabilitation goals.[54]

Significant to the field of rehabilitation counseling, Kahng and Mowbray[39] found that positive social roles and higher levels of income were related to higher ratings of self-esteem for people with mental health conditions, underscoring the importance of participation in vocational services (e.g., overcoming social isolation) and the outcome of successful job placement (e.g., providing means for competence in role fulfillment and self-care). Self-esteem and positive self-concept have also been linked to better rehabilitation outcomes and community participation, greater physical and mental health, and higher life satisfaction;[32] where, conversely, lower levels of these attributes have been associated with decreased help-seeking, increased social isolation, presence of psychopathology, and greater stigmatization.[1,28,64]

Subscribing to the multidimensional model of self-esteem means that measuring self-esteem is not an "all or none" technique; and the presence of a disability, alone, does not predict poor outcomes or impact on a person's self-esteem.[8,64] Disability may affect a singular domain of a person's self-concept, meaning that one's deficits in self-esteem may be linked to only that domain, as well. Research has shown that, despite lower self-concept, perceived competence, or self-esteem in the intellectual domain for children with learning disabilities, many students maintain positive feelings of overall self-worth or self-concept.[1] Zeleke[89] found, in comparing students with learning disabilities and those with average and high achievement in mathematics, that there existed a significant difference in self-esteem only in the area of mathematics, whereas there was no difference in relation to academic or global self-esteem. Similarly, Gans and colleagues[31] found that, despite lower self-concept in specific academic areas, the global self-concept of students with disabilities was on par with those students without disabilities. To explore further this phenomenon, consider the next case scenario of Chase.

CASE STUDY
CHASE

Chase is a high school junior classified as having a specific learning disability related to mathematics, as well as attention-deficit/hyperactivity disorder. He is involved in mainstream classes, but goes to a resource room for math instruction and has an additional period every day for one-on-one assistance with study skills. This is a little embarrassing to him because he wants to be "as good as" his friends and take all his classes with them. Chase is a member of the wrestling team and is active with the school's Habitat for Humanity chapter; sports appear to be a good way to focus his attention. His parents assist him with his homework and studying, and they have been working on teaching him how to handle money. Teachers would describe Chase as "a good kid" and his coach would say, "he's a heck of a wrestler."

The primary location of Chase's difficulties is in the area of mathematics, with some attention difficulties that are remediated with individualized instruction and participation in wrestling. His self-esteem appears to be decreased as a result of his lower level of competence in math, but also because it separates him from his peer group for part of the school day, causing the negative self-comparison. On the positive side, Chase excels in athletics, has a supportive family and peer group, and he is held in high regard by the school staff. It is anticipated that if you asked Chase to rate his overall "happiness" and high school experience that he would focus on the positive aspects, rather than his singular difficulty in math. Social/Parental support and competence in other areas beyond the academic domain have been found to be contributors to overall enhanced self-esteem.[33,65] In the context of school, students' perceived image of self will have an impact on their academic performance, but early positive learning experiences should assist students with developing efficacy and esteem necessary for academic perseverance.[76]

Now that the constructs of self-concept and self-esteem have been expanded, with some applicability to individuals with disabilities, the following section will explore further the consequences of disability on an individual's identity and esteem.

THE INTERPLAY OF DISABILITY WITH SELF-CONCEPT AND SELF-ESTEEM

The process of self-concept development, with its related self-esteem associations, relies on information from a variety of sources, including performance accomplishments, evaluations of others, self-evaluations, and emotional reactions, to form one's self-identity. This course of development occurs throughout the lifespan and within a person's personal and cultural contexts. The process of identity formation is complex enough given the typical course of human development and social interactions. Compound it, though, with the period of upheaval that typically comes with an acquired disability, or the societal stigma and devaluation that can come with any disability, and the process becomes imminently more convoluted.

Within the context of the disability experience, individuals are left to integrate the "self with a disability" into their current construct of self or deal with the discrepancy between others' perceptions of their capabilities and what they know to be true. Threats to self-concept and self-esteem can come from internal appraisals of lowered capabilities or from the imposition of environmental and attitudinal barriers. Mpofu and Harley contended that "whether the disability is newly acquired or congenital in nature, the development and preservation of a value system that integrates disability concepts in an adaptive and positive manner is essential to dealing with disability issues intrapersonally and within the individual's environment."[56, p.147] The formation of self means everyone must create a unique narrative identity, "a personal evolving story of the self that an individual consciously and unconsciously creates to bind together many different aspects of the self."[23, p.148] Specific to a person with a disability is creating the narrative identity of a disability identity.

Disability identity refers to creating a positive sense of self with a disability, as well as a feeling of connection to and kinship with other members of the disability community.[23] Those living with mental health conditions or substance use disorders may define this as recovery—the establishment of a meaningful life and positive sense of identity, despite the presence of the condition.[73] Identification with the disability community allows a person to incorporate group membership into one's identity from which he or she can draw self-worth, combat discrimination, and engage in collective action.[59] Collective action can range from employing strategies to emphasize strengths and problem solve[58] to disability pride and activism, which is an outgrowth of the Disability Rights Movement.[19] These group activities seek to improve the status and esteem of the disability community, which can thereby raise the self-esteem of those who affiliate with the group.[8]

Although disability can play a prominent role in the self-identity of a person with a disability, it need not be the defining feature of the person's existence. As such, the importance of the disability identity will wax and wane with the environment, situation, and context, whereas it may be salient in times of social activism, but not so when a person is relaxing with family.[23] The following sections highlight three specific examples of the impact of disability and social perceptions on the self-concept and self-esteem of an individual.

MENTAL HEALTH CONDITIONS AND SELF-STIGMA

The stigma of disability is felt significantly by people with mental health conditions given poor portrayals of these individuals in the media and the perception of danger and unpredictability associated with these conditions.[57,87] Public stigma can be conceived in terms of three components: stereotypes, prejudice, and discrimination. Stereotypes are social acknowledgements of held beliefs—efficient heuristics by which to conceptualize groups of individuals. "Stereotypes are considered 'social' because they represent collectively agreed upon notions of groups of persons. They are 'efficient' because people can quickly generate impressions and expectations of individuals who belong to a stereotyped group."[86, p. 236] However, not all stereotypes result in prejudice. The cognitive and affective response of prejudice results from *agreement* with stereotypes, which may result in anger, fear, blame, and other emotional responses towards the stigmatized group. Discrimination is a behavioral reaction to the internalized prejudice, which can be manifest as withholding opportunities (e.g., jobs to people with disabilities) or hostile behavior.[44] Public stigma may also be imbedded as institutional stigma, in which rules, policies, and procedures restrict the rights of individuals with psychiatric disabilities.[48]

Individuals in society may develop negative perceptions about people with psychiatric disabilities; however, these perceptions do not necessarily change when the person develops the condition.[48] This may result in the development of self-stigma regarding a person's own mental health. Once a person is diagnosed as having a mental health condition, it can be predicted that one will develop negative self-esteem related to the social perceptions and devaluation associated with the illness, making these devaluations relevant to one's own self.[16] The development of self-stigma follows much of the same process as developing affective and behavioral responses to stereotypes. Corrigan and colleagues[17] identified the four phases of self-stigma development:

> *stereotype awareness*: the person is aware of the general negative beliefs about mental health held by one's culture;

> *stereotype agreement*: the person endorses the same stereotypes perceived to be common in the public;

> *self-concurrence*: the person believes that culturally internalized beliefs in fact apply to him/her;

> *self-esteem decrement*: the person's self-esteem is diminished due to concurrence with the negative belief.

Several factors may influence the degree to which a person applies a negative stereotype to oneself. The strength with which one identifies with the disability group or culture may directly correlate to the degree to which the person believes the stereotype applies to oneself.[37] The perceived legitimacy of the stereotype also impacts the degree to which the person will apply the stereotype. When people perceive negative responses as legitimate, such as "people with mental illness are unpredictable and unreliable," they are apt to agree with the stigma, possibly limiting their efficacy in this example for seeking and retaining employment.[25] Finally, contingencies of self-worth, or the domains upon which a person determines his or her self-esteem, can contextually and temporally affect a person's adherence to self-stigma. If the stereotypes are directly related to central life domains, such as competence and the approval of others, then this will have a more distinct impact on one's self-esteem and self-valuation.[86]

Studies have linked self-stigma to diminished self-esteem, undermined adherence with services, and interfering with the attainment of rehabilitation goals.[16,28] Self-stigma and fear of public stigma have led to individuals with mental health conditions not seeking services or dropping out of treatment prematurely.[44] Individuals may feel demoralized because of the stigma, limiting their options to alleviate distress and develop strategies to cope with the stigma.[61] Another impact of the imposition of self-stigma is that individuals will restrict their social networks and opportunities in anticipation of rejection due to the stigma.[86] The outcomes of these behaviors include increased social isolation, decreased opportunity for employment, and reduced income, which can in turn lead to further decrements in self-esteem and self-efficacy. According to Ilic and colleagues,[37] the development of a positive identity related to psychiatric disabilities and the mental health community, as well as strategies to manage this identity, is one way that individuals can cope with stigma and isolation. They report that those who hold individuals with mental health conditions in positive regard and align with the community in a positive way experience better mental health. Additionally, employing coping strategies, known as identity management strategies, can improve personal resources for dealing with stigma-related stressors.

SOCIAL INTERACTIONS, THE PERCEPTIONS OF OTHERS, AND THE "MASTER STATUS"

We recall from the above sections that self-concept and self-esteem do not develop in a vacuum; they are, at least in part, reliant on the judgments of others and the greater environmental and social context. The research reflects that social interaction between people with and without disabilities can span the spectrum from negative devaluing interactions, to 'non-person' experiences, to contact that is highlighted by acts of kindness and goodwill. The overriding standard for many of these interactions is ill-conceived or stereotyped perceptions of others.

The hallmark of social goals is to be accepted, to fit in, to be 'one of the crowd'—to quote Rudyard Kipling in his poem *If*, "that all men count with you, but none too much." The goals of people with disabilities are often no different. But, by and large, society chooses to use disability as their primary identifier.[88] Oliver, as cited in Watson,[85] noted that people with disabilities are identified either through (a) the presence of an impairment, (b) the experience of socially or environmentally imposed restrictions, or (c) self-identification as a person with a disability. Disability is viewed as their defining characteristic, or master status, which results in an overriding stigmatized identity.[11] Some individuals feel boxed into their disability label by others or by their own internalized ableism.[40] Other individuals with disabilities attempt to reject the disability identity as part of their self-concept for fear that they will be labeled or identified as their disability first and foremost, rather than 'John Q. Citizen' who just happens to have a disability. However, findings suggest that individuals who fail to self-identify as a person with a disability experience lower self-esteem and quality of life.[18,23]

Galvin[30] conducted a qualitative, multinational study exploring the process of disability identity formation and the situations that colored the experiences of people with acquired disabilities. Issues of independence, work, and appearance/sexuality were the areas that were most impacted by the identity transformation. Many individuals reported they wanted to avoid representations of disability that focused on pity, weakness, and loss, and focus more on the reconstruction of self and a positive image. A shift in frame of reference was needed to start to focus on interdependence over independence, acknowledging that *all* humans rely on others and structures in society for resources and support, not just people with disabilities. There was also a theme of rejecting work as the singular way to define oneself as a member of society, that it is not a requirement of living or being counted as a human being. Individuals in the sample looked for new ways to define themselves beyond work and roles that are 'required' by society.

Perception of the capabilities of people with disabilities is another obstacle to social interactions. Individuals without disabilities make attributions of limitations, need for charity, and personal responsibility based on their impression of the disability.[22] These perceptions can shape the interaction and impact on the individual with disability's self-concept or esteem. For example, in hypothesizing the reasons why individuals with minor physical disabilities had lower self-esteem than those with significant physical limitations, Miyahara and Piek[55] posited that those with greater physical disability most likely engendered greater empathy and less insensitive discrimination from others. Those with less physical impairment may have their limitations masked or hidden; leading others to believe that lack of effort is the cause for lack of competence. It is not necessarily their actual lack of ability that resulted in lowered ratings of self-esteem, but rather the perception of others that they were 'slackers' that resulted in the decrement.

Those with non-visible or 'hidden' disabilities do not escape the negative perceptions and devaluation of others. Charmaz[11] found that individuals, who did not have visible symptoms and disabilities and appeared 'healthy,' had difficulty garnering credibility with health care practitioners. This healthy appearance was confusing to family and friends who could not understand the limitations imposed by a debilitating condition, given their pre-illness conception of the individual. Individuals with fibromyalgia[21] and chronic fatigue syndrome[39] encounter skepticism and disbelief related to their limitations, especially in the absence of empirical evidence of impairment. Similar devaluations are experienced by those with intellectual impairments and traumatic brain injury, in that they look "normal" to people (as a physical evaluation); therefore, people are not empathetic to their cognitive limitations.

On the other end of the spectrum are interactions with those in society who are overly nice and inappropriately helpful, seeking to make an affiliation or kinship with people with disabilities. These people viewed individuals with disabilities as heroic or extraordinary for participating in typical activities of daily life. Unwelcome social interactions came from those who praised individuals using a wheelchair for performing routine tasks or for simply being out in public independently.[7] Several respondents in Galvin's[30] study indicated individuals they encountered felt people with disabilities should be applauded for doing ordinary activities, when to the people with disabilities that is exactly what they were—routine tasks, like riding a bus. Participants felt demeaned by the praise. In some cases, good intentions on the part of individuals result in a devaluing or negative experience for a person with a disability. Wheelchair users felt that strangers and salespeople would go to incredible lengths to serve their needs, although sometimes it was overwhelming, not requested, or even painful.[7] Respondents noted several occasions when well-intended employees of restaurants and other establishments would make physical accommodations for their wheelchair, such as rearranging tables or carrying the person up the stairs; however, these experiences often lead to unnecessary and embarrassing attention drawn to the person in the wheelchair.

Negative and 'non-person' experiences permeate the stories of individuals with disabilities. Participants in the study conducted by Sheldon and colleagues[74] reported they were stared at because of their spinal cord injury and wheelchair use, sometimes being laughed at for spilling or incontinence. In their qualitative study with wheelchair users, Cahill and Egglston[7] reported that many users were not ignored, as is often reported, but rather were treated as though not there. This included being talked about or talked past to a preferred companion not in a wheelchair, as well as feelings of boundary encroachment or claimed kinship. In these latter instances, individuals in wheelchairs were approached with inappropriate questions about the function and cost of their wheelchair, or others would attempt to ally with the individual on the basis that they "know someone" who uses a wheelchair. However, a man on the autism spectrum, profiled by Dunn and Burcaw,[23] reported that he was bullied by classmates in school, but preferred the negative treatment to receiving no attention at all.

As can be gleaned from the above examples, oftentimes it is the unfamiliarity of the person *without* a disability, and the subsequent anxiety he or she experiences in the social interaction with the person with a disability, that is the basis for awkward or inappropriate social interactions.[9] It is also not necessarily that people with disabilities experience the stigma of disability in a negative way at all times, as the experiences cover the spectrum. What was evident is that many of the negative experiences were not derived from discrimination, but from ignorance of disability etiquette, social boundaries, and respect for autonomy.[7] That is why the basis for interactions with people with disabilities should be founded on the fundamental principles that Beatrice Wright[88] articulated decades ago: treat people with disabilities as *persons first*, with the respect, privacy, and dignity we would ask for ourselves.

BODY IMAGE AND DISABILITY

Physical and visible disability, whether congenital or acquired, can impact a person's self-concept with regard to one's body image, which can then cloud interactions and relationships with others. Body image describes how one sees, thinks, feels, and acts in relation to his or her body, incorporating how a person views oneself and interprets the perceptions of others.[74] On a personal level, positive body image is composed of:

- ➤ favorable opinions about one's body;

- ➤ body acceptance;

- ➤ respecting the body through healthy practices; and

- ➤ protecting oneself by rejecting unrealistic ideal body images.[2]

The presence of a disability, messages received from prevailing society, and the reactions of others can present a barrier to obtaining and maintaining this positive body image. Pande and Tewari[63] found several of the factors that related to distress for people with physical disabilities, among others, were deviant body image, dependency on others, and interpersonal relations.

Loss of function is a prominent feature in altered body image. With disabilities like spinal cord injury, individuals feel disconnected between their functioning body parts and those affected by the injury, in a way that makes them feel as though they are not whole.[74] Sexual encounters have been noted to be an area of difficulty for people with physical or known disabilities because of the reactions of others. Kattari[40] investigated the sexual experiences of people with physical disabilities in regard to how they negotiate sexual partners. Respondents indicated that disability was at the forefront of many sexual interactions because of one's own embarrassment, the need to negotiate physical or communication barriers, or partners not seeing past disability to the individual. Ways to alleviate discomfort and increase connection to one's partner included open communication, adapting sexual practices, and finding new ways to create intimacy.

Oftentimes, reconciling body image following an acquired disability requires the person come to terms with aspects that cannot be changed and focus on assets rather than shortcomings; appreciating all aspects of the body (e.g., health, personality), instead of just physical appearance, allows a person to broaden his or her outlook on the definition of beauty.[2] The strength of psychological coping resources, not the severity of the condition, predicts more positive outcomes for those with visible disabilities, as well as having family and social environments that support a view that self-esteem is not contingent on appearance.[79]

Difficulties with social and interpersonal experiences resulting from the impact of disability on self-concept and self-esteem form the basis for counseling strategies. The following section will cover implications and interventions in counseling practice.

INTERVENTIONS FOR COUNSELING

The code of ethics for rehabilitation counselors calls for professionals to respect the rights, dignity, and autonomy of the individual and to seek to reduce environmental and attitudinal barriers.[13] It is responsible, ethical practice for rehabilitation counselors to develop and implement interventions aimed at facilitating self-concept and self-esteem development in individuals with disabilities, as a means to the goal of improving overall quality of life for consumers. Interventions can be targeted toward change within the person or environment. The following sections delineate specific strategies and interventions for rehabilitation counseling practice.

CHANGE WITHIN THE PERSON

One must recognize self-concept is a product of self-determination, autonomy, and personal choice for counseling interventions to succeed. Consumers have the capability to make decisions about how they view themselves and react to an environment that attempts to label and define who they are.[85] Several strategies can be employed by an individual to protect and/or enhance their self-concept. counselors should work with consumers on using these strategies effectively.

➢ Self-concept should develop through a person's life narrative.[23,85] Traditionally, people define themselves by group memberships or role assignments in life. However, defining oneself in this way, lends itself to the risk of labeling. Consumers should be encouraged to tell their life story, which is more fluid and less confining to a label. Through this process, consumers should be encouraged to think about their life story positively, perhaps incorporating disability identity into their narrative.[23] This may involve revising a negative memory from the past in a positive way so as to boost the self-concept or envisioning a future self through positive storytelling.[71]

➢ Considering the multidimensional nature of self-concept, people are in a position to lower or heighten the importance of certain aspects of their self-concept over others.[35,41] Their self-esteem is also likely to vary across the different dimensions. Consumers should be encouraged to place more importance on experiences that support valued aspects of the self-concept, which leads to higher rather than lower self-esteem. Similarly, when a person feels a threat to self-concept due to feedback, labeling, or other evaluative processes, they may wish to lower the importance or centrality of the specific area being targeted. This, in turn, helps to preserve and enhance their self-concept.[35] Lannin and colleagues[44] suggested one way that counselors can assist consumers with psychiatric disabilities to counteract some of the negativity associated with the label of mental health conditions is through "mental illness coming out," wherein a person can disclose his/her condition and take pride in it as part of one's identity. Broadcasting one's disability can create a sense of power for the individual, but also educate and sensitize others to mental health conditions.[16] Additionally, counselors can use various assessments related to well-being and quality of life to explore salient aspects of a person's self-concept/worldview to assist in his or her response to disability and goal setting.[45]

➢ Self-verification and social comparisons may also serve as tools to preserve the self-concept. Self-verification may occur by soliciting or paying attention to feedback from others that confirms specific self-perceptions. While individuals with high self-esteem are inclined to seek positive feedback, those with low self-esteem often seek negative self-verifying feedback.[35] Interventions should focus on assisting consumers to verify their self-concept in a positive way that promotes higher self-esteem. Social comparisons may be used as one type of strategy to self-verify. According to Marini,[49] "downward comparisons" are often used by people as a way to feel better about themselves. Individuals will compare themselves to others (hypothetical or real) whom they believe are in a situation below their own. By making this comparison, they perceive their own situation more favorably. In making this type of comparison, it is important for individuals to be sensitive towards those with whom the comparisons are being made. Individuals may also make an upward identification to someone they perceive to be in better health, as a means of providing hope.[45]

➢ As discussed earlier, incorporating disability into one's identity can be important to that person achieving satisfaction in life and connecting with the disability community.[23] Research indicates those who recognize and identify with their disability have greater self-esteem, better mental health, and more adaptability to situations.[37,58] One way for consumers to take pride in their disability is through collective action with others in the disability community. Nario-Redmond and colleagues[59] found those most likely to make an impact in society by challenging the status quo were those who claimed disability as a centrally defining feature of themselves. Collective action and identity serves a purpose for the individual, but also for all people with disabilities. First, by associating with others with disabilities, individuals can learn adaptive strategies, educate themselves on services/resources, and make helpful social comparisons/identifications to motivate them toward goals.[83] Additionally, as a group supporting one another, membership and participation in the disability community can facilitate collective action against stigma and discrimination at a personal and institutional level.[37] Therefore, counselors can seek opportunities for consumers to connect with the disability community, at the level of comfort and ability of the consumer, to draw benefits and contribute through this affiliation.

CHANGE WITHIN THE ENVIRONMENT

Counseling interventions aimed at "change within the environment" should focus on addressing perceptions and attitudes toward people with disabilities, demystifying disability, and improving social interactions among people with and without disabilities. The following techniques are recommended:

> Strategies for erasing public stigma at a personal level include interventions of advocacy, education, and contact.[15] Advocacy strategies use public demonstration and media to address the stigmatizing images of people with disabilities. Educational approaches are aimed at providing factual information to counteract and replace negative stereotypes of people with disabilities. For example, increased mental health literacy may change how people view mental health. For people with psychiatric disabilities, this may decrease their own feelings of self-stigma and increase their likelihood to seek treatment.[15,28] However, the public service message should avoid a medical/biological approach to describing mental health conditions, as this was found to enhance the perceptions of the dangerousness of people with these conditions.[37] The most effective means for combating and reducing prejudice is personal contact with members of the stigmatized group, with improvements in attitudes most pronounced when contact is with a person that moderately challenges prevailing stereotypes. Evans-Lacko and colleagues[28] found that countries with greater comfort in talking to people with mental illness had lower stigma and higher empowerment for people with psychiatric disabilities.

> Given the link between positive self-esteem and valued social roles, the quality of services in rehabilitation can be enhanced by increasing the number of positive social roles in which the person can engage, including support groups, education, and work.[39,64] Offering a variety of services from which to choose, furnishing adequate information regarding those services, and providing opportunities for active participation and decision-making in the service delivery process will provide the conditions for consumer

direction,[42] thereby enhancing the consumer's sense of competence and role attainment.

> Public disability awareness education should focus on disability etiquette and respecting the boundaries of individuals with disabilities.[81] Inappropriate, embarrassing, or uncomfortable social interactions often result from not placing respect for the individual above adhering to the laws or striving to be politically correct. Basic social rules should include asking if a person wants assistance, not just providing it (sometimes against the person's will!), addressing the person with a disability directly and not speaking about them to a companion without a disability, and providing accommodations in a discreet manner. Workplaces and social environments should strive to create inclusive cultures where the language and practices are disability-appropriate.[34]

REFERENCES

[1]Arens, A. K., & Hasselhorn, M. (2014). Age and gender differences in the relation between self-concept facets and self-esteem. *Journal of Early Adolescence, 34,* 760-791.

[2]Bailey, K. A., Gammage, K. L., van Ingen, C., & Ditor, D. S. (2015). "It's all about acceptance": A qualitative study exploring a model of positive body image for people with spinal cord injury. *Body Image, 15,* 24-34.

[3]Baumeister, R. F. (1995). Self and identity: An introduction. In A. Tesser (Ed.), *Advanced social psychology* (pp. 51-97). Boston, MA: McGraw-Hill Inc.

[4]Bishop, M., Shepard, L., & Stenhoff, D. M. (2007). Psychosocial adaptation and quality of life in multiple sclerosis: Assessment of the disability centrality model. *Journal of Rehabilitation, 73*(1), 3-12.

[5]Bogart, K. R. (2014). The role of disability self-concept in adaptation to congenital or acquired disability. *Rehabilitation Psychology, 59,* 107-115.

[6]Brabcova, D., Zarubova, J., Kohout, J., Jost, J., & Krsek, P. (2015). Effects of learning disabilities on academic self-concept in children with epilepsy and on their quality of life. *Research in Developmental Disabilities, 45-46,* 120-128.

[7]Cahill, S. E., & Eggleston, R. (1995). Reconsidering the stigma of physical disability: Wheelchair use and public kindness. *The Sociological Quarterly, 36,* 681-698.

[8]Chalk, H. M. (2016). Disability self-categorization in emerging adults: Relationship with self-esteem, perceived esteem, mindfulness, and markers of adulthood. *Emerging Adulthood, 4,* 200-206.

[9]Chan, F., Cardoso, E. D., & Chronister, J. A. (2009). *Understanding psychosocial adjustment to chronic illness and disability: A handbook for evidence-based practitioners in rehabilitation.* New York, NY: Springer.

[10]Chang, H. J., Yurchisin, J., Hodges, N., Watchravesringkan, K., & Ackerman, T. (2013). An investigation of self-concept, clothing selection motivation, and life satisfaction among disabled consumers. *Family and Consumer Sciences Research Journal, 42*(2), 162-176.

[11]Charmaz, K. (1995). The body, identity, and self: Adapting to impairment. *The Sociological Quarterly, 36,* 657-680.

[12]Charmaz, K. (1993). *Good days, bad days: The self in chronic illness and time.* New Brunswick, NJ: Rutgers University Press.

[13]Commission on Rehabilitation Counselor Certification. (2017). *Code of professional ethics for rehabilitation counselors.* Schaumburg, IL: Author.

[14]Coopersmith, S. (1981). *Antecedents of self-esteem* (2nd ed.). San Francisco, CA: Freeman.

[15]Corrigan, P. W., Druss, B. G., & Perlick, D. A. (2014). The impact of mental illness stigma on seeking and participating in mental health care. *Psychological Science in the Public Interest, 15*(2), 37-70.

[16]Corrigan, P. W., Larson, J. E., & Rüsch, N. (2009). Self-stigma and the "why try" effect: Impact on life goals and evidence-based practices. *World Psychiatry, 8,* 75-81.

[17]Corrigan, P. W., Watson, A. C., & Barr, L. (2006). The self-stigma of mental illness: Implications for self-esteem and self-efficacy. *Journal of Social and Clinical Psychology, 25,* 875-884.

[18]Dagnan, D., & Sandhu, S. (1999). Social comparison, self-esteem, and depression in people with intellectual disability. *Journal of Intellectual Disability Research, 43*(5), 372-379.

[19]Darling, R. B., & Heckert, D. A. (2010). Orientations toward disability: Differences over the lifecourse. *International Journal of Disability, Development and Education, 57,* 131-143.

[20]Datta, P. (2014). Self-concept and vision impairment: A review. *British Journal of Visual Impairment, 32*(3), 200-210.

[21]Dennis, N. L., Larkin, M., & Derbyshire, S. W. G. (2013). 'A giant mess'—Making sense of complexity in the accounts of people with fibromyalgia. *British Journal of Health Psychology, 18,* 763-781.

[22]Dunn, D. S. (2015). *The social psychology of disability.* New York, NY: Oxford University Press.

[23]Dunn, D. S., & Burcaw, S. (2013). Disability identity: Exploring narrative accounts of disability. *Rehabilitation Psychology, 58,* 148-157.

[24]Elbaum, B., & Vaughn, S. (2003). For which students with learning disabilities are self-concept interventions effective? *Journal of Learning Disabilities, 36*(2), 101-108.

[25]Elkington, K. S., Hackler, D., McKinnon, K., Borges, C., Wright, E. R., & Wainberg, M. L. (2012). Perceived mental illness stigma among youth in psychiatric outpatient treatment. *Journal of Adolescent Research, 27*, 290-317.

[26]Ellis-Hill, C. S., & Horn, S. (2000). Change in identity and self-concept: A new theoretical approach to recovery following a stroke. *Clinical Rehabilitation, 14*, 279-287.

[27]Epstein, S. (1973). The self-concept revisited: Or a theory of a theory. *American Psychologist, 28*(5), 404-416.

[28]Evans-Lacko, S., Brohan, E., Mojtabai, R., & Thornicroft, G. (2012). Association between public views of mental illness and self-stigma among individuals with mental illness in 14 European countries. *Psychological Medicine, 42*, 1741-1752.

[29]Ferro, M. A., & Boyle, M. H. (2013). Brief report: Testing measurement invariance and differences in self-concept between adolescents with and without physical illness or developmental disability. *Journal of Adolescence, 36*(5), 947-951.

[30]Galvin, R. D. (2005). Researching the disabled identity: Contextualising the identity transformations which accompany the onset of impairment. *Sociology of Health & Illness, 27*, 393-413.

[31]Gans, A. M., Kenny, M. C., & Ghany, D. L. (2003). Comparing the self-concept of students with and without learning disabilities. *Journal of Learning Disabilities, 36*, 287-295.

[32]Geyh, S., Nick, E., Stirnimann, D., Ehrat, S., Michel, F., Peter, C., & Lude, P. (2012). Self-efficacy and self-esteem as predictors of participation in spinal cord injury—an ICF-based study. *Spinal Cord, 50*, 699-706.

[33]Gniewosz, B., Eccles, J. S., & Noack, P. (2012). Secondary school transition and the use of different sources of information for the construction of the academic self-concept. *Social Development, 21*, 537-557.

[34]Golden, L. (2013). *Diversity leaders: 6 things to NEVER say about disabilities.* Retrieved from http://www.diversityinc.com/things-not-to-say/diversity-leaders-6-things-never-to-say-about-disabilities/

[35]Hattie, J. (2004). *Models of self-concept that are neither top-down or bottom-up: The rope model of self-concept.* Retrieved from University of Auckland, New Zealand from https://cdn.auckland.ac.nz/assets/education/hattie/docs/hattie-models-of-self-concept-(2004).pdf

[36]Higgins, E. T. (1987). Self-discrepancy: A theory relating self and affect. *Psychological Review, 94*(3), 319-340.

[37]Ilic, M., Reinecke, J., Bohner, G., Röttgers, H., Beblo, T., Driessen, M...Corrigan, P. W. (2011). Protecting self-esteem from stigma: A test of different strategies for coping with the stigma of mental illness. *International Journal of Social Psychiatry, 58*, 246-257.

[38]Jang, J. S. (1998). Self-esteem, delinquent peers, and delinquency: A test of the self-enhancement thesis. *American Sociological Review, 63*, 586-598.

[39]Kahng, S. K., & Mowbray, C. T. (2005). What affects self-esteem of persons with psychiatric disabilities: The role of causal attributions of mental illness. *Psychiatric Rehabilitation Journal, 28*, 354-361.

[40]Kattari, S. K. (2014). Sexual experiences of adults with physical disabilities: Negotiating sexual partners. *Sexuality and Disability, 32*, 499-513.

[41]Kling, K. C., Ryff, C. D., & Essex, M. J. (1997). Adaptive changes in the self-concept during a life transition. *Personality and Social Psychology Bulletin, 23*(9), 981-990.

[42]Kosciulek, J. F. (1999). The consumer-directed theory of empowerment. *Rehabilitation Counseling Bulletin, 42*, 196-213.

[43]Kuzucu, Y., Bontempo, D. E., Hofer, S. M., Stallings, M. C., & Piccinin, A. M. (2014). Developmental change and time specific variation in global and specific aspects in self-concept in adolescence and association with depressive symptoms. *Journal of Early Adolescence, 34*, 638-666.

[44]Lannin, D. G., Vogel, D. L., Brenner, R. E., & Tucker, J. R. (2015). Predicting self-esteem and intentions to seek counseling: The internalized stigma model. *The Counseling Psychologist, 43*, 64-93.

[45]Larsen, P. D. (2016). Psychosocial adjustment. In P. Larsen (Ed.), *Lubkin's chronic illness* (9th ed., pp. 43-62). Burlington, MA: Jones & Bartlett.

[46]Leon, L. C., & Matthews, L. R. (2010). Self-esteem theories: Possible explanations for poor interview performance for people experiencing unemployment. *Journal of Rehabilitation, 76*(1), 41-50.

[47]Leonard, N. H., Beauvais, L. L., & Scholl, R. W. (1999). Work motivation: The incorporation of self-concept-based processes. *Human Relations, 52*, 969-998.

[48]Livingston, J. D., & Boyd, J. E. (2010). Correlates and consequences of internalized stigma for people living with mental illness: A systematic review and meta-analysis. *Social Science & Medicine, 71*, 2150-2161.

[49]Marini, I. (2012). Theories of adjustment and adaptation to disability. In I. Marini, M. J. Millington, & N. M. Glover-Graf (Eds.), *Psychosocial aspects of disability: Insider perspectives and counseling strategies* (pp. 115-143). New York, NY: Springer Publishing.

[50]Markus, H. R., & Kitayama, S. (1991). Culture and the self: Implications for cognition, emotion, and motivation. *Psychological Review, 98*(2), 224-253.

[51]Markus, H., & Wurf, E. (1987). The dynamic self-concept: A social psychological perspective. *Annual Review of Psychology, 38*, 299-337.

[52]Marsh, H. W., & Craven, R. G. (2006). Reciprocal effects of self-concept and performance from a multidimensional perspective: Beyond seductive pleasure and unidimensional perspectives. *Perspectives on Psychological Science, 1*(2), 133-163.

[53]Mikula, P., Nagyova, I., Krokavcova, M., Vitkova, M., Rosenberger, J., Szilasiova, J...van Dijk, J. P. (2016). Self-esteem, social participation, and quality of life in patients with multiple sclerosis. *Journal of Health Psychology.* Advance online publication. doi: 10.1177/1359105315621778

[54]Miller, J. F. (2000). *Coping with chronic illness: Overcoming powerlessness,* 3rd ed. Philadelphia, PA: F. A. Davis, Co.

[55]Miyahara, M., & Piek, J. (2006). Self-esteem of children and adolescents with physical disabilities: Quantitative evidence from meta-analysis. *Journal of Developmental and Physical Disabilities, 18,* 219-234.

[56]Mpofu, E., & Harley, D. A. (2006). Racial and disability identity: Implications for the career counseling of African Americans with disabilities. *Rehabilitation Counseling Bulletin, 50*(1), 14-23.

[57]Nairn, R., Coverdale, S., & Coverdale, J. H. (2011). A framework for understanding media depictions of mental illness. *Academic Psychiatry, 35,* 202-206.

[58]Nario-Redmond, M. R., Noel, J. G., & Fern, E. (2013). Redefining disability, re-imagining the self: Disability identification predicts self-esteem and strategic responses to stigma. *Self and Identity, 12,* 468-488.

[59]Nario-Redmond, M. R., & Oleson, K. C. (2015). Disability group identification and disability-rights advocacy: Contingencies among emerging and other adults. *Emerging Adulthood, 4,* 207-218.

[60]Olney, M. F., & Kim, A. (2001). Beyond adjustment: Integration of cognitive disability into identity. *Disability and Society, 16*(4), 563-583.

[61]Owen, J., Thomas, L., & Rodolfa, E. (2013). Stigma for seeking therapy: Self-stigma, social stigma, and therapeutic processes. *The Counseling Psychologist, 41,* 857-880.

[62]Ownsworth, T., Desbois, J., Grant, E., Fleming, J., & Strong, J. (2006). The associations among self-awareness, emotional well-being, and employment outcome following acquired brain injury: A 12-month longitudinal study. *Rehabilitation Psychology, 51*(1), 50-59.

[63]Pande, N., & Tewari, S. (2011). Understanding coping with distress due to physical disability. *Psychology and Developing Societies, 23,* 177-209.

[64]Paterson, L., McKenzie, K., & Lindsay, B. (2012). Stigma, social comparison and self-esteem in adults with an intellectual disability. *Journal of Applied Research in Intellectual Disabilities, 25,* 166-176.

[65]Peixoto, F., & Almeida, L. S. (2010). Self-concept, self-esteem and academic achievement: Strategies for maintaining self-esteem in students experiencing academic failure. *European Journal of Psychology in Education, 25,* 157-175.

[66]Phoenix, T. L. (2001). Who am I?: Identity formation, youth, and therapeutic recreation. *Therapeutic Recreation Journal, 35*(4), 348-355.

[67]Ponsford, J., Kelly, A., & Couchman, G. (2014). Self-concept and self-esteem after acquired brain injury; A control group comparison. *Brain Injury 28*(2), 146-154.

[68]Raine, R., Carter, S., Sensky, T., & Black, N. (2004). General practitioners' perception of chronic fatigue syndrome and beliefs about its management, compared with irritable bowel syndrome: Qualitative study. *BMJ, 328,* 1354-357.

[69]Reeve, D. (2002). Negotiating psycho-emotional dimensions of disability and their influence on identity constructions. *Disability and Society, 17*(5), 493-508.

[70]Sanders, K.Y. (2006). Overprotection and lowered expectations of persons with disabilities: The unforeseen consequences. *Work, 27,* 181-188.

[71]Sanitioso, B., Conway, M. A., & Brunot, S. (2006). Autobiographical memory, the self, and comparison processes. In S. Guimond (Ed.), *Social comparison and social psychology: Understanding cognition, intergroup relations and culture* (pp. 55-75). Cambridge, England: Cambridge University Press.

[72]Self Research Centre (2007). *Unidimensional vs. multidimensional perspectives.* Retrieved from http://self.uws.edu.au//Research%20Focus/unidimensional_vs_multidimension.htm

[73]Shea, J. M. (2009). Coming back normal: The process of self-recovery in those with schizophrenia. *Journal of the American Psychiatric Nurses Association, 16,* 43-51.

[74]Sheldon, A. P., Renwick, R., & Yoshida, K. K. (2011). Exploring body image and self-concept of men with acquired spinal cord injuries. *American Journal of Men's Health, 5,* 306-317.

[75]Smedema, S. M., Catalano, D., & Ebener, D. J. (2010). The relationship of coping, self-worth, and subjective well-being: A structural equation model. *Rehabilitation Counseling Bulletin, 53,* 131-142.

[76]Sze, S., & Valentin, S. (2007). Self-concept and children with disabilities. *Education, 127,* 552-557.

[77]Taleporos, G., & McCabe, M. P. (2001). The impact of physical disability on body esteem. *Sexuality and Disability, 19*(4), 293-308.

[78]Thomas, S. (2011). Using personal construct theory to explore self-image with adolescent with learning disabilities. *British Journal of Learning Disabilities, 39,* 225-232.

[79]Tiggemann, M. (2015). Considerations of positive body image across various social identities and special populations. *Body Image, 14,* 168-176.

[80]Triandis, H. C. (1989). The self and social behavior in differing cultural contexts. *Psychological Review, 96,* 506-520.

[81]United Spinal Association. (2015). *Disability etiquette: Tips on interacting with people with disabilities.* Retrieved from http://www.unitedspinal.org/disability-etiquette/

[82]Vash, C. L. (1981). *The psychology of disability.* New York, NY: Springer.

[83]Verhaeghe, M., Bracke, P., & Bruynooghe, K. (2008). Stigmatization and self-esteem of persons in recovery from mental illness: The role of peer support. *International Journal of Social Psychiatry, 54,* 206-218.

[84]Waterman, A. S. (1992). Identity as an aspect of optimal psychological functioning. In G. R. Adams, T. P. Gullotta, & R. Montemayor (Eds.), *Adolescent identity formation* (pp. 50-72). Thousand Oaks, CA: Sage Publications.

[85]Watson, N. (2002). Well, I know this is going to sound very strange to you, but I don't see myself as a disabled person: Identity and disability. *Disability & Society, 17,* 509-527.

[86]Watson, A. C., & Larson, J. E. (2006). Personal response to disability stigma: From self-stigma to empowerment. *Rehabilitation Education, 20,* 235-246.

[87]Wood, L., Birtel, M., Alsawy, S., Pyle, M., & Morrison, A. (2014). Public perception of stigma toward people with schizophrenia, depression and anxiety. *Psychiatric Research, 220*(1-2), 604-608.

[88]Wright, B. A. (1983). *Psychical disability—A psychosocial approach* (2nd ed.). New York: Harper & Row.

[89]Zeleke, S. (2004). Difference in self-concept among children with mathematics disabilities and their average and high achieving peers. *International Journal of Disability, Development and Education, 51,* 253-269.

CHAPTER 6

COPING

ANDREA PERKINS NERLICH

SAGE ROSE

I get up. I walk. I fall down.
Meanwhile, I keep dancing.

Native American proverb

Lazarus noted, "When a major loss appears imminent, it can be a difficult time for that person and others close to him or her. It is not just the amount of stress itself that is important, but how one copes with it. Effective coping allows people to keep stress levels moderate and to live with stress without significant psychic and psychological damage."[37, p. 52] The experience of adapting to and living with a disability can be full of these moments of stress and challenge, both for the individual and for the individual's support system. It is necessary for counselors and professionals to have a perspective into coping mechanisms and strategies that will assist the person in attaining an optimal quality of life. To this end, the following chapter will address:

➢ general concepts related to coping, from a historical and contemporary perspective;

➢ the intersection of coping and the disability experience;

➢ specific strategies to facilitate coping;

➢ coping from a family perspective; and

➢ implications for counseling.

COPING

Throughout the literature, most coping researchers agree that coping is essential to understanding how stress affects the well-being of individuals. At the same time, little agreement can be reached about how to conceptualize or measure the theoretical underpinnings of coping, leaving us with multiple theories explaining the same phenomena.[76] Freud[18] was one of the first to conceptualize coping, suggesting it was a defense for internal threats against the ego. A disagreement between Freud and his student, Alfred Adler, led to a shift in the concept of coping, with Adler[1] describing the construct as protection from external environmental threat. It was not until 1936 when Anna Freud[18] determined coping was a function of defending against both internal and external threats.

From the beginning, coping has been an indefinable construct; even today, the theory of coping continues to evolve and grow through the work of researchers and clinicians. Following Anna Freud, Lazarus[80] moved the focus away from coping as a defense mechanism and toward coping as an active appraisal process. He did not present coping as an enduring trait, where the personal disposition of coping style most strongly affects the individual's coping responses to a given situation, but more as a cognitive transaction between the individual (internal) and the environment (external). Lazarus and Folkman defined coping as "constantly changing cognitive and behavioral efforts to manage specific external and/or internal demands that are appraised as taxing or exceeding the resources of the person."[38, p. 141] These demands were also known as unspecified stressors or stressful events that taxed the mind or body.[73] In their transactional coping model, appraisals were the initial response to the stressor or demand, and occurred in sequence as primary appraisals and secondary appraisals. The presence of the stressor on its own will not predict the impact it has on the person; rather, how it is perceived initially, and in reference to perceived resources, will determine the extent to which it is a threat to the person.[74]

Primary Appraisals

People are continuously evaluating what is happening to them and what the impact will be on their well-being.[39] Whether we cope, and how we cope, are based on the first appraisal of the stressful encounter. Primary appraisals are judgments about the initial situation. For example, determining whether an event is irrelevant, positive, or stressful is important in determining whether the stressor will exceed one's resources or how much is perceived to be at stake at that time.

Primary appraisals focus on whether the stressor will be harmful, a threat, or a challenge.[39] Harm is an already experienced damage to the body, mind, or social relationship. A threat is the harm that might occur in the future if something is not done, and challenge is the potential for mastery over the stressor. Although challenge does not have the negative connotation that harm and threat do, challenge is seen as part of the stress appraisal process, because there is potential to experience harm in order to experience challenge. Effective coping must be put into motion for the stressful event to be experienced as a challenge. The key to the appraisal is that the stressor must activate the person's motivation to act based on one's perception it will hinder valued goals.[48] Occasionally, one may appraise a circumstance as more challenging and less threatening, indicating a situational appraisal.

Situational appraisals reflect one's perceived possibility to have control in a specific stressful encounter, as opposed to others having control. These types of appraisals closely resemble Bandura's[3] conceptualization of outcome expectancies, where a prediction is made about whether one will be successful in accomplishing a task. Successfully accomplishing a task may be exceedingly stressful if high stakes are tied to the task, such as passing a licensing exam or changing one's career. If the person determines there is high risk associated with that situation, then the secondary appraisal proceeds in which coping resources are examined.

SECONDARY APPRAISALS

Secondary appraisals are the evaluation of available coping resources and possible options in a stressful situation. Secondary appraisals become significant when the primary appraisal has been made and the next step is to ask what can be done. Coping resources, such as physical, social, psychological, and material availabilities, are evaluated regarding the demands of the situation.[33]

Physical resources are the output of energy or stamina. For example, if a student is at risk of failing an upcoming exam (primary appraisal), the student may think of ways to expend more time studying for that class (secondary appraisal) to be more prepared for the exam. Social resources are social support systems that can provide emotional comfort. In the context of the risk of failing an exam, the student may seek emotional support from a close friend or relative to discuss the possibility of failing. Psychological resources include belief systems that can be utilized to maintain hope, self-esteem, and perseverance. These internal, dispositional coping resources are traits, strengths, and skills that allow people to feel a sense of control and optimism in the situation.[42] Many individuals who are characterized as persevering or resilient can draw upon inner resources to help them through difficult times. Material resources reflect actual access to money, tools, and other objects that may be relevant to the context. A student failing a class may purchase additional resources, such as a textbook companion, study guide, or the help of a tutor. Secondary appraisals may reflect the use of internal and external resources to deal with a stressful encounter.

PROBLEM-FOCUSED AND EMOTION-FOCUSED COPING

Once the situation has been appraised as exceeding the resources of the individual, coping is the process by which the person responds to the demands of the stressful encounter or event.[38] Coping responses mediate the stress between the environment and the self (problem-focused coping) and/or the emotions that are brought on by stress (emotion-focused coping). Problem-focused and emotion-focused coping typically occur together and can facilitate one another by reducing negative emotions to solve problems or by using problem-focused coping to make a threat seem less distressful. Problem-focused coping includes efforts to diminish or remove the threatening event and may include strategies such as defining the problem, weighing potential strategies, and following a plan of action. Problem-focused coping is directed at controlling sources of the stress. Emotion-focused coping relies on attempts to reduce negative feelings that develop in response to a threat and may include social, material, and psychological processes. Processes include seeking emotional support and positive reappraisal, but also denial and avoidance.

Research has explored the relationship between context and coping and has found that problem-focused coping is most effective in controllable situations.[48] Findings are less clear when it comes to emotion-focused coping, with some studies showing this style of coping occurs when faced with uncontrollable stressors,[61] while other findings show the opposite.[7] Lazarus and Folkman suggested that coping processes are neither adaptive nor maladaptive, that coping processes should be kept separate from coping outcomes.[38] However, the adjustment process to stressors is recursive, in that positive outcomes to coping enhance one's personal resources and lead to better future outcomes; on the other hand, poor outcomes become future stressors, depleting resources and the ability to cope.[33]

APPROACH VS. AVOIDANT COPING STYLES

Coping has been defined as a process of dealing with stress. In contrast to the processes mentioned above, a second paradigm does not differentiate between problem solving and emotion control; rather the focus is on whether the individual was active in resolving the stressful encounter. Roth and Cohen[69] suggested approach and avoidance coping are two basic orientations towards threatening situations or events. Both methods of coping may occur, even if one is a more desired approach over the other.

Individuals often prefer one orientation over the other. A student who turns in incomplete homework due to a lack of understanding may then start to skip class to avoid showing his learning difficulties. An approach-oriented coping method would be for the student to set up weekly appointments with the instructor to go over the material not understood. Choosing one method over the other, however, is not always so simple.

To further differentiate approach and avoidance methods of coping, Roth and Cohen[69] provided examples of costs and benefits indicating why certain strategies become useful or disadvantageous to the individual. Approach coping is an engaged coping strategy where the goal is to reduce or eliminate the internal and/or external demands of a stressor. Approach coping benefits include possible resolution of the stressful situation and experiencing a ventilation of affect through the removal of the stressor; however, there is a cost involved. While resolving the situation, the person may experience increased distress and worry, as cognitive and emotional activity is continuously focused on the stressful event. Some individuals do not have the emotional resources to withstand this continuous interaction with the stressor.

Avoidance coping is a disengaged coping strategy where the goal is to avoid or withdraw from the stressor and the emotional consequences. Avoidant coping has the benefit of promoting temporary stress reduction that may allow for the possibility of renewed perseverance and courage to come through; but if avoidance is continued, there is less chance appropriate actions toward resolution will be engaged. With avoidant coping, a sense of emotional numbness is a possibility along with disruptive avoidance behaviors that develop to keep threatening cognitions and feelings out of awareness.[69] In ideal contexts, both approach and avoidant coping methods would operate with benefits being maximized and costs minimized.

Furthering this model, the Responses to Stress model proposes conscious efforts to deal with stressors using three primary strategies of coping.[56] Primary control engagement coping aims to control the situation through problem solving, help seeking, and expressing one's feelings. Secondary control engagement strategies aim at gaining mastery over thoughts and feelings to adapt to the situation, akin to emotion-focused coping. Disengagement coping involves avoiding the stressor and its effects by physically avoiding the source of the stressor, minimizing it, or wishful thinking. Similarly, these approaches can be used in combination to combat the stressor.

COPING AND POSITIVE PSYCHOLOGY

For the past 25 years, positive psychology has been providing an alternative to the deficit model, encouraging practitioners and researchers to focus on a strengths-based approach to well-being. Positive psychology has had applications to many areas, but is particularly powerful for research in disability because of the emphasis on strengths over limitations. Building on one's strengths is achieved by encouraging individuals to exercise positive beliefs and behaviors to manage challenges and cultivate a sense of agency in perceived uncontrollable circumstances. Positive psychology constructs have been found to predict successful adaptation to a range of disabling conditions.[49] Hope and optimism are two positive psychology constructs often used in this research because they share a strong theoretical relationship with coping.

Hope is a cognitive motivational process involving a global view of positive expectations[82] and is based on a reciprocal interaction between one's will (agency) and ways (pathways) toward goal achievement.[61] Those with higher hope have higher levels of well-being because they experience fewer mental health symptoms,[83] more positive therapeutic results, and less depression.[15] Research indicates that hope is a partial mediator between career adaptability and life satisfaction for individuals with a mild intellectual disability.[72] Career adaptability is the ability to cope with changes in work-related tasks and roles. Similarly, Livneh and Martz[42] found individuals with a spinal cord injury (SCI) had better psychological adjustment regarding their condition when they used an engagement coping style. Maintaining this type of coping was beneficial regardless of a person's level of hope. However, if fewer problem-solving styles of coping were utilized, then having a hopeful outlook was essential for the psychological adjustment to SCI. This is reflective of past research producing similar results for psychological adjustment and SCI. Smedema, Catalano, and Ebener[77] found individuals with spinal cord injuries were more likely to experience positive self-worth and well-being if they used positive methods like hope, humor, and proactive coping to make meaning of their disability. Those who used negative coping styles were less likely to experience successful response to their disability. Focusing on hope and humor can facilitate problem-focused coping styles.

Like hope, optimism is a dispositional trait defined as a generally positive outlook on life and the expectation good things will happen in the future. Optimists rely on active coping that is problem-solving oriented. Unlike optimists, pessimists disengage when stressors become too much.[16] Optimism can buffer against the stress of experiencing challenging conditions, like chronic illness.[23] Optimism has been shown to be indirectly associated with negative perceptions about illness,[31] and negative illness coherence in individuals.[25] In a study investigating the well-being of individuals with rheumatoid arthritis, researchers found stress and pessimism were correlated with lower psychological well-being, and being optimistic with an active coping style was associated with higher levels of the construct.[84] Cognitive and behavioral methods of coping were found to be the best methods to buffer stress and facilitate well-being.

Research on hope and optimism strongly suggests that maintaining positive perceptions about the future is a way to help individuals make meaning from their disability and facilitate adaptation. However, it is consistent in the literature that an active coping style is necessary for maintaining a greater sense of well-being in individuals with disabilities. The discussion above portrays coping as a complex, multidimensional process involving the person—with his or her own dispositions—and external demands and resources, in appraising stressful situations.[36] Coping cannot be separated from context, but rather understood as a relationship between the person and the environment. With this, we will further explore the intersection of coping and the disability experience, as it applies to individuals and their families.

COPING AND DISABILITY

As explained above, there are several avenues by which individuals attempt to overcome difficult situations in their life, but the goal is the same—the alleviation of stress to a state of better well-being. The experience of disability, congenital or acquired, is a challenging situation that may be fraught with stress, uncertainty, and setback. Through counseling and the development of efficacious coping strategies, the person will be better able to achieve goals and reach a desired quality of life. The literature is replete with examples of the "ingredients" essential for people with disabilities to adjust to or cope with their conditions. The onset and course of a disease or disability can impact the lived disability experience, as well as interpersonal encounters. The following examples will elucidate the experiences of people with disabilities.

Although born with their condition, those with congenital disability must still adjust to their condition as they interact with people and environments. In a study focusing on the experiences of people with cerebral palsy, Sandström[71] noted participants' concerns to be perceptions of their bodies, being different, and restricted autonomy. Social consequences of their disability included being treated as different by others, including special treatment that kept them from experiencing the true consequences of life, and experiences of discrimination due to perceptions of incompetence. Autonomy was threatened by dependence on others to fulfill necessary care tasks. Hayter and Dorstyn[24] found that many with spina bifida had positive emotional adjustment to their disability, despite physical challenges; but, higher levels of anxiety from difficult childhood experiences and cumulative medical stressors impeded this.

In their study of individuals living with multiple sclerosis (MS) and their caregivers, Edmonds and colleagues[11] identified important adjustment issues, including loss of mobility, lack of independence, and changes in relationships. One respondent commented on the importance of independence: "Keeping my independence, not allowing MS to completely dominate my life; having support workers is a way of helping me to keep my independence, not losing it."[11, p. 104] A significant change was in the roles individuals held within the family structure, feelings of loss associated with not being able to maintain those roles, and feelings of being a burden to the family. Loss of personal independence and employment led to feelings of loss related to self-esteem, social contact, and income. There was a difference in the coping process between those with episodic and progressive forms of MS, in that individuals with progressive forms needed to reincorporate back into their identity the limitations consistently imposed by their worsening condition.

Elkington and colleagues[13] reported on the experiences of youth with psychiatric conditions, with many participants alluding to feelings of stigmatization due to their disability. While there were some differences in experiences based on age and diagnostic group, participants perceived being labeled in a negative way, as though there exists an "us vs. them" dichotomy in society through both attitudes and structural discrimination. This label resulted in changes to their relationships with family and friends, ranging from rejection to lack of trust to others becoming more open and understanding. Not only did youth need to navigate the feelings of others toward them, but also their own internalized stigma regarding mental health conditions and its accompanying challenges to self-worth. Some youth chose to withdraw and not disclose their condition, while others found no shame in their identity, embracing it as a common experience many encounter and something that made them stronger.

The impact of disability can also be felt across cultures, with similar approaches used for coping. In a sample of individuals with various physical disabilities in India, Pande and Tewari[62] analyzed themes related to major stressors and the accompanying coping strategies employed to alleviate the distress. Stressors included deviant body image, dependency on others, educational and occupational barriers, relationship problems, attitudinal barriers, and inability to fulfill traditional gender roles. Ego-related stressors, including feelings of inadequacy, helplessness, and shame/guilt, however, were the most significant. These experiences are consistent with those reported by a domestic sample of individuals with spinal cord injury.[20] Common approaches for dealing with these stressors included taking action, positive reinterpretation, acceptance, denial, seeking emotional support, and turning to religion, with most of these approaches representing problem-focused coping techniques.

These examples bring to light the variety of experiences across individuals with disabilities, even within other cultures. In the case of persons with congenital disabilities, their difficulties focus on social engagement and competence. Those with acquired disabilities are trying to recapture some of what has been lost and make sense of their new self-concept. However, both groups of individuals spoke of wanting interconnectedness with others, maintaining autonomy and independence, and engaging in meaningful activities. These themes form the basis of the following discussion on coping strategies and their efficacy, as well as coping interventions for people with disabilities.

STRATEGIES FOR COPING

Snyder[79] asserted that, in times of duress, positive and negative behaviors simultaneously operate to assist individuals with negotiating their new realities. At these times, "a person will maintain beliefs that distance himself or herself from information that has negative implications for the self-image, but will simultaneously adhere to positive, optimistic beliefs that enhance the self-image."[14, p. 375] Following a disability or illness, people expect to resume life unaffected by their limitations, but as they test their bodies, they realize they must make trade-offs or lower goals until they match their lessened capacities.[19] At times, they may raise their hopes and goals as they meet with successes. In this way, formation of identity is implicitly linked with the self-efficacy of the individual. The following sections will review additional themes from the coping literature, as they relate to the experience of disability.

Succumbing vs. coping frameworks. Beatrice Wright[90] introduced the response to disability through the coping versus succumbing frameworks. On one end of the response continuum, succumbing is characterized by a focus on the negative aspects of one's disability and its consequences, devaluing one's own life and precluding successful adaptation.[77] The other end of the continuum, coping, allows the person to focus less on the losses and consequences and more on intrinsic values and retaining assets. Through coping, disability is seen as just one aspect, among many, that comprise a person and one's life experience.[10] A positive outcome of coping and evidence of a successful adaptation to disability would be to view it as a growth experience.[43]

Accommodative and assimilative coping. The process of incorporating disability into the self-image and adjusting to the disability experience has been theoretically proposed by many over the years,[48] especially in relation to how individuals will attain an optimal quality of life. Two additional coping styles have been proposed to understand the response of a person to the stress of a disabling condition.[44] Accommodative coping is directed at changing one's personal goal standards in accordance with perceived deficits. Assimilative coping involves active attempts by the person to alter unsatisfactory situational constraints in accordance with one's preferences. These are similar to the concepts of importance change and control change in Bishop's[5] disability centrality model.

Individualistic vs. collective coping. Stemming from social identity theory, which states individuals are motivated to achieve positive self-regard, it is posited individuals look to maintain their positive identity through their personal attributes, as well as group membership.[59] In line with this perspective, individuals will gravitate toward groups that maintain their positive status and avoid groups that threaten it. Typically, coping with stress by emphasizing one's personal strengths does not contradict coping through social means, but the negative stigma imposed on disability status may cause individuals with disabilities to distance themselves from disability and others who have it.[58] Individualistic coping, which assists those from stigmatized groups to pass as "normal," includes avoiding disability group activities, concealment of disability, and downplaying the importance of disability as part of the self.[59] The danger in such action is individuals might not avail themselves of services or eschew treatment for fear of stigmatization from the disability identity.[65]

Collective strategies, which focus on managing stigma to enhance the status of the group and not just the individual, encourage disability identification and collective action for social change; these include advocacy, legal reform, reclaiming disability as a cultural heritage, and group pride. This conceptualization of disability views it as not merely a medical condition, but also a socially-contrived barrier. Galvin[19] suggested those who continue to experience marginalization because of their disability may do so because they are constrained by the individualistic view of disability as a personal problem, with the only way to cope as striving for the normative goals of society. Through collective coping and group identification, individuals will be able to claim disability as a life-enriching part of identity and seek to improve society for others like them.

EFFICACY OF COPING STRATEGIES

Empirical research has demonstrated some mixed findings on the utility of actual strategies used to accomplish these tasks of adjustment and self-identity reformation. The focus of attention in the literature related to the efficacy of strategies has primarily been on the use of problem-focused vs. emotion-focused coping strategies—but, also, which strategies within these categories are considered to be adaptive vs. maladaptive, successful vs. unsuccessful. Response to disability, however, cannot be polarized between "coping well" and "not coping", but, can be found somewhere along this continuum.[10] The type of coping strategy used has been found to explain more of the variance in psychological adjustment than other mediating variables such as age, severity of injury, or time since injury. Although, specific personality factors and the availability of support and resources may impact one's ability to activate certain coping responses. These internal coping resources include sense of coherence, internal locus of control, hopeful outlook, and perceived control.[42]

Livneh and Martz[42] found in a systematic review that problem-focused coping has been associated with better adaptation, reduced anxiety, lower overall psychosocial impairment, and increased life satisfaction and well-being among individuals with spinal cord injury. Lo Buono and colleagues[44] found individuals who had strokes, who used active, accommodating coping styles, were better able to adjust their goals, make new meaning from their situation, and transform their personal identity, although this was fortified by extraverted personality traits and social support from one's family. Perceived distress among individuals with physical disabilities was positively correlated with emotion-focused coping and negatively correlated with problem-focused coping, suggesting active coping was a more adaptive way of coping with disability-related stressors.[62]

Victorson and colleagues[87] found emotional venting, escape-avoidant techniques, disengagement strategies, denial, and self-blame were found to exacerbate distress in the long-run for individuals experiencing traumatic physical injuries, despite some initial usefulness following injury. For example, venting, an emotion-focused technique, requires a large expenditure of emotional capacity, thereby diminishing a person's defense for intrusive thoughts and feelings. It may also inhibit the active exploration of more constructive coping mechanisms. In investigating the functions of denial within the disability literature, Livneh[40] found it provided a protective function soon after diagnosis to distort the present reality, instill hope, and control emotional flooding. Denial, however, can be considered adaptive or maladaptive depending upon its duration and use. While it serves to buffer and gradually accommodate a person to the realities of a traumatic experience, it becomes a hindrance when it impedes the person from moving toward rehabilitation progress.

As these studies indicate, a variety of techniques can be used successfully in the short- and long-term to adjust and cope with the disability experience. No coping strategies are universally successful under all conditions,[56] with each form being adaptive under some circumstances and counterproductive in others, depending on the nature of the situation and how the response is executed.[62] The intent of or motive behind the specific coping strategy used is more significant than the actual technique itself.

The key to successful intervention is determining which coping strategies promote positive gains within the individual, although attending to this singular perspective would be short-sighted in determining the true efficacy of coping strategies. Marin and colleagues[47] contended the discrepancy in the literature regarding which strategies are adaptive versus those that are maladaptive lies in the fact the effectiveness of any given strategy depends on the response of others to the use of that strategy. Once a coping mechanism is used, our desire to continue using it will be guided by the response of others or our perception of their response.

The coping themes identified above—interconnectedness with others, maintaining autonomy and independence, and engaging in meaningful activities—represent an active, and even social, approach to coping. What can be surmised from this, however, is that individuals with disabilities rely on both problem-focused and emotion-focused strategies to negotiate their daily lives. It would, therefore, behoove counselors to explore with their consumers their motivations and goals for meaningful life and develop a repertoire of integrated techniques to achieve desired outcomes. To this end, the following potentially powerful strategies counselors can explore with their consumers, will be discussed:

> social comparison;

> disability identity and stigma resistance;

> social support;

> leisure coping; and

> encouraging hope.

Social comparison. Social comparison—relating one's own characteristics to those of others—has been linked to coping.[63] For example, in situations where individuals have low esteem, they will often make a comparison to others who are worse-off in an effort to improve feelings of well-being. Several types of social comparisons exist. As in the example above—considered a *downward contrast*—a person facing a health threat will make a comparison with someone who is in a lesser position to contrast her experiences. In another situation, the individual may actually identify with the target person perceived as worse-off, making a *downward identification*, evoking further negative feelings about the self. Conversely, an individual facing a health threat may make an *upward identification* in which he identifies with a person who is in better health as a way to view oneself with a potentially promising future. An *upward contrast* may induce feelings of frustration when he sees another person with a disability doing better than he is. Downward identification and upward contrast can be viewed as negative coping techniques, as the former compares oneself to the "feared self" and the latter to the "unattainable self." Downward contrast and upward identification are the most positively interpreted, leading to a hopeful future.[36]

Social comparisons can add to stress when individuals realize they cannot keep up with the pace of others, leading to increased feelings of difference.[71] There is also danger when a person makes a collective downward identification toward a disability group, allowing that unfavorable view to influence one's behavior. For example, a person with a psychiatric diagnosis may wish to avoid the stigma of psychiatric disability by distancing himself from others with the condition or keeping the condition a secret. He faces a double-edged sword where he disparage himself for needing help because of his condition (self-stigma), while avoiding seeking help because of the stigma it elicits (public stigma).[35] Ilic and colleagues[26] found secrecy, selective disclosure, and overcompensation to be harmful coping strategies, whereas positive in-group stereotyping, community involvement, and humor were effective. Therefore, engaging in the community and finding positive examples can allow individuals to challenge public and self-stigma perceptions.

Upward identification and downward contrast can be useful in establishing hopeful role models, a future orientation, or a sense of competence. Upward comparisons to people who are successfully managing a similar condition should be sought to provide the most powerful vicarious learning experiences, and indicate not only an emotional approach to enhancing self-concept, but also a problem-focused approach by gathering information.[10] Individuals with spinal cord injury indicated seeing others with more severe injuries successfully coping was a critical turning point to making them realize they needed to change and strive.[45] One method for facilitating contact with individuals similar to your consumer would be through support groups, rehabilitation programs, and leisure/recreation activities. Changing one's perceptions about disability is the first step to a person developing a better self-concept. However, it does little to change the actual prejudice and discrimination toward those with disabilities. This can be accomplished through activism.

Disability identity and stigma resistance. Disability identity relates to positive self-beliefs related to one's disability, as well as an affinity for the disability community.[10] Time with disability and its impact on one's independence tend to greatly vary the response to disability, with those in the early stages of impairment feeling the most diminished sense of self.[19] Individuals learn to redefine themselves over time and challenge their poor perceptions and those of others. On a personal level, individuals begin to develop self-worth, pride, and personal meaning in relation to their disability.[10] Continued exposures to a society not designed for equal acceptance leads to an affirmation that those with disabilities should have the same rights as others. This sentiment is a precursor to an awareness of group discrimination, which leads to a desire for communal attachment with others with disabilities. Therefore, embracing one's disability identity as a source of pride will allow the individual to address stigma through coping strategies and group affiliation.

Hiding one's disability may have an adverse effect on self-esteem, even if done to avoid discrimination.[26] While it may result in attainment of short-term goals, like employment, by not being authentic, non-disclosure may result in a more global impact to the person's self-concept. Additionally, not confronting the discrimination and avoiding disclosure contributes to maintaining the stigmatization of people with disabilities as a group by ignoring their plight.[86] Nario-Redmond and colleagues[58] found that engaging in action-oriented strategies, like endorsing social change and working to overcome disability, predicted a more positive sense of self as a group member. Personally valuing disability as a source of pride over stigma predicted a more positive sense of self as an individual.

Coping strategies specifically designed to resist stigma include, not attributing stereotypes about disability to oneself, challenging discrimination, regaining control of one's identity, and improving one's self-concept.[56] Those who are able to externalize the negative perceptions, rather than adopt them, are able to resist the mistreatment and oppression they experience.[19] Individuals who highly identify with a stigmatized group will challenge externally-imposed definitions and limitations and work to improve the status of the group, whereas those who are less identified will work to only improve their own situation.[58] Counselors can work with consumers to gauge their trajectory of positive disability identity formation. Individuals can explore their own narratives through counseling to develop a disability identity. Those who have affirmed their identity and desire to integrate with the disability community or pursue social change can be linked with social and advocacy groups to explore these avenues.

Social supports. Support can be conceived as a form of physical, informational, emotional, or financial/material aid from a member of a person's social network.[10] Social support has often been viewed as a buffer in the process of coping with a disability,[89] with socio-emotional support being the most powerful predictor of reduced psychological distress.[86] Objective social support refers to the extent to which others provide tangible assistance, whereas subjective social support is the extent to which others will mobilize to provide assistance in the time of crisis.[28] Social support must first be perceived before a person can use it to facilitate coping.[74] Perceived subjective support has been found to be predictive of adjustment to stressful life events, higher physical and psychosocial well-being, and the development of resilience for people with disabilities.[4, 41]

The literature regarding the mediating effects of interpersonal contact on stress and coping suggests it serves the adaptive function of facilitating processing, cognitive reappraisal, and finding meaning in the experience.[47] Social support has demonstrated positive results across a number of disabling conditions. Individuals with spinal cord injury reported higher levels of body acceptance when they had greater social support, especially from others with an injury.[4] Youth with psychiatric disabilities found having a non-judgmental person in whom they trusted facilitated self-disclosure; this held true even when the person was a "virtual friend" over the Internet, as the connection to someone who understood resulted in more positive feelings regarding the diagnosis.[13] Peer support appears to be a common salient factor across disability groups, as well. People with MS used peer support to exchange information about self-identity and empowerment.[75] Individuals with spinal cord injury in a sports program found peer support from other athletes with disabilities was instrumental in their resilience and adaptation process.[45] Those with psychiatric disabilities relied on peer contact to maintain positive self-evaluations; however, peer support only buffered self-esteem in instances where individuals did not experience high levels of stigmatization.[86] This finding relates back to the fact that those who self-stigmatize or are fearful of stigmatization may avoid associating with others (peers) with mental health conditions.

It is evident that it is not merely the presence of social support to the person, but the quality of the interaction. Supportive systems provide a barrier against stress and negative emotions, whereas dysfunctional, negligent, or abusive systems can thwart positive adjustment.[48] Care should be taken to investigate the social network of the individual and capitalize on creating supportive, positive connections for the person. This may also include counseling interventions with support persons, family members, and rehabilitation professionals so they can learn to support the coping efforts of the person with a disability. Information and resources can also be provided to the individual about seeking additional social supports through support groups, recreational groups, disability agencies, and faith-based communities.

Leisure coping. Given the medical orientation of acute care rehabilitation and the vocational orientation of rehabilitation counseling, the importance of establishing and pursuing leisure goals for individuals with disabilities can, at times, be undervalued. With the exception of utilizing sport as a treatment for those experiencing traumatic injury, like in the case of the Wounded Warrior Project,[45] concerted focus on the benefits of leisure for people with disabilities has been peripheral; although, the therapeutic value of leisure coping and leisure participation is vast. Leisure need not only equate with athletics or physical pursuits in recreation. Leisure activities can also include reading and hobbies, arts, volunteering, recreation, and religious observance. A distinction should be made, however, between leisure activities and therapeutic arts and modalities. The leisure activities discussed in this section are informal or structured activities that are not supervised or prescribed by trained clinicians. Therapeutic activities, such as creative arts therapy or physical therapy, require facilitation by trained and qualified practitioners to ensure no harm comes to participants. For example, legal case study research has demonstrated arts interventions by underqualified practitioners can cause serious harm to those with mental health complexities.[46]

Leisure, in general, allows a person with an acquired disability to create a bridge between one's former and current self in that it allows the individual to reconnect with the past and find continuity within one's self-concept. It can be seen as a way to "return to normal," connecting to the former self in valued ways while accepting the current limitations. Leisure has been shown to help sustain effort and generate hope in the face of difficulties. Leisure plays a role in facilitating coping, establishing a positive identity, and fostering self-acceptance.[8] Engaging in activities that lead to better self-efficacy for physical performance will provide valuable information about the self and future potential in the identity reformation process.[45] The main benefits to leisure for people with disabilities, as expressed in the literature, are palliative coping, mood enhancement, and social connection. The following examples will explore this further.

In a study of leisure-generated meanings for individuals with mental health conditions, Iwasaki and his team[29] found meanings gained from leisure contributed to stress-coping, recovery, adjustment, and active living. Leisure-generated meaning predicted leisure satisfaction and lower boredom, which can lead to individuals continuing their participation because of the value they assign to the activities. Meaning was found to be related to physical health and well-being, as active living is seen as a defense against the sedentary lifestyle common in this at-risk population; but attention should also be given to the expressive, spiritual, social, and cultural benefits of leisure activities and their associated personal meaning for the individual.

The reported benefits of leisure activities for a group of individuals with visual impairments aligned with the difficulties youth navigate to achieve resilience, including relationship, identity, power and control, and social justice.[30] Participation allowed individuals to interact with like-minded, challenged peers. In achieving accomplishment through sports participation, youth developed a sense of pride, confidence, and self-belief. This self-confidence fueled their desire to face their fears and anxieties regarding the world at large. Sports participation allowed these blind youths to challenge stereotypes and lowered expectations, contrasting the concept of people with disabilities lacking strength and competence.

Since many individuals with spinal cord injury experience a traumatic event, the transformative nature of sports participation is a framework for investigating resilience, adaptation to trauma, and the development of positive self-image. Machida and colleagues[45] analyzed the narratives of wheelchair rugby players to find that participation provided multiple forms of support (e.g., social, vicarious learning, "tough love"), the motivation to overcome challenges, confidence to overcome adversity on and off the court, and an emotional outlet. Perceived benefits included: physical fitness, returning to a valued role (e.g., athlete), providing a distraction, and a sense of achievement. The mentoring from other athletes who had overcome similar, and sometimes greater, challenges modeled life tactics, coping skills, and attitudes to develop resilience.

These findings underscore the utility and benefit of leisure programming for people recovering from or living with a disability. Overall, participation in leisure activities allowed individuals to experience a connection to their past, manage stress, affirm personal values and beliefs, and attain positive physical and psychological states. It should be noted, however, that leisure participation can add to stress, as planning, possibility of injury, and dealing with accessibility issues were also noted, but were often outweighed by the benefits.[8]

The main point of importance with leisure programming with consumers is that the activity be personally relevant and congruent with their personality and defined quality of life indicators.

Encouraging hope. The coping strategies individuals select are said to have an impact on their subjective well-being and overall quality of life.[55] Post-traumatic growth typically includes changed perceptions of the self and changed interpersonal relationships, which may reflect a greater appreciation for the "small things in life" and a desire to make the most out of life's moments.[32] Psychosocial resistance resources stem from personality characteristics and the social environment within which we live. The psychological resources of efficacy, hope, optimism, and resilience—which combine to form a construct referred to as psychological capital—have demonstrated greater well-being and performance outcomes for individuals.[2] As mentioned earlier in this chapter, hope and optimism assist in coping with stressors. Those who experience high levels of stress and are able to avoid its negative effects are thought to possess a personality difference. Kobasa[34] postulated a personality trait, called hardiness, buffered against the psychological effects of stress. Hardiness is characterized by challenge, control, and commitment. This component of control, in conjunction with perceived freedom, is the core of self-determination.

Hope is useful in two ways following a traumatic event.[78] First, hope entails agency, or goal-directed energy, which provides motivation to pursue goals. Hope also encompasses pathways thinking, which allows the person to visualize possibilities, plan ways to achieve goals, and actively realize the goals. In relation to psychosocial impairment following injury and disability, research indicates that agency has a palliative effect shortly following injury and, over time, pathways thinking attenuates the impact of the loss.

Research suggests greater life satisfaction and a positive life orientation is reported in people when they reprioritize their values to be more in line with their limitations, have good emotional health, maintain valued roles and relationships, engage in meaningful leisure pursuits, and make a contribution to others.[19,29,42,62] Methods such as positive reframing, using humor, and demonstrating mastery allow people to transcend the negative aspects of disability.[26,43,88] Given these findings, rehabilitation environments and strategies should be constructed with an aim toward fostering the components of hardiness—especially control—and facilitating hope through agency and pathways thinking. Although these are seemingly intrinsic personality traits, providing relevant information, planning solutions, and linking with resources are all ways to facilitate hope and hardiness within our consumers by allowing for a greater sense of control over the situation.

FAMILY RESPONSE TO DISABILITY

As described earlier, coping does not occur in solitary, as the individual is influenced by the perceptions of others. Disability also impacts the family as a unit, necessitating a systemic coping response to deal with the shift in structure and responsibility. According to theoretical models, families must integrate two dimensions of family behavior to produce a response to stressors and challenges: cohesion and adaptability.[60] Family cohesion can be defined as the emotional bond between members, whereas adaptability is the ability of the marital or family system to change its structure, roles, and rules in response to stress. The varying levels of these factors comprise family types, which are a set of basic attributes that explain how a family system typically operates or behaves. Families with more balanced, flexible structures are better able to adapt to stressors, whereas unbalanced, rigid families fail to adapt and may actually contribute to more stress.[9] Positive changes in families are predicated on pre-injury family functioning, such as better pre-injury communication, better use of resources, role flexibility, greater activity, and less conflict and control.[6]

All families experience stress and undergo change, regardless of whether a member of the family system has a disability. For example, the introduction of a new child into the system will trigger the need to reorganize, mobilize resources, and change typical modes of operation. These types of normative demands (e.g., family life cycle changes, marriage, birth) usually do not present a high risk to the stability of the family, unless there are limited resources or they co-occur with other stressors, so families competently weather them.[64] It is the non-normative demands, like the birth of a child with a disability or the experience of a traumatic injury, that increase the risk of families to experience stress. It should be cautioned here, however, to not think of the disability as the stressor; or that disability within a family structure can only be a negatively-valenced experience.[52] Although not typically a choice most would make, many parents of children with disabilities report the experience has been a positive one[51] and they are able to manage successfully against adversity.[66] It is the prevailing societal model, however, that views disability as unalterably negative.

Stressors that family systems of those with disabilities experience can come from many sources. Socioeconomic status, time constraints/demands, lack of childcare access and respite, mental health of family members, and challenges within service systems can pose barriers to families.[52] Family sense of coherence and cohesion impact the family unit's ability to be emotionally and cognitively equipped to evaluate situations and respond.[67] Any one of these factors, on its own, appears surmountable by a family. But, when these stressors cascade, accumulate, and compound to a point where resources and capacities to meet demands are exceeded, the family may struggle to adapt.[64]

FAMILY RESPONSE AND RESILIENCE

The family response to stress through coping can be defined as: "families engage in active processes to balance *family* demands with *family capabilities* as these interact with *family* meanings to arrive at a level of *family* adjustment or adaptation."[64, p. 350] The Double ABCX Model of Family Stress, which forms the basis for most research on how families respond, postulates that difficulties do not arise from a single factor—like disability—but rather from the "pile up" of stressors, taxing the family to a state of maladjustment.[66] In the five factors of the model, Factor A represents the stressor of the injury itself; however, it is a given that the injury is not the only stressor that impacts the family. Factor aA incorporates the impact of the injury along with other accumulating stressors. The other factors consist of the family's crisis meeting resources and ability to mobilize/accept help (Factor bB); coping strategies involved in creating meaning out of the experience (Factor cC); and the level of adaptation achieved by the family (Factor xX). This model forms the basis for family resilience.[6]

Resilience has been defined as both a personality trait and a process. Patterson[64] argued for the differentiation of these concepts, earmarking resiliency as the former and resilience as the latter. Using this delineation, family resiliency would relate to a family's capacity to handle life circumstances, and family resilience would refer to the processes by which families adapt and gain mastery following crisis. The Resiliency Model for Family Stress, Adjustment and Adaptation focuses on the family's attempt to navigate toward control and competence.[70] The resilience process involves adjustment (protective factors that help the family unit maintain function when faced with risk factors) and adaptation (recovery factors that aid the family unit in adapting to crisis). Therefore, to become resilient, the family amasses protective and recovery factors to combat against the accumulating risk factors. Peer and Hillman[66] investigated resilience through an extensive literature review and determined three factors associated to family wellness in the face of disability: coping style, social support, and optimism. These three concepts, and those related to them, will now be explored.

Coping style. Coping has an interpersonal context. In addition to emotion- and problem-focused coping, relational coping exists among dyads within the family unit. Relational coping is used to preserve relationships, comfort members, and make appraisals in times of stress.[54] As mentioned earlier, the perceptions of others regarding the coping technique one employs contributes to its continued use. Marin and colleagues[47] found that, even when individuals in a family used similar coping strategies, the contextual factors surrounding their use impacted their effectiveness. Certain methods of coping were predictive of distress. For instance, relationship-focused coping was found to be associated to greater levels of distress when it was executed in a context of perceived negative spouse responses. Cognitive restructuring was only effective when conditioned on positive responses from one's spouse, but caused distress when negative responses were reported. The relationship between problem-focused strategies and distress, however, was not influenced by the perceptions of spouses.

Individuals in the family develop resilience and this resilience feeds family resilience. Family resilience has been defined as consisting of three concurrent coping processes as the unit adapts to adversity: searching for meaning, maintaining control, and maintaining valued identities.[21] Meaning-making builds resiliency by redefining threat as a challenge and reconstituting a coherent family identity and structure for effective coping.[54] Implementing collaborative problem-solving and problem-focused coping strategies allows families to actively engage and exact more control of difficult situations. Altering the situational demands of the moment and using problem-focused planning prevents the stressful situation from recurring.[66] Members of families should also be wary of sacrificing too many valued activities or too much personal time, whether it be for work, leisure, or family pursuits, in order to free up time to address the therapeutic and service needs of their family member with a disability. Families in which these "trade-offs" were made too frequently reported lower levels of family life congruence and family cohesion.[50]

Social support and resources. It is often noted that it takes a village to raise a child. This concept extends to support needs of families with a member with a disability. It is a basic human drive to cultivate resources to sustain one's family; this is accomplished by developing and maintaining ties to one's community. Whereas, individual resilience relies on the support of the family, family resilience relies on this social support and community resources.[54] These resources are built up and mobilized in times of crisis. Social contact, and the exchange of valuable information that comes from it, correlates to higher perceived life satisfaction and quality of life.[89] For example, developing kinship with other families navigating the disability services system will allow family members to conserve energy they would have devoted to accomplishing the task alone. Families with better functioning search for information about disability and services and seek social support through both formal and informal resources.[22]

Optimism (and other positive psychology constructs). Although the response to difficulty in one's life can result in negative emotions, positive emotions can co-exist. Positive emotions, as a response to negative events, build enduring coping resources; they are not merely seen as an end result of weathering a challenge, but as a means to achieve psychological growth and improved well-being.[85] "Dispositional optimism, or the tendency to expect positive outcomes when confronting problems in life, appears to be a key factor in protecting individuals from stress."[66, p. 94] Optimism has been supported as a resilience factor, as it facilitated the ability to process health information, maintain hope, and use and restore coping resources. Similar to optimism, other positive psychology constructs have demonstrated a protective and restorative effect with stress. Weaker sense of coherence in parents of children with disabilities led to greater feelings of helplessness.[67] Higher levels of self-efficacy lead to a greater sense of competence and personal control; this results in families attending to the needs of the family unit, as well as the self-care and well-being needs of each individual.[22] Parents with greater self-efficacy demonstrated better health, more satisfaction with relationships, better mental health, and less anxiety. Interventions aimed at increasing optimism, sense of coherence, and self-efficacy will allow families to surmount difficulties more effectively through better control and a positive mindset.

ASSISTING FAMILIES

Oftentimes, disability is seen as an inherently negative event families must navigate or "make the best of." However, much of the hardship lies in systems and environments that are not created to lend support. Inflexible employment conditions, lack of inclusive childcare settings, and the additional time demands of keeping medical/service appointments and therapy regimes can lead to a tipping point of emotional or energy imbalance.[52] Professionals can play a role in stemming this tide. First, by assisting parents and families with reframing the experience of disability *for them*. This will facilitate a focus on the positive, over the potential negative, of the situation. A positive mindset will allow families to strengthen their bonds, enrich their social networks, and develop an approach-oriented response to coping.[50] Second, families and professionals must advocate for better systemic support for families with a member with a disability through policy reform and service structures. The goal should be on helping families *change the odds* rather than just beating them by leveling the playing field for all families to succeed.[52] Lastly, to achieve this, professionals must conduct appropriate, individualized assessment with families to determine their treatment/service needs, current and needed levels of social support, need for advocacy and education, and current levels of resilience.[57] Exploring the current state of protective and risk factors within the family, including their levels of cohesion and well-being, will provide the basis for a customized service plan to enhance quality of life for the family and its individual members.

INTERVENTIONS FOR COUNSELING

Coping may not be a natural attribute of all people. The foregoing sections have provided a basis for interventions that can be used to facilitate the coping strategies of our consumers with disabilities and their families. Psychosocial education programs are recommended for those people who overuse certain coping mechanisms to refine their approach and resume progress. Following a traumatic experience, suitable interventions include brief, solution-focused counseling, information giving, coping skills training, and trauma debriefing.[87] The following are further suggestions for use in counseling practice.

COPING SKILL DEVELOPMENT

Psychoeducational groups, coping skills training, behavioral techniques, and cognitive techniques have been used to improve self-efficacy and coping skills and combat the negative effects of disability.[77] Problem-solving therapy is a form of brief therapy that overlays with hope theory; improves an individual's problem-solving (coping) skills; and increases personal agency and, in turn, hope.[53] This intervention begins with examining the client's problem orientation and formulating the approach to the problem through the client's lens, assisting him to envision alternatives, implement them, and evaluate their success. Hope theory and problem-solving therapy draw similarities from their reliance on examining behaviors and cognitions, encouraging client's active participation in overcoming challenges, and promoting skills that will increase agency and goal attainment.[53] A client will conceptualize a number of viable routes to reaching a desired goal, which improves hopeful thinking that there is "more than one way to reach the end," and motivates the client to continue to work toward attainment of the goal.

Emotion-focused coping methods, which can complement problem-focused approaches, can also be fostered within individuals. Decatastrophizing, a cognitive technique used to modify maladaptive perceptions, can be used to assist a person in viewing disability as manageable.[77] Using narrative techniques, the focus of counseling can be aimed at helping a person "re-author" their own story to account for other alternatives and empower them toward a more positive perception.[88] Reduction of self-stigmatizing perceptions and beliefs may allow a person to engage in activities and treatment more readily to develop further approach-oriented coping strategies.

ENGAGEMENT IN VALUED ACTIVITIES

Psychosocial problems may influence one's pace and progress in rehabilitation programs. Physical and activity limitations can give rise to some of the psychosocial difficulties.[12] Attention should be paid to psychosocial prevention and support services early in the rehabilitation process, as psychosocial and activity limitation can have a reciprocal deleterious impact on one another.[33] Leisure can be used as a conduit for the energy once directed toward work in those individuals who are no longer able to participate in the competitive workplace. Leisure activities provide similar rewards of belonging, activity, and accomplishment.[45] Leisure activities provide a new or continuing context for the accomplishment of goals and positive adaptation. These types of experiences can include volunteering, learning new skills, and recreational exercise.

ENCOURAGING HOPE AND RESILIENCE

Edmonds and colleagues[11] advocated a focus on hope, rather than on successful adaptation, as an outcome. In their study of people with progressive multiple sclerosis, they found hope strategies could be directed toward slowing down the disease course, maintaining key bodily functions, and preventing admission to care facilities. Families and other psychosocial environments, such as school and rehabilitation settings, create the contexts in which hope is learned through role modeling and the messages supplied. Although not empirically proven, worship and prayer may engender positive emotional experiences, such as relaxation, hope, and forgiveness, and religious faith could contribute to optimism, which might promote physical and emotional well-being.[37] Dunn[10] advocated the following steps individuals can take, perhaps through the assistance of family and professionals, to cultivate resilience:

➤ Accepting change as part of life.

➤ Being decisive, through implementing problem-focused and task-focused strategies.

➤ Maintaining a hopeful outlook.

➤ Reframing stressful events to keep a balanced perspective.

➤ Connecting with others in the community for support.

RESOURCES, INFORMATION, AND SUPPORT

The best way to learn to cope adaptively across the lifespan and varying situations is to provide individuals with a repertoire of adaptive coping skills early in rehabilitation, as initial efforts in coping are predictive of success in the post-injury years.[68] Support and resources given in early rehabilitation efforts will allow survivors of trauma to develop the necessary self-efficacy for coping and resilience in the face of future challenges.[89] Providing necessary information and facilitating the process of pathways thinking will allow individuals living with an injury or disability to be empowered toward recovery. Interacting with those who have experienced disability can provide key wisdom related to navigating service systems, dealing with stigma, and hoping for positive outcomes in the future. For example, engaging in self-help groups can enhance self-esteem and engender strong in-group feelings to promote positive disability identity.[86] As a systems intervention, Curtiss and colleagues[9] suggested enrollment in a family support group as an effective intervention to provide coping and social support in light of new responsibilities.

REFERENCES

[1]Adler, A. (1929). *Problems of neuroses: A book of case histories.* London: Kegan Paul, Trench, & Treubner.

[2]Avey, J. B., & Luthans, F., Smith, R. M., & Palmer, N. F. (2010). Impact of positive psychological capital on employee well-being over time. *Journal of Occupational Health Psychology, 15,* 17-28.

[3]Bandura, A. (1977). Self-efficacy: Toward a unifying theory of behavioral change. *Psychological Review, 64,* 359-372.

[4]Bailey, K. A., Gammage, K. L., van Ingen, C., & Ditor, D. S. (2015). "It's all about acceptance": A qualitative study exploring a model of positive body image for people with spinal cord injury. *Body Image, 15,* 24-34.

[5]Bishop, M. (2005). Quality of life and psychosocial adaptation to chronic illness and disability: Preliminary analysis of a conceptual and theoretical synthesis. *Rehabilitation Counseling Bulletin, 48,* 219-231.

[6]Carnes, S. L., & Quinn, W. H. (2005). Family adaptation to brain injury: Coping and psychological distress. *Families, Systems, & Health, 23*(2), 186-203.

[7]Carver, C. S., Pozo, C., Harris, S. D., Noriega, V., Scheier, M. F., Robinson, D. S...& Clark, K. C. (1993). How coping mediates the effects of optimism on distress: A study of women with early stage breast cancer. *Journal of Personality and Social Psychology, 65,* 375–390.

[8]Cook, L. H., & Shinew, K. J. (2014). Leisure, work, and disability coping: "I mean, you always need that 'in' group". *Leisure Sciences, 36,* 420-438.

[9]Curtiss, G., Klemz, S., & Vanderploeg, R. D. (2000). Acute impact of severe traumatic brain injury on family structure and coping response. *Journal of Head Trauma Rehabilitation, 15,* 1113-1122.

[10]Dunn, D. S. (2015). *The social psychology of disability.* New York, NY: Oxford University Press.

[11]Edmonds, P., Vivat, B., Burman, R., Silber, E., & Higginson, I. J. (2007). Loss and change: Experiences of people severely affected by multiple sclerosis. *Palliative Medicine, 21,* 101-107.

[12]Eide, A. H., & Røysamb, E. (2002). The relationship between level of disability, psychological problems, social activity, and social networks. *Rehabilitation Psychology, 47,* 165-183.

[13]Elkington, K. S., Hackler, D., McKinnon, K., Borges, C., Wright, E. R., & Wainberg, M. L. (2012). Perceived mental illness stigma among youth in psychiatric outpatient treatment. *Journal of Adolescent Research, 27,* 290-317.

[14]Elliott, T. R., & Kurylo, M. (2000). Hope over acquired disability: Lessons of a young woman's triumphs. In C. R. Snyder (Ed.), *Handbook of hope: Theory, Measures, and applications* (pp. 373-386). San Diego, CA: Academic Press.

[15]Elliott, T. R., Witty, T. E., Herrick, S., & Hoffman, J. T. (1991). Negotiating reality after physical loss: Hope, depression, and disability. *Journal of Personality and Social Psychology, 61*, 608–613.

[16]Fontaine, K. R., Manstead, A. S. R., & Wagner, H. (1993). Optimism, perceived control over stress, and coping. *European Journal of Personality, 7*, 267-281.

[17]Freud, A. (1936). *The ego and the mechanisms of defense.* New York, NY; International Universities Press.

[18]Freud, S. (2014). *The neuro-psychoses of defense.* [Kindle version]. (Originally published in 1894.)

[19]Galvin, R. D. (2005). Researching the disabled identity: Contextualising the identity transformations which accompany the onset of impairment. *Sociology of Health & Illness, 27*, 393-413.

[20]Graf, N. M., Marini, I., & Blankenship, C. J. (2009). One hundred words about disability. *Journal of Rehabilitation, 75*(2), 25-34.

[21]Grant, G., Ramcharan, P., & Flynn, M. (2007). Resilience in families with children and adult members with intellectual disabilities: Tracing elements of a psycho-social model. *Journal of Applied Research in Intellectual Disabilities, 20*, 563-575.

[22]Guillamón, G., Nieto, R., Pousada, M., Redolar, D., Muñoz, E., Hernández, E…Gómez-Zúñiga, B. (2013). Quality of life and mental health among parents of children with cerebral palsy: The influence of self-efficacy and coping strategies. *Journal of Clinical Nursing, 22*, 1579-1590.

[23]Gustavsson-Lilius, M., Julkunen, J., Keskivaara, P., Lipsanen, J., & Hietanen, P. (2012). Predictors of distress in cancer patients and their partners: The role of optimism in the sense of coherence construct. *Psychology and Health, 27*, 178–195.

[24]Hayter, M. R., & Dorstyn, D. S. (2014). Resilience, self-esteem and self-compassion in adults with spina bifida. *Spinal Cord, 52*, 167-171.

[25]Hurt, C. S, Burn, D. J., Hindle, J., Samuel, M., Wilson, K., & Brown, R. G. (2014). Thinking positively about chronic illness: An exploration of optimism, illness perceptions and well-being in patients with Parkinson's disease. *The British Psychological Society, 19*, 363-379.

[26]Ilic, M., Reinecke, J., Bohner, G., Röttgers, H., Beblo, T., Driessen, M…Corrigan, P. W. (2011). Protecting self-esteem from stigma: A test of different strategies for coping with the stigma of mental illness. *International Journal of Social Psychiatry, 58*, 246-257.

[27]Irving, L. M., Cheavens, J., Snyder, C. R., Gravel, L., Hanke, J., Hilberg, P., & Nelson, N. (2004). The relationships between hope and outcome at pre-treatment, beginning, and later phases of psycho- therapy. *Journal of Psychotherapy Integration, 14*, 419–433.

[28]Iso-Ahola, S. E., & Park, C. J. (1996). Leisure-related social support and self-determination as buffers of stress-illness relationship. *Journal of Leisure Research, 28*, 169-187.

[29]Iwasaki, Y., Coyle, C., Shank, J., Messina, E., & Porter, H. (2013). Leisure-generated meanings and active living for persons with mental illness. *Rehabilitation Counseling Bulletin, 57*, 46-56.

[30]Jessup, G. M., Cornell, E., & Bundy, A. C. (2010). The treasure in leisure activities: Fostering resilience in young people who are blind. *Journal of Visual Impairment & Blindness, 104*, 419-430.

[31]Karademas, E. C., Kynigopoulou, E., Aghathangelou, E., & Anestis, D. (2011). The relation of illness representations to the 'end-stage' appraisal of outcomes through health status, and the moderating role of optimism. *Psychology and Health, 26*, 567–583.

[32]Kastenmüller, A., Greitemeyer, T., Epp, S., Frey, D., & Fischer, P. (2012). Posttraumatic growth: Why do people grow from their trauma? *Anxiety, Stress, & Coping, 25*, 477-489.

[33]Kendall, E., Catalano, T., Kuipers, P., Posner, N., Buys, N., & Charker, J. (2007). Recovery following stroke: The role of self-management education. *Social Science & Medicine, 64*, 735-746.

[34]Kobasa, S. (1979). Stressful life events, personality and health: An inquiry into hardiness. *Journal of Personality and Social Psychology, 37*, 1-11.

[35]Lannin, D. G., Vogel, D. L., Brenner, R. E., & Tucker, J. R. (2015). Predicting self-esteem and intentions to seek counseling: The internalized stigma model. *The Counseling Psychologist, 43*, 64-93.

[36]Larsen, P. D. (2016). Psychosocial adjustment. In P. Larsen (Ed.), *Lubkin's chronic illness* (9th ed., pp. 43-62). Burlington, MA: Jones & Bartlett.

[37]Lazarus, R. S. (2006). *Coping with aging*. Cary, NC: Oxford University Press.

[38]Lazarus, R. S., & Folkman, S. (1984). *Stress appraisal, and coping*. New York: Springer.

[39]Lazarus, R. S., & Folkman, S. (1987). Transactional theory and research on emotions and coping. *European Journal of Personality, 1*, 141-170.

[40]Livneh, H. (2009). Denial of chronic illness and disability: Part I. Theoretical, functional, and dynamic perspectives. *Rehabilitation Counseling Bulletin, 52*, 225-236.

[41]Livneh, H., & Martz, E., (2011). The impact of perceptions of health control and coping modes on negative affect among individuals with spinal cord injuries. *Journal of Clinical Psychology Medical Settings, 18*, 243-256.

[42]Livneh, H., & Martz, E. (2014). Coping strategies and resources as predictors of psychological adaptation among people with spinal cord injury. *Rehabilitation Psychology, 59*(3), 329-339.

[43]Livneh, H., & Martz, E. (2016). Psychosocial adaptation to disability within the context of positive psychology: Philosophical aspects and historical roots. *Journal of Occupational Rehabilitation, 26*, 13-19.

[44]Lo Buono, V., Corallo, F., Bramanti, P., & Marino, S. (2015). Coping strategies and health-related quality of life after stroke. *Journal of Health Psychology, 22*, 16-28.

[45]Machida, M., Irwin, B., & Feltz, D. (2013). Resilience in competitive athletes with spinal cord injury: The role of sports participation. *Qualitative Health Research, 23*, 1054-1065.

[46]MacPherson, H., Hart, A., & Heaver, B. (2015). Building resilience through group visual arts activities: Findings from a scoping study with young people who experience mental health complexities and/or learning difficulties. *Journal of Social Work, 16*, 541-560.

[47]Marin, T. J., Holtzman, S., DeLongis, A., & Robinson, L. (2007). Coping and the response of others. *Journal of Social and Personal Relationships, 24*, 951-969.

[48]Marini, I. (2012). Theories of adjustment and adaptation to disability. In I. Marini, M. J. Millington, & N. M. Glover-Graf (Eds.), *Psychosocial aspects of disability: Insider perspectives and counseling strategies* (pp. 115-143). New York, NY: Springer Publishing.

[49]Martz, E., & Livneh, H. (2016). Psychosocial adaptation to disability within the context of positive psychology: Findings from the literature. *Journal of Occupational Rehabilitation, 26*, 4-12.

[50]McConnell, C., Parakkal, M., Savage, A., & Rempel, G. (2015). Parent-mediated intervention: Adherence and adverse effects. *Disability and Rehabilitation, 37*, 864-872.

[51]McConnell, M., Savage, A., Sobsey, D., & Uditsky, B. (2015). Benefit-finding or finding benefits? The positive impact of having a disabled child. *Disability & Society, 30*, 29-45.

[52]McConnell, D., & Savage, A. (2015). Stress and resilience among families caring for children with intellectual disability: Expanding the research agenda. *Current Developmental Disorder Reports, 2*, 100-109.

[53]Michael, S. T., Taylor, J. D., & Cheavens, J. (2000). Hope theory as applied to brief treatments: Problem-solving and solution-focused therapies. In C. R. Snyder (Ed.), *Handbook of hope: Theory, measures, and applications* (pp. 151-166). San Diego, CA: Academic Press.

[54]Millington, M. J., & Madden, R. H. (2015). Counseling in the context of family identity. In M. J. Millington & I. Marini (Eds.), *Families in rehabilitation counseling: A community-based rehabilitation approach* (pp. 21-46). New York, NY: Springer Publishing.

[55]Montel, S. R., & Bungener, C. (2007). Coping and quality of life in one hundred and thirty-five subjects with multiple sclerosis. *Multiple Sclerosis, 13*, 393-401.

[56]Moses, T. (2015). Coping strategies and self-stigma among adolescents discharged from psychiatric hospitalization: A 6-month follow-up study. *International Journal of Social Psychiatry, 61*(2) 188-197.

[57]Mpofu, E., Levers, L. L., Mpofu, K., Tanui, P., & Hossain, Z. S., (2015). Family assessment in rehabilitation service provision. In M. J. Millington & I. Marini (Eds.), *Families in rehabilitation counseling: A community-based rehabilitation approach* (pp. 251-266). New York, NY: Springer Publishing.

[58]Nario-Redmond, M. R., Noel, J. G., & Fern, E. (2013). Redefining disability, re-imagining the self: Disability identification predicts self-esteem and strategic responses to stigma. *Self and Identity, 12*, 468-488.

[59]Nario-Redmond, M. R., & Oleson, K. C. (2015). Disability group identification and disability-rights advocacy: Contingencies among emerging and other adults. *Emerging Adulthood, 4*, 207-218.

[60]Olson, D. H. (1993). Circumplex model of marital and family systems. In F. Walsh (Ed.), *Normal family processes* (3rd ed., pp. 104-137). New York: Guilford Press.

[61]Pakenham, K. I. (1999). Adjustment to multiple sclerosis: Application of a stress and coping model. *Health Psychology, 8*(4), 383-392.

[62]Pande, N., & Tewari, S. (2011). Understanding coping with distress due to physical disability. *Psychology and Developing Societies, 23*, 177-209.

[63]Paterson, L., McKenzie, K., & Lindsay, B. (2012). Stigma, social comparison and self-esteem in adults with an intellectual disability. *Journal of Applied Research in Intellectual Disabilities, 25*, 166-176.

[64]Patterson, J. (2002). Integrating family resilience and family stress theory. *Journal of Marriage and Family, 64*, 349-360.

[65]Pattyn, E., Verhaeghe, M., Sercu, C., & Bracke, P. (2014) Public stigma and self-stigma: Differential association with attitudes toward formal and informal help seeking. *Psychiatric Services, 65*, 232-238.

[66]Peer, J. W., & Hillman, S. B. (2014). Stress and resilience for parents of children with intellectual and developmental disabilities: A review of key factors and recommendations for practitioners. *Journal of Policy and Practice in Intellectual Disabilities, 11*, 92-98.

[67]Pisula, E., & Kossakawska, Z. (2010). Sense of coherence and coping with stress among mothers and fathers of children with autism. *Journal of Autism and Developmental Disorders, 40*, 1485-1494.

[68]Pollard, C., & Kennedy, P. (2007). A longitudinal analysis of emotional impact, coping strategies, and post-traumatic psychological growth following spinal cord injury: A 10-year review. *British Journal of Health Psychology, 12*, 347-362.

[69]Roth, S., & Cohen, L. J. (1986). Approach, avoidance, and coping with stress. *American Psychologist, 41*, 813-819.

[70]Russo, T. J., & Fallon, M. A. (2015). Coping with stress: Supporting the needs of military families and their children. *Early Childhood Education Journal, 43*, 407-416.

[71]Sandström, K. (2007). The lived body—Experiences from adults with cerebral palsy. *Clinical Rehabilitation, 21*, 432-441.

[72]Santilli, S., Nota, L., Ginevra, M.C., & Soresi, S. (2014). Career adaptability, hope and life satisfaction in workers with intellectual disability. *Journal of Vocational Behavior, 85,* 67-74.

[73]Selye, H. (1976). *The stress of life* (revised edition). New York: McGraw-Hill.

[74]Sirois, F. M., & Gick, M. L. (2016). An appraisal-based coping model of attachment and adjustment to arthritis. *Journal of Health Psychology, 21,* 821-831.

[75]Skår, A. B. R., Folkestad, J., Smedal, T., & Grytten, N. (2013). "I refer to them as my colleagues": The experience of mutual recognition of self, identity, and empowerment in multiple sclerosis. *Disability and Rehabilitation, 36,* 672-677.

[76]Skinner, E. A., Edge, K., Altman, J., & Sherwood, H. (2003). Searching for the structure of coping: A review and critique of category systems for classifying ways of coping. *Psychological Bulletin, 129,* 216-269.

[77]Smedema, S. M., Catalano, D., & Ebener, D. J. (2010). The relationship of coping, self-worth, and subjective well-being: A structural equation model. *Rehabilitation Counseling Bulletin, 53*(3), 131-142.

[78]Smedema, S. M., Chan, Y. J., & Phillips, B. (2014). Core self-evaluations and Snyder's Hope Theory in persons with spinal cord injuries. *Rehabilitation Psychology, 59,* 399-406.

[79]Snyder, C. R. (2001). *Coping with stress: Effective people and processes.* Cary, NC: Oxford University Press.

[80]Snyder, C. R., & Dinoff, B. L. (1999). Coping: Where have you been? In C.R. Snyder (Ed.), *Coping: The psychology of what works* (pp. 3-19). Cary, NC: Oxford University Press.

[81]Snyder, C. R., Harris, C., Anderson, J. R., Holleran, S. A., Irving, L. M., Sigmon, S. T...& Harney, P. (1991). The will and the ways: Development and validation of an individual-differences measure of hope. *Journal of Personality and Social Psychology, 60,* 570-585.

[82]Snyder, C. R., Lehman, K. A., Kluck, B., & Monsson, Y. (2006). Hope for rehabilitation and vice versa. *Rehabilitation Psychology, 51,* 89–112.

[83]Snyder, C. R., Sympson, S. C., Ybasco, F. C., Borders, T. F., Babyak, M. A., & Higgins, R. L. (1996). Development and validation of the State Hope Scale. *Journal of Personality and Social Psychology, 70,* 321–335.

[84]Treharne, G. J., Lyons, A. C., Booth, D. A., & Kitas, G. D. (2007). Psychological well-being across 1 year with rheumatoid arthritis: Coping resources as buffers of perceived stress. *The British Psychology Society, 12,* 323-345.

[85]Trute, B., Benzies, K. M., & Worthington, C. (2012). Mother positivity and family adjustment in households with children with a serious disability. *Journal of Child and Family Studies, 21,* 411-417.

[86]Verhaeghe, M., Bracke, P., & Bruynooghe, K. (2008). Stigmatization and self-esteem of persons in recovery from mental illness: The role of peer support. *International Journal of Social Psychiatry, 54,* 206-218.

[87]Victorson, D., Barocas, J., Farmer, L., Burnett, K., & Ouellette, A. (2005). Maladaptive coping strategies and injury-related distress following traumatic physical injury. *Rehabilitation Psychology, 50,* 408-415.

[88]Vogel, D. L., Shechtman, Z., & Wade, N. G. (2010). The role of public and self-stigma in predicting attitudes toward group counseling. *The Counseling Psychologist, 38,* 904-922.

[89]Wilson, L., Catalano, D., Sung, C., Phillips, B., Chou, C., Chan, J. Y. C., & Chan, F. (2013). Attachment style, social support, and coping as psychosocial correlates of happiness in persons with spinal cord injuries. *Rehabilitation Research, Policy, and Education, 27,* 186-205.

[90]Wright, B. A. (1983). *Psychical disability—A psychosocial approach* (2nd ed.). New York: Harper & Row.

CHAPTER 7

DEALING WITH UNCERTAINTY

MICHELLE MARMÉ

We can never know what will happen to us next.
We can try to control the uncontrollable
by looking for security and predictability,
always hoping to be comfortable and safe.
But the truth is that we can never avoid uncertainty.
This not knowing is part of the adventure.
It is also what makes us afraid.[11]

We make plans to visit our parents at the end of the month, to attend a conference in September, or to join friends at Disney World in January. With each, we assume all factors will be in place to allow us to accomplish these plans. Implicit in these beliefs, we anticipate our health, finances, family, work situations, transportation, weather, and world events will allow these plans to happen. At the base of these assumptions may be a belief in a reliable, predictable universe. At another level is an assumption we will be able to respond competently to whatever surprises or detours might arise, without affecting our ability to follow through on those plans. When we are reminded that many of these factors are outside our immediate control, however, we must confront our awareness that much in life is uncertain.

At varying levels, uncertainty is experienced throughout each day through our interactions with others, in planning activities, or in making decisions. We say hello to a neighbor, set a meeting for later in the week, or decide to accept a job offer. We encounter each occurrence with some level of confidence of the outcome: the neighbor's response will be correspondingly pleasant, the meeting will be held, and the job decision will prove to be a sound one. When the actual experience does not comply with our expectations, our sense of balance, of justice, and our confidence in our ability to trust our assessments of life events is shaken. The degree of insult to one's sense of confidence varies. The certainty with which we approach subsequent situations may be diminished, even if just a bit.

In this chapter, a broad, constructivist view of uncertainty and its role in our lives is provided. The concept of uncertainty is explored both in a general context of daily existence, as well as with specific attention to its role in the experience of chronic illness and disability (CID). Readers are invited to reflect upon their own beliefs about uncertainty and constructs related to it, such as stress, faith, fear, competency, resilience, optimism, hope, trauma-related growth, and a continuum between perceiving uncertainty as a danger or as an opportunity.[25] Although culturally, data-oriented, scientific method-inclined practitioners may be most interested in collecting information to reduce uncertainty, a broader understanding of the ways uncertainty operates in our lives is suggested. While uncertainty is considered with respect to strategies that target "reducing uncertainty," the chapter advocates strategies for "managing uncertainty." From a fuller understanding of the types and functions of uncertainty, the concepts associated with it, and the various components of its definition, the rehabilitation professional is better able to understand the role of uncertainty in shaping one's behavior. With this robust appreciation, the rehabilitation professional may develop more effective strategies for assisting individuals in meeting their needs in responding to the inevitable uncertainty in their lives.

THE NATURE OF UNCERTAINTY

A review of the literature reveals that increasing attention among psychological[9,15,18,23,24,27,30] and allied medical[8,14, 22,25,26,28] areas focus on the concept of uncertainty as an issue of research or pedagogical concern, particularly with respect to people with chronic illness and disability.[10] While the primary focus of much of this research appears to be on ways to reduce uncertainty, other avenues of response are highlighted in this chapter that address efforts to provide more person-responsive interventions.

Uncertainty is defined variously: at times as a cognitive process, at times as an emotional process. As a cognitive process, it involves perceptions, assessments, judgments, and decision making. As an emotional process, implications of competing feelings of fear and safety, doubt and confidence, suspicion and trust, helplessness and potency are involved. Both cognitive and affective responses are highly idiosyncratic and are related directly to the individual's previous experiences of loss, success, risk, conflict, confidence, stress, and anxiety.

Mishel[25] provides the foundational definition of uncertainty for our purposes: "the inability to determine the meaning of illness-related events and occurrences in situations where the decision maker is unable to assign definite values to objects, events and/or is unable to accurately predict outcomes because sufficient cues are lacking."[p. 256] She further addresses components of uncertainty as related to the cognitive process of constructing meaning. As such, she opens the door to the myriad ways individuals may interpret events, based upon their individual histories of dealing with stress, ambiguity, fear, and conflicting information.

The definition of uncertainty is further enhanced by Hannibal and Bishop[14] and Carey[8] who equate the experience of uncertainty as one of stress, affecting one's psychological, cognitive, physical, and spiritual dimensions. Seminal works on the psychological aspects of CID consider constructs such as the following: ambiguity,[15] illness uncertainty,[35] intolerance of uncertainty and fear of the unknown,[9] habituation to uncertainty,[15] and strengths-based approaches to coping, optimism, hope, and spirituality.[10,30,23,24] By extension, perhaps we should consider constructs such as adherence to treatment recommendations, adjustment, accommodation, adaptation, acceptance, coping, and the incorporation of CID into one's identity as consequences to one's coping with uncertainty, rather than separate entities? The following section will provide a fuller understanding of the components of uncertainty.

THE COMPONENTS OF UNCERTAINTY

Conceptual frameworks for understanding the components of uncertainty are considered to follow two major avenues of research. One research model originates in nursing education research[24] while the other was developed from a communications framework, focusing on communication practices/skills between health care providers and patients.[2,3,4,5,6] The distinct contributions of each will be described. While the overlap of topics is significant, it appears each line of research developed independently of the other.

Western cultures value certainty, rationality, linear thinking, predictability, and scientific, mechanistic orientations. Stability, control, and the power of the self in affecting change are valued. As a result, the beliefs that "uncertainty is to be feared" and "accurate, concrete answers are to be valued" are built into Western culture and psyche.[25, p. 257] It is understandable, therefore, that when uncertainty is encountered, we resist those elements outside our control. These events assault our sense of confidence and mastery, as well as our convenient fictions surrounding the belief that we can do anything if we put our minds to it. We associate uncertainty with a lack of control, a need to fight or flee in response. The literature seems to confirm a basic universal: uncertainty is stress.[14,21,28] These cognitive assessments trigger a series of physical responses that, in short term, may be helpful: we become more alert, more focused, have increased energy and strength to cope; ancillary bodily processes give precedence to cognitive, sensory, and physical responses so we can respond to the danger. Longer term, however, these mechanisms cause harm to our physical and psychological functioning.[8,14]

Mishel's[25,26] reconceptualization of uncertainty in illness is of distinct relevance to this chapter. Building upon the definition shared previously, the strength of her work rests upon several points. While her early work focused upon the uncertainty relative to the acute phase of illness (i.e., following the pattern from symptoms, to diagnosis, to treatment, to cure), she expanded her work to address the continual, constant uncertainty involved in chronic illness (i.e., variable symptoms, prolonged assessment often followed by variable diagnoses, conflicting information about treatment, leading to no certain cure). Her early formulations offered formative concepts including the following:

> ➤ Adaptation was defined as the idealized end state;

> ➤ People will perceive uncertainty along a continuum from danger to opportunity; and

> ➤ Regardless of person's perception of uncertainty as danger or opportunity, coping behaviors will be attempted to manage the psychic

tumult of the situation as it is perceived, to achieve some state of equilibrium.[26]

After the original formulation of her theory, Mishel[25] observed that the "longer people lived with continual uncertainty, the more positively they evaluated the uncertainty that they experienced."[p. 257] Further, the data suggested individuals developed new views of life over time, strongly influenced by the response and support of health care providers and social resources. This change over time is regarded as an evolution in the appraisal of uncertainties, both specific and general, from psychic demands for continuity and return to normal to increasing openness and comfort with the unfolding experience of life. She interpreted her data as suggesting that, one moves from "a sense of disorganization to increasing comfort and sense of competence in responding to life as it is."[p. 258] The validation that growth and change are possible outcomes of this transitional response to uncertainty was a significant step forward. This shift is exemplified in the shift from the individual's seeking to return to previous levels and ways of functioning to growth that results from meeting daily challenges and performing desired tasks in novel ways.

Importantly, she stated "the person with a new orientation toward life is a far-from-equilibrium system, the new life is *fragile,* and it is maintained by continually expressing a *negative appraisal* of uncertainty into the environment in exchange for the view that uncertainty allows for multiple choices; thus, uncertainty may lead in multiple directions, among which is *opportunity*. The person functions to maintain this new view of life, relying upon two environmental forces: support resources and health care professionals."[24, p. 260] This is to say that, as people work to embrace a probabilistic world view, they seek support and confirmation from those most valued in their world at that time: family, friends, and the health care providers surrounding them. Consequently, it is essential that health care providers, family, and friends understand the concepts presented in this chapter and adhere to them personally to ensure the individual receives essential support, bolstering the notion of uncertainty as an opportunity to thrive.

Accepting uncertainty allows one to consider multiple possibilities, as nothing is certain or universal.[24] With a shared understanding among social and health care supports, the individual is supported in shifting from a perception of uncertainty as an unnatural, aversive enemy to understanding it as an inherent part of reality and life, to be incorporated into one's daily experience.

Turning now to complementary research conducted in the area of social science research, specifically in the area of communication, the concept of uncertainty is considered along a number of dimensions keenly relevant to any consideration of the experience of chronic illness and disability.[5,24] According to Babrow, Hines, and Kasch,[3] uncertainty exists when "the details of situations are ambiguous, complex, unpredictable or probabilistic; when information is unavailable or inconsistent; and when people feel insecure in their own state of knowledge or the state of knowledge in general."[p.42] Uncertainty results when individuals doubt their understanding of the situation and/or doubt their capacity to understand the situation accurately. The assessment of when one has *enough information* to feel confident about the situation at hand is a fluid process, varying with the person and the moment. When individuals and their families discuss medical issues with their physician and other health care providers, uncertainty is a likely response, as they wonder whether they have heard and/or understood the information provided accurately or have the required knowledge to accurately interpret the significance of this information.

An overview of research on uncertainty and the role of communication in the process of creating, maintaining, and coping with uncertainty is presented in a special issue of the *Journal of Communication*.[5] Three theoretical perspectives are presented that address ways of dealing with uncertainty: uncertainty reduction, problematic integration, and uncertainty management. To better understand and apply these theories, as well as to explore their implications for counseling practice, some key elements of uncertainty must first be considered.

Uncertainties may be experienced in multiple areas of one's life. The challenge in responding to these uncertainties may be a factor of the multiplicity of areas involved and the significance of each to the individual. Additionally, the individual must manage the plethora of responses to uncertainty by those around them. Brashers[5] suggested that uncertainty should be considered along the following dimensions:

➤   as multi-layered,

➤   as interconnected, and

➤   as temporal.

In describing uncertainty as multi-layered, Brashers and Babrow[6] offered the following: "uncertainty may be about the self (e.g., one's own beliefs, values, abilities, and behaviors), others (e.g., others' beliefs, values, abilities, and behaviors), relationships (e.g., the quality and durability of relationships), and other features of a context (e.g., rules, social norms, and procedures)."[p.245]

To illustrate this point, consider an individual newly diagnosed with nonHodgkin's lymphoma. For the individual, questions may arise concerning the diagnostic skills and treatment knowledge of the oncologist, one's own ability to manage the side effects of chemotherapy, the ultimate effectiveness of the treatment, one's spouse's capacity to be supportive throughout the process of treatment, the financial resources to maintain day-to-day necessities if unable to work, insurance resources available to provide for the recommended treatment, and what the response of others will be to a person diagnosed with cancer. Inherent in balancing this multitude of concerns is the stress that results from dealing or not dealing with numerous areas of concern for which clarity is either elusive or fleeting.

Multiple uncertainties need to be identified so their unique and combined effects on communication can be better understood. The idea that these multiple sources of uncertainty are interconnected suggests that, as uncertainty or clarity is found on one issue, additional questions of uncertainty may arise at other levels. Following the example of the person diagnosed with non-Hodgkin's lymphoma, the development of additional symptoms and diagnoses may preclude the continuance of one treatment plan and affect the choice of treatment options available. Consequently, while some areas of uncertainty previously resolved reemerge as concerns, those of less immediate concern may recede into the background. Concerns about losing one's hair, for example, may become secondary to renewed concerns about surviving the cancer.

Brashers[5] also advised that the duration of the experience of uncertainty merits consideration. Uncertainties may be short-lived, intermittent, or ongoing. Micro-interactional forms of uncertainty, for example, occur in direct conversation with others, both as speaker and as listener. As speaker, one is assessing what the listener is able or ready to hear and understand. When the speaker has bleak news to deliver, perhaps a diagnosis for which treatment options are limited and/or painful, the speaker may attempt to increase the uncertainty of the message to soften the effect on the individual. For the listener, one may have difficulty processing highly technical information and terms and/or emotionally-charged information. The listener may be hesitant either to ask questions that may seem simplistic (to the speaker) or to ask questions for which the answer may be difficult to accept.

Short-term uncertainty may surround the occurrence of a specific event, such as "How well will I be able to tolerate the first round of chemotherapy?" On-going uncertainty spans the duration of a chronic illness or disease process, whereas one issue is resolved and others surface. An example of on-going uncertainty is illustrated by this situation: a young woman diagnosed with bulimia reported having experienced significant periods in her life when the symptoms and issues surrounding bulimia had been relatively dormant. In response to a series of life events she experienced as stressful, bulimic thinking and behaviors resurfaced. As she worked toward regaining control over these thoughts and behaviors, she was concerned about numerous aspects of her illness related directly to issues of uncertainty. How might she respond to a return of symptoms in the future? If she "recovered too quickly," would her family and friends understand the legitimacy of bulimia or regard her recent bout with bulimic symptoms as attention-getting behaviors, rather than part of a serious illness? During her counseling sessions, an exploration of these concerns, these uncertainties, allowed her to move ahead in her recovery. It is asserted that her progress would have been hampered had these concerns, and their interplay, not been explored.

For others with chronic illnesses that have inconsistent patterns and experience periods of remission or plateaus in functioning, worries may surround their present ability to handle the normative daily activities during periods of remission that may have been abandoned during illness.[5] Consequently, even periods of good health may contribute to the experience of uncertainty in that one cannot depend upon sustained good health. The subtle meanings of uncertainty may shift over time as people become accustomed to various aspects of the uncertainty of the situation,[25] such as fluctuations in function. To illustrate this point, a person with chronic inflammatory joint disease may decide to schedule appointments in the middle of the day, allowing them to meet after having time to loosen joints and before exhausting the energy available for the day.

An individual's response to uncertainty may vary markedly along a continuum from attempts to reduce the amount of uncertainty experienced to attempts to manage one's experience of chronic uncertainty and, in some situations, to increase the perception of uncertainty. Attempts to minimize levels of uncertainty serve to reduce the complexity and ambiguity of the situation so that one is better able to make decisions. Efforts to manage the level of uncertainty experienced represent attempts to restore a sense of control over a situation perceived as threatening. It is also important to note the individual may choose to increase the perception of uncertainty as a strategy to maintain a sense of hope and optimism, or to carry on a course of action or to attempt tasks that otherwise would seem of limited promise. An example of the latter would be people participating in a highly controversial treatment, believing the actual cure rates may be higher than previously reported or, at least, that they might be the exception to the more conservative projections.

Hines[16] suggested there are two general areas of uncertainty for those coping with serious illness: uncertainties in probabilistic orientations and uncertainties in evaluative orientations. Uncertainties within probabilistic orientations are produced by efforts to understand biomedical, social, and psychological outcomes of the medical conditions and treatment options. Some people may want to know their chances: of survival, of impairment, or of returning to life as they know it. Others may actively avoid information on these topics, believing that their "chances" of a desirable outcome might be enhanced by not knowing what the objective estimates are.

A curvilinear relationship between one's beliefs about the probability of a target event occurring and one's perception of uncertainty is thought to exist.[2] Uncertainty is lowest when the probability of the target event happening is thought to be 0% or 100% and highest when the probability of occurrence approaches 50%. When one feels confident an event will or will not happen, or is likely, then one can make firm plans as to ways to respond. The clarity allows the individual to regain a sense of order and control of the situation. Uncertainty, confusion, and stress would be expected to be highest when all events seem equally probable. In such situations, one does not know for what he or she should be preparing and anticipating.

A separate set of uncertainties involves the assessment of the desirability of potential outcomes. For an individual whose mobility might be enhanced significantly by a knee joint replacement, the initial judgment might be to move ahead with the surgery. If that person is 75 years old, living independently in a small community, and otherwise in sound health with only some reservations concerning the rigors of surgery and rehabilitation, the impression may still be to proceed with the surgery. If that person also is experiencing mild/moderate cognitive decline, other assessments of the desirability of the knee replacement may be made. In all scenarios, the actual condition of the knee remains constant, while the advisability of surgery varies along with the other variables mentioned. The evaluations will be influenced by varying perspectives on age, independence, support system, specifics of the individual's cognitive status, as well as the degree of deterioration of the knee, among other factors.

Brashers[5] stated that "understanding the various types of uncertainty enhances our ability to describe and explain its influences on behavior and to develop strategies for improving people's lives."[p. 479] When issues of uncertainty are involved, interactions with others demand an appreciation of the many dimensions involved for the individual: the individual meanings attached to both cognitive and affective dimensions of uncertainty; the individual's needs with respect to increasing/maintaining/reducing the level of uncertainty involved; the layers of uncertainty and the interconnectedness of these layers; and the temporal dimensions of uncertainty and their relative order of importance at the moment. One must also remain mindful of the rapidity with which these variables may be shifting for the individual. As Hines[16] suggested, "efforts to develop successful interventions must account for the interconnectedness of multiple uncertainties at particular points in time."[p. 500] In subsequent sections, the strategies for making these observations and determining responses will be explored.

THE EFFECTS OF UNCERTAINTY

As people experience changes in their lives, even positive changes such as going away to college or taking a new job, the meanings assigned to these situations and the experience of such changes may affect individuals in profound ways, both physically and psychologically. Sleeping and eating patterns may be disrupted. Immune systems may weaken. Tension-related ailments, such as headaches and muscle strains, may appear. Individuals may become more rigid in their thinking, have trouble remembering details, and be less able to concentrate and make decisions. They may be confident in one plan at one moment and equally supportive of another, perhaps contradicting plan, shortly afterward. They may be insistent on keeping parts of their lives as consistent as possible or postpone the event generating this confusion. They may appear agitated, restless, demanding, or sad. At other times, they may appear energetic, hopeful, and enthusiastic. The temptation to control as much of their lives as possible may be very compelling. Over-learned strategies for coping may be employed, regardless of their efficacy for the current situation.

Psychological effects of uncertainty. The psychological effects of uncertainty are complex. The sequelae may reflect as much about the individual's previous experiences with similar themes of loss, control, and competency, as it does with one's skills for dealing with the current situation. People may initially rely on the coping skills and strategies that have been effective for them in the past. Hines [16] suggested people may have a preferred strategy for responding to uncertainty and stress. He stated "some persons may have coped with most or all uncertainties in their lives by choosing to ignore them and to avoid discussing them with others. Other persons may have coped with (health) uncertainties by actively seeking information about the medical aspects of their condition, discussing their uncertainties with others, and scheduling appointments with physicians. If that has worked for the individual in the past, they are likely to continue to use it."[p. 503] With respect to the experience of disability and chronic illness, those coping skills used previously may not be a sufficient response for the current situation.

The awareness and experience of uncertainty pose substantial challenges to the individual's perception of safety and trust, both of self or others. The experience of a traumatic injury or of a chronic illness may call one's sense of identity (who one is, how one is perceived by others, and how one functions in the world) into question.[31] Through coping, the person is seeking to regain ownership of his previous identity while, on the other hand, coming to terms with the new, externally imposed identity. As the individual struggles, the stress experienced in grappling with either reality is substantial.

With so much internal upheaval, various aspects of communication may be affected. The energy required either to find out all one can about a topic or to avoid acknowledging certain kinds of information may be significant and exhausting. People may ask the same question many times, of the same or various people, perhaps reflecting the difficulty they are having in absorbing the information or perhaps seeking a more satisfying answer. As is characteristic of the experience of stress, individuals may evidence trouble taking in information, retaining information, and/or being able to apply it to their current situations.

Although Brashers [5] suggested uncertainty management is not directly linked to anxiety, intuitively one could expect feelings of anxiety to arise in the face of uncertain symptoms, diagnoses, and treatment recommendations. As individuals attempt to understand the implications of what is happening to their bodies, symptoms often associated with depression may develop: rigidity in thinking, intrusive (likely, deprecating) thoughts, changes in appetite or sleep patterns, withdrawal from usual activities and customary support systems. The constant shifting of expectations–vacillating between hope and disappointment, confidence and self-doubts, clarity and confusion–may contribute to an inconsistency in the individual's mood and perspectives.[33] Rehabilitation practitioners must meet individuals where they are functioning and accommodate the interactional hurdles and needs of the individuals as they make their way in dealing with uncertainty. As one would with any individual overwhelmed by the information being provided and discussed, break the sessions down into manageable chunks, write down critical information, review, and allow many opportunities to revisit complex and emotionally-charged information and plans.

Physical/physiological components of uncertainty. Most experiences of uncertainty result in stress to the physical aspect of the individual. Incremental amounts of stress may be useful in daily function and performance. Prolonged and intermittent stress is not, for most people; physiologically prolonged stress wreaks havoc on the body.

Whether the uncertainty is short-term, fluctuating, or prolonged, the physical system is stressed. The human body responds to stress by readying itself to act. The endocrine system increases activity. Heart rate, respiratory rate, and muscle tension increase. Pupils dilate. Sensations of pain decrease. Intestinal activity and immune systems decrease. These changes are helpful to the individual who needs to respond to an immediate threat or danger. When this state of preparedness is prolonged, however, the capacity of the body to protect itself from infection becomes compromised. The body shifts from a position of preparedness to one of exhaustion.[25] In-depth descriptions of the body's physiological response to acute and prolonged stress are outside the scope of this chapter. For additional information, readers can consult Carey,[8] Hannibal and Bishop,[14] and Peters, McEwen, and Friston.[28]

In his book, *Listening to Prozac*, Kramer[20] provided an interesting explanation of the concept of "reaction sensitivity" that merits consideration at this point. His research on the origins and treatment of anxiety and depression suggested these disorders are the result of problems in the biological regulation of mood. His theory states that people may develop a rejection-sensitivity through any number of genetic or environmental pathways relatively early in life. Experiences of disappointments, loss, or abandonment early in life may generate a change in the person's physiological response to situations perceived as threatening in some way. What is initially an adaptive, cognitive, and physiological response to a hostile stimulus persists after the termination of exposure to that stimulus. Subsequently, the physical systems generalize their responses to stimuli perceived as threatening at any level, even though the current events may or may not approximate the earlier threats.

The relevance of Kramer's[20] work on reaction sensitivity to the effects of uncertainty for individuals with chronic illness and disability rests in the notion that, when a challenge or threat is perceived by the individual, the physical response may be immediate and pronounced. The response may be related more directly to the sense of threat that the organism experienced previously, than to any set of circumstances in the present. The inaccuracy of this "emotional thermostat" suggests the individual's response to the current situation may well be out of proportion with the objective circumstances being experienced. While the individual may have been able to deal productively with rejection sensitivity prior to the onset of disability or chronic illness, the additional stress may overwhelm the individual's coping system, and the physical response to the current situation may seem out of balance, either under-responding or over-responding to expected levels. Kramer's work overlaps with Hannibal and Bishop's[14] assertion that "stress-induced cortisol secretion may facilitate the formation of a fear-based memory, ... likely to intensify with repetition of similarly-perceived situations, and culminating in a "sensitized physiological stress response."[p. 5]

CONSTRUCTIVE RESPONSES TO UNCERTAINTY

THEORIES OF COPING WITH UNCERTAINTY

Communications specialists have developed theories to address ways individuals deal with uncertainty in their lives.[4,5,16] Consider these models carefully and listen for which model people may be operating from in your conversations. With practice, you may be able to meet the individual in their current belief system and help them move to one that reduces the experience of stress more effectively. Given the pertinence of these models to this discussion, a brief description of the three primary perspectives follows

Uncertainty Reduction Theory. Uncertainty Reduction Theory is predicated on the belief that there is a human drive to reduce uncertainty, to explain the world, and to render it predictable. Uncertainty is viewed as "something large and bad that will become smaller as a result of external forces intentionally applied."[4, p. 465] Broadly defined, it asserts that the most productive way to deal with uncertainty is to gather as much information about the topic as possible so that uncertainty is minimized. This position is appealing in that it seems clearly formulated and highly logical. It further asserts that to deal with uncertainty in any other way is faulty, that one may be avoiding the situationally-correct conclusions and, perhaps worst of all, said to be in "denial."

Problematic Integration Theory. Hines[16] stated Problematic Integration (PI) Theory addresses situations where "probabilities and values are discrepant, where factors are ambiguous, when persons are ambivalent about alternatives or outcomes, and occasions when what is wanted is impossible."[p. 471] Within PI theory, the idea of "uncertainty" is more complex. It refers to the probability of an outcome, an event, an attribute, or other characteristic of the situation. The struggle is to integrate beliefs about the likelihood of an event, the desirability of that likelihood, and the desirability of the event.

Uncertainty Management Theory. Uncertainty Management Theory suggests that, depending upon the specific characteristics of the situation, people may experience uncertainty in varying ways, not simply as an uncomfortable tension-demanding reduction. One may wish to reduce, maintain, or, in fact, increase the level of uncertainty, depending upon whether it is viewed as a "large, bad thing to be reduced or a small, good thing to be nurtured."[4, p. 465] This situation is seen as fluid, allowing the individual maximal flexibility for responding to the stimulus situation. This framework explains why an individual may cycle rapidly from elaborate efforts for gathering information about the target situation to minimizing the need to consider the situation at all.

These theories work from the premise that the experience of uncertainty may result in a range of emotional responses: negative, neutral, and positive. The appraisal of each is significant in understanding the individual's response to uncertainty. When a negative emotional response results, the uncertainty is viewed as a danger or a threat. The individual seeks to reduce or contain the degree of threat to oneself by allowing only as much information or awareness of the situation as the person can tolerate. Feelings of anxiety and fear may result. The individual may respond by doing nothing when overwhelmed, or may respond to these feelings as a catalyst for action. A neutral emotional response occurs when the outcome is perceived as inconsequential. A positive emotional response is found when the experience is framed as beneficial. People who are uncertain, yet believe that a positive outcome is possible, feel hope and optimism. An example of this might be the response of an individual who has been diagnosed with cancer and offered encouraging information about treatment options and expectations for cure.

Brashers[5] offered a framework for conceptualizing how individuals can manage uncertainty, whether to increase, decrease, or maintain uncertainty. Key components of this framework include the following, and are briefly described below:

➢ seeking and avoiding information;

➢ adapting to chronic uncertainty; and

➢ obtaining assistance with uncertainty management through social support.

SEEKING AND AVOIDING INFORMATION

People seek information to collect data, opinions, and perspectives about a situation. Their goal may be to substantiate a position or to discredit information previously offered. The information need not be accurate to be useful, provided it supports the position individuals want to believe and offers an acceptable level of coherence. They may be direct or indirect in soliciting information, selecting their sources of information carefully, depending upon their goal in those communications.

Individuals may avoid situations or resources that might provide information that would challenge or disprove the beliefs they want to hold. Avoidance may shield people from feeling overwhelmed and allow them to maintain a sense of hope. Avoidance takes many forms. Direct avoidance of information may manifest as not reading information provided by health care professionals or not attending appointments at which information might be presented. Selective attention and selective ignoring provide opportunities for people to hear some of the information while suppressing details too psychologically threatening. Social withdrawal may serve the person by limiting access to others who may not be able to support the individual's belief system. Other forms of avoidance may include thought suppression, intentional forgetting, discounting the veracity of negative information, and discrediting the source of the information. These processes may be engaged consciously or unconsciously. It is essential to consider that these behaviors serve a purpose for the individual in managing the uncertainty of one's situation. As rehabilitation professionals, it is essential we understand the behaviors the individual is using to cope and realize the significance of these behaviors for the person at that stage of the process.

ADAPTING TO CHRONIC UNCERTAINTY

Adapting to chronic uncertainty requires individuals to develop a tolerance for the ambiguity that exists in their lives. Various behaviors may signal this process is developing: trusting significant others, developing skills in decentralizing the uncertainty-producing event in their lives, or relying on faith or a sense of a Higher Power being involved during their lives. These behaviors have been identified as being helpful in the lives of people with HIV in tolerating and appreciating uncertainty.[5] These individuals indicated that, as an alternative to achieving predictability in their lives, they changed the way they planned their lives and made decisions. By making shorter-term plans and engaging in events that provided immediate consequences, they reduced a significant level of stress in their lives. Another strategy promoting adaptation to chronic uncertainty was developing structures and routines for those aspects of their lives for which they could. Becoming more comfortable in making decisions based upon more limited facts and becoming satisfied with a "good enough" solution was also identified as an important coping strategy.

ASSISTED UNCERTAINTY THROUGH MANAGEMENT SOCIAL SUPPORT

The significance of social support to one's psychological and physical health is widely accepted. Supportive others may facilitate the messages, beliefs, and behaviors that increase and decrease certainty and uncertainty for the individual. Other people offer a significant source of influence on how an individual appraises uncertainty as either a danger, an opportunity, as inconsequential, or as a normal part of life. Sometimes unwittingly, others become significant collaborators in the individual's assessment of uncertainty.

As the individual questions, directly or indirectly, the support person's experience, thoughts, and impressions of a topic of significance to them, the nuances of language and the stories, regardless of their objective relevance, become critical sources of information for the individual seeking to make sense of the uncertainty being experienced. Increasingly, research supports the significant influence of health care providers' responses as key to expanding and reinforcing the individual's attempts to engage with uncertainty and adapt cognitive processes that restrict uncertainty as a danger and source of stress.[28]

From a behavioral perspective, individuals may display responses that, at first consideration, may seem odd or unrelated, given the situation. Activities might include writing lists; organizing photographs; sorting through papers; cleaning closets; or watching movies, perhaps the same one, many times. For health care workers, these behaviors may be regarded or categorized as irrational or evidence of maladaptive responses to the situation. Perhaps a more functional way to consider these organizing behaviors may be to consider them as attempts to gain control, order, and a sense of safety and predictability in an emotionally-overwhelming situation.

RESPONDING CONSTRUCTIVELY TO UNCERTAINTY

Most therapeutic approaches hold that meaning is created by the individual and it does not inherently rest in the object or event itself. Each emphasizes the importance of observing and facilitating an examination of beliefs and meanings attached to events by the individual. Cognitive behavioral perspectives may be particularly directive in guiding the individual reflection and assessment of those beliefs, while challenging their objective accuracy. These theoretical approaches provide a foundation from which to consider constructive ways of dealing with uncertainty.

Uncertainty is a key factor in the experience of life, although it may hold additional significance for those experiencing disability and chronic illness. It lurks throughout the process of noticing symptoms, finding confidence in one's ability to accurately describe symptoms and their development, and seeking medical treatment. In the search for a diagnosis, one encounters a multitude of diagnostic tests, conflicting information about ways to proceed, and difficulty dealing with answers for which one may not have the medical expertise to interpret. The exploration of treatment options may be daunting: those currently available; those that may treat the primary condition, with some potential to harm other areas of function; those under investigation; or those outside the mainstream of medical treatments. Searching for or avoiding a prognosis may be equally uncertain endeavors.

Rehabilitation professionals may observe the effect of uncertainty on the individual's ability to attend to information, process it, or sustain a commitment to a treatment plan. For many, uncertainty surrounds financial issues related to health care options being available. Questions and doubts surround one's expectations of the response of others to having been diagnosed. Questions surface about whether one's treatment team is the "best." At various points, one wonders about what might have been done to prevent this situation from ever arising or to have noticed the symptoms and sought appropriate treatment sooner.

Primary to responding effectively to the uncertainty being experienced by another is to understand the complexity of the concept of uncertainty. Once one recognizes the pervasiveness of this in the human condition, counselors become more skillful in listening to and observing how others are experiencing uncertainty in their lives. The focus of intervention follows the individual's needs to maintain a sense of psychological safety rather than a struggle to "help" the individual to resolve the uncertainty in ways that might seem more appropriate for the rehabilitation professional, rather than the individual.

For individuals experiencing chronic illness and disability, as well as those who comprise their support systems, the issue of uncertainty needs to be recognized and addressed. Expect it. Listen. Accept their perceptions as the most relevant. Adopt an attitude of openness and patience to questions being posed repeatedly. Examine why these questions are repeated. Attention is warranted to help clients gain a fuller understanding of the various components of uncertainty presented in this chapter. Attention is also warranted to validate the significance of uncertainty in their experience and to de-pathologize the process for them.

STRATEGIES FOR HELPING CLIENTS MANAGE UNCERTAINTY

For those interacting with the person who has a disability or chronic illness, some strategies may enhance both the functioning of the individual and the success of communications.

INCREASE AWARENESS OF OUR OWN PROJECTIONS

For those involved in the health care and rehabilitation community, it is vital to examine our own issues, biases, and understandings of the ways we experience uncertainty on a personal level. Distinguishing between how we imagine we might respond to uncertainty in the situation faced by another and what the other person is communicating to us as to what they need, in that moment, is essential.

Since much traditional academic work follows a systematic, scientific method for decision-making, it may be more likely that our perspectives and needs collide with the needs of persons experiencing uncertainty in their own lives. For example, in situations where uncertainty is a key factor, gathering as much background and research information as possible might seem (to the practitioner) the most reasonable strategy for addressing uncertainty. For many people, however, the need to keep the situation as uncertain as possible may be their way of dealing with potentially overwhelming circumstances. This is evidenced by the clients who do not read the educational handouts given to them throughout treatments, who may forget appointments, or who fail to follow through on plans that are made. These behaviors may be a clue to the rehabilitation or mental health counselor that these individuals are coping with the situation by limiting the amount of information they acquire about their disease process. These behaviors become meaningful issues to explore with the individual in a supportive way, recognizing them as coping strategies to maintain hope, rather than perhaps dismissing or criticizing them as evidence of noncompliance.

FACE OUR OWN FEARS

Recognize the function our own behavior is serving to protect us from the uncertainty we are observing in others. Be mindful that we may be protecting our own sense of vulnerability in the face of the confusion and fear being experienced by the other. As health care professionals, we must reflect upon our own responses to individuals and their behaviors and situations.

MODEL PROBABILISTIC THINKING & PROVIDE SUPPORT

Looking again to Mishel,[25,26] consider this reminder: For this new orientation toward life to be maintained, both the social resources in a person's life and the health care providers must believe in the probabilistic paradigm, rather than the mechanistic paradigm. Reflect upon your own response to uncertainty, what your thoughts, physical response, and behaviors are in response to the uncertain situation, as well as general functioning. Practice the skills of moving along Mishel's continuum from perceiving uncertainty as a danger toward regarding uncertainties as expected, as opportunities for growth.

Support individuals in developing and/or strengthening a sense of trust in themselves, their health care systems, and their support systems. Help them to make peace with concerns about their past behaviors and choices: acknowledging they tried "hard" enough, were sufficiently creative and industrious in exploring their options, have read enough, been thorough enough, and cared enough to have found the best information.

Explore the client's previous experiences with uncertainty. To better understand the response of clients to the uncertainties they are encountering in the present, explore with them their response to thematically-similar situations in the past: situations in which the information available was limited, conflicting, or unclear; where the possible outcomes were undesirable; and where concerns of disappointment, abandonment, loss, and risk were primary. In doing so, the counselor can develop an understanding of the client's reaction sensitivity to these themes and help the client to understand similarities between how he or she coped with those earlier experiences and which strategies could be most helpful in the present. Help them to learn to think in terms of differing ways to achieve shorter-term goals, rather than the linearity of regarding one path or set of behaviors to achieve a goal.

Anticipate that individuals and their significant others may feel overwhelmed and may have difficulty remembering the many therapies and therapists with whom they interact, or may have difficulty following conversations regarding their care and conditions. Provide photos and names of the staff involved in their care, along with the discipline each represents. Have the individuals keep a notebook for recording dates, with whom and what has been discussed. These can also be used for keeping relevant articles. Encourage the individual to review these notes so they can write down questions and concerns to ask later. Particularly in the early interactions, therapists may want to be the scribe for these entries to model the behavior and alleviate some of the confusion for the individual.

Strength-based approaches to counseling and psychology identify several key constructs of universal importance in counseling relationships: encouragement, optimism, hope, posttraumatic growth, and spirituality and resilience.[32] These will be identified briefly below, with greater expansion on spirituality and resilience to follow.

Encouragement. Encouragement refers to "positive feedback that focuses primarily on effort or improvement rather than outcomes."[13, p. 1] Fundamental to Adlerian and other subsequent theories of healthy psychological functioning, encouragement involves recognizing, accepting, and conveying faith in individuals purely because they exist. According to Wong,[34] encouragement is "the expression of affirmation through language or other symbolic representations to instill courage, perseverance, confidence, inspiration, or hope in a person within the context of addressing a challenging situation or realizing a potential."[p.3] Encouragement refers to attitudes, as well as to specific behaviors, of respect and support. An attitude of encouragement is essential to assisting the individual as one struggles from a fragile stage of uncertainty to developing a belief in one's abilities to respond meaningfully to what happens. As people seek to incorporate more positive beliefs about themselves and their situation, they are continually seeking support from the people in their environment. This applies most specifically to the rehabilitation and health care workers with whom they interact.

Optimism. Optimism is defined by Rand and Shea[29] as one's tendency to focus on the positive aspects of life and events for people in general, although not specifically with respect to people with CID. Marmé[24] noted evidence of a self-fulfilling component between one expecting to find good things to happen and an increased likelihood that they will find just that. As one's conceptualization of uncertainty shifts from aversion to acceptance, the body's assessment of the threat level decreases and the physiological response may decrease accordingly.[32] Events remain constant; how one responds, changes. As the individual develops both enhanced persistence for acting on his environment and heightened passion for life, *grit* is said to develop. Grit is considered an essential element of *flourishing.* [32]

Seligman[32] suggested optimism allows people to "see bad events as temporary, changeable, and restricted"[p. 42] and as a major contributor to growth. Throughout much of Seligman's[30,32] work on positive psychology, strategies are described for helping people develop skills of optimism, hope, and posttraumatic growth. Through developing an optimistic perspective, he believes people become capable of resisting *learned helplessness*. An example of such an exercise, a Gratitude Journal, invites the individual to keep a notebook and every night, write down 3 things that happened or were experienced that day for which the person is grateful. They may be little things, a passing moment or a small achievement. The point is to become more mindful of what opportunities and gifts come into our lives each day.

Hope. Hope intuitively seems essential to sustaining motivation. The construct of hope has been widely researched among numerous populations. Research supports connections between a sense of hope and factors such as engagement in meaningful life activities and self-reports of greater life satisfaction.[10] Further, high-hope individuals are found to be more effective in reaching their goals.[12] Coduti and Schoen[12] suggested that hope develops through the process of identifying short term, concrete goals, and achieving them. When the steps to goal achievement fail to result in success, then prompt and careful attention must be directed toward refining the plan and attaining that goal; or, as necessary, revising the goal to one more readily achievable. In so doing, the individual benefits in several ways:

➢ developing a history of successes while operating within the new circumstances;

➢ when success is not found immediately, to develop probabilistic thinking skills while defining new paths to success;

➢ as necessary, learning that the original goal may not have been as functional as newly defined intermediate goals; and

➢ with support and reinforcement, develop a stronger sense of optimism, hope, persistence, and efficacy.

Lockshin[22] shares his perspectives as a physician on the topic of chronic illness and uncertainty. Particularly meaningful passages are shared here:

Chronic illness lacks the certainty of unequivocal diagnosis and cure. Time passes, facts change. Assumptions need to be revised. Pathways merge and intertwine in hidden networks, like the underground network that reveals itself only to those imaginative enough to intuit the <u>fairy ring</u>.[p. 38]

Omnipresent, not invalidating, uncertainty does not excuse inaction. It calls upon imagination, innovation, to address what is known, factors that may change and cautiously developing plans that creatively move in a growth direction.[p. 202]

> As long as you have hope, uncertainty may be tolerable, acceptable, and welcome. So long as you know you have a plan [for improving the life situation], you offer hope.[p. 59]

While searching for vagueness in an otherwise bad situation, uncertainty can "bend" to be a reason for hope.[25] The relationship between the constructs of hope and optimism are interrelated, enhancing one another.

Posttraumatic Growth. Experiencing adverse life events can be a catalyst for a person to learn to cope with life's challenges, develop new skills and insights, and be positively transformed by them.[17] This may contribute to the cognitive and emotional shifts noted among people who have been dealing with uncertainty for longer periods of time. Roepke and Seligman[30] noted that positive changes can follow adverse experiences. They noted these changes may occur in the following areas: improved relationships, deeper spirituality, greater appreciation for life, increased personal strength, and a sense of new possibilities. Sanguine posttraumatic growth is far more likely when external support is provided early in the process, and when the individual is supported in reviewing life events as challenges and normative, rather than catastrophic and bitter. This appears to support the necessity of early intervention of rehabilitation workers, rather than postponing involvement until after the individual may have developed a more cynical, fatalistic outlook. Marmé[24] cautioned that care must be taken to refer to the traumatic event as a catalyst for growth without implying the trauma itself was a good thing. Posttraumatic growth is also consistent with Mishel's[25,26] formulation that, if one perceives uncertainty as an opportunity, then openness to new understandings, behaviors, and experiences is enhanced. In keeping with the author's interpretation of Mishel's work, optimism, hope, and regarding uncertainty as opportunity are prerequisites to posttraumatic growth.

ENCOURAGE EXPLORATION OF SPIRITUALITY

It is anticipated that, at some stage in addressing the uncertainties in life, people will be addressing existential concerns: death, freedom, existential isolation, meaninglessness, and future-becoming-present.[7,36] By exploring with the individual one's sense of spirituality and meaning, as well as thoughts, concerns, and questions on these key issues, we may be able to help the client grapple with the spiritual aspects of his or her existence. The exploration of issues of faith and meaning in life are integral in the individual's effort to come to terms with the ambiguity of life.[1]

Hunter-Hernandez, Costas-Muniz, and Gany[17] suggested spirituality is a resource that supports adaptation and resilience toward an improved quality of life for patients with cancer and other chronic illnesses. They regarded spirituality as a bridge between coping and resilience. They defined resilience as the "ability of humans to cope and adapt when faced with tragedy, trauma, adversity, hardship, and life stressors while maintaining normal psychological and physical functioning."[p.2] While the focus of their work is on Latinos and cancer, their attention to spirituality and religiosity as factors in confronting cancer has much to offer our discussion.

ACKNOWLEDGE CHALLENGES TO COPING THROUGH COMMUNICATION

Communication about serious illness or approaching death requires interactions with others who may misjudge the uncertainties the person finds of utmost concern. In a study of dialysis patients and nurses from dialysis units, distinct differences were demonstrated in the uncertainties of greatest concern to patients who had been involved in treatment for some time and those the nurses working with them anticipated to be of greatest concern to those patients.[16] The nurses anticipated patients would consider consoling and encouraging comments helpful. Although these responses appear to be helpful and desired by people in the early experience of dialysis treatment, this did not appear to be the case for those who had been involved in dialysis for longer time periods. Those patients who had started to develop substantial health problems found these responses hindered communication about the issue most pertinent to them: Is dialysis worthwhile given compounding health problems? The significance of these findings is that one might expect an increased likelihood that patients' concerns would not be heard and addressed and that, instead, nurses would focus their interactions with patients on issues no longer relevant to them.

If uncertainty involves the individual having insufficient information, it is likely to be managed by attempts to seek additional information. However, misunderstandings or disagreements about the form of uncertainty being experienced are likely to undermine the success of coping efforts. Hines[16] offered the example of doctors who assume uncertainty is rooted in a lack of information; these professionals may be inclined to provide even more information to the patient. If, however, the patient's uncertainty stems from attempting to deal with information too complex to process, the doctor's action may be counterproductive and serve to overwhelm the individual even more.

It should be noted that all people involved in the life of the person with disability and chronic illness issues are managing different forms of uncertainty, continually shifting in kind and degree. This marks a significant factor in the complexity of communication in health care settings. Each stakeholder in a conversation or conference may be using different, perhaps conflicting strategies, for managing their various forms of uncertainty. Coping strategies that may be helpful include relying on an authority for guidance, such as one's physician or therapist, or drawing on some simple decision rules.

Be mindful of the restrictions/hollowness of our assurances. Be alert to the individual's needs for increasing, maintaining, or decreasing the level of uncertainty. At times, encouragement may be a very powerful response. At other times, however, the individual might benefit more from an open discussion of the pros and cons of continuing treatment or deciding the best course of action to pursue. Assurances often come with a "one size fits all" imprecision. Our mandate is to listen and observe the individual more closely, more carefully. Those interacting with the person with chronic illness and disability are attempting to manage different sets of uncertainties, each from their own perspective. These varying and perhaps conflicting concerns need to be recognized and explored in conversations with families and friends, and in the counselor's own supervision, to maximize the productivity of communications.

Lockshin,[22] reflecting upon his years of practice as a physician, noted some key factors in communication: "By statement, by posture, inflection, and data, the certainty with which we communicate implies confidence that what is true today [or appears to be true today] will always be true... When we offer certainty, we direct the client's thinking in a narrow conceptual direction, restricting the conceptualization of the outcomes and possibilities."[p. 16] Further, he pointed out that, as we mature personally and professionally, for most, the need to appear certain lessens. We become more comfortable in situations and courses of action that are vulnerable to many variables, working in wonderfully powerful combinations, allowing for results that could not otherwise be imagined.

The act of raising the same questions and issues repeatedly and/or with different people, may serve the person's need to hear different answers, thus maintaining uncertainty, as well as a sense of hope and optimism. As suggested earlier in this chapter, the individual may be seeking reinforcement of tentatively held beliefs. There may be issues of concern other than those specifically mentioned. A productive response may be to explore special meanings of the terms used, expectations for prognosis, and other factors with the individual.

CONSIDER SUPPORT GROUPS

The appropriateness of referral to support groups must be considered carefully. The dynamics of the group must be considered with respect to the intensity and volume of information provided, as well as the certainty with which emotionally-laden information is provided. Depending upon the individual's needs for certainty and ambiguity, the varying coping mechanisms of the group members may significantly threaten the individual's feelings of hope and optimism necessary for a person to sustain himself. It is essential that those referring clients to support groups and, those participating in the groups, understand the complexity of this process and to respond insightfully to individuals dealing with their own and others', perhaps superficially-similar, situations.

Based upon some of the literature reviewed for this chapter, creation of a group focusing specifically on *dealing with uncertainty* may be useful to participants and their families. As an educational/emotional processing group, activities may focus on various, non-threatening topics of shared interests in which the group works to develop creative, novel ways to accomplish tasks of interest to the group. Ideally, this could be directed by members of the team across allied health care specialties, in part modeling this approach with respect to how the group is managed and in their interactions with colleagues.

CONSIDERATIONS FOR REHABILITATION PROFESSIONALS

Rehabilitation professionals may have the closest and most consistent relationship with people as they grapple with the various aspects of uncertainty. Consequently, you must model probabilistic thinking, modeling a widening perspective toward approaching issues large and small in the individual's life, as well as reinforcing hope, spirituality, resilience, and opportunities for growth in your interactions with the individual. You play an essential role in the lives of the people with whom you work and serve as a guide to the families and friends of your clients. They will be observing your responses to uncertainty in situations as they arise and follow your lead in learning how to embrace the inevitable uncertainties of life.

Additionally, you are responsible for assisting the social supports for the people with whom you work, as well as your colleagues, in understanding the role of uncertainty in people's lives. Most likely, you will need to teach, both through direct conversation and modeling, how this perspective operates in people's lives. Feedback to the people with whom you work, their support systems, and colleagues that promote a probabilistic world view will encourage them to adjust their perceptions. This may be accomplished when you encourage all stakeholders to consider multiple ways to accomplish valued activities, emphasizing alternatives for accommodating limitations, and fostering a sense of power in the process of finding new paths. These actions require creativity on all parts. Almost by definition, this then shifts the dynamic to one in which all are involved authentically, meaningfully in the creation of novel approaches to accomplishing desired tasks. These skills will serve the individual and their social system in working from a position of strength, creativity, cooperation, and mastery. Uncertainty will no longer need to be feared or aversive. The skills of embracing uncertainty and working collaboratively toward desired goals will be life-enhancing.

FINAL COMMENTS ON DEALING WITH UNCERTAINTY

Previously, the obvious question may have been, what can we do to facilitate the individual's confrontation with uncertainty? Additional questions may have been: what can we do to minimize the person's uncertainty? How do we facilitate the person dealing with what is happening? We hope that those questions have modified a bit so that you are considering the very important role, for individuals, their families, and health care providers, that dealing with uncertainty serves for people with chronic illness and disability.

In this chapter, we have attempted to describe the construct of uncertainty, the varying forms it may take, and functions it may serve for people, particularly those with chronic illness and disability. We provided complementary research findings from various streams of psychological and communications-oriented fields. We offered strategies for working more effectively with uncertainty for both the individual and the clinician. We urge the reader to consider uncertainty as far more complex than a target to be reduced. Uncertainty must be reconsidered, much as denial, for the function it is serving for the individual. Like denial, the ways one processes the inevitable and complicated uncertainties in one's life provide an opportunity for the individual to acknowledge as much information as can be processed safely.

REFERENCES

[1]Anandarajah, G., & Hight, E. (2001). Spirituality and medical practice: Using the HOPE questions as a practical tool for spiritual assessment. *American Family Physician, 63*, 81-89.

[2]Babrow, A. S. (1992). Communication and problematic integration: Understanding diverging probability and value, ambiguity, ambivalence and impossibility. *Communication Theory, 2*, 95-130.

[3]Babrow, A. S., Hines, S. C., & Kasch, C. R. (2000). Managing uncertainty in illness explanation: An application of problematic integration theory. In B. Whaley (Ed.), *Explaining illness: Research, theories and strategies* (pp. 1-67). Hillsdale, NJ: Erlbaum.

[4]Bradac, J. J. (2001). Theory comparison: Uncertainty reduction, problematic integration, uncertainty management, and other constructs. *Journal of Communication, 51*(3), 457-476.

[5]Brashers, D. E. (2001). Communication and uncertainty management. *Journal of Communication, 51*(13), 477-496.

[6]Brashers, D. E., & Babrow, A. (1996). Theorizing communication and health. *Communication Studies, 47*, 243-251.

[7]Bruyere, S. (1986). An existential approach to rehabilitation counseling. In T. R. Riggar, D. R. Maki & A. W. Wolf (Eds.), *Applied rehabilitation counseling* (pp. 125-134). New York: Springer Publishing Company.

[8]Carey, J. (2012). Stress. In *Brain facts: A primer on the brain and nervous system* (7th ed, pp. 36-38). Washington, D.C: Society for Neuroscience.

[9]Carleton, R. N. (2016). Into the unknown: A review and synthesis of contemporary models involving uncertainty. *Journal of Anxiety Disorders, 39*, 30-43.

[10]Chan, J., Chan, F., Ditchman, N., Phillips, B., & Chou. C. (2013). Evaluating Snyder's hope theory as motivational model participation and life satisfaction for individuals with spinal cord injury: A path analysis. *Rehabilitation Research, Policy, and Education, 27*(3), 171-185.

[11]Chodron, P. (2002). *Comfortable with uncertainty*. Boston, MA: Shambhala Publications, Inc.

[12]Coduti, W. A., & Schoen, W. (2014). Hope model: A method of goal attainment with rehabilitation services clients. *Journal of Rehabilitation, 80*(2), 30-40.

[13]Evans, T. (2005). The tools of encouragement. *CYC-Online, 73*. Retrieved from www.cyc-net.org/cyc-online/cycol-0205-encouragement.html

[14]Hannibal, K. E., & Bishop, M. D. (2014). Chronic stress, cortisol dysfunction, and pain: psychoneuroendocrine rationale for stress management in pain rehabilitation. *Physical Therapy, 94*(12), 1816-1825.

[15]Hillen, M. A., Gutheil, C. M., Strout, T. D., Smets, E. M. A., & Han, P. K. J. (2017). Tolerance of uncertainty: Conceptual analysis, integrative model, and implications for healthcare. *Social Science and Medicine, 180*, 62-75.

[16]Hines, S. C. (2001). Coping with uncertainties in advance care planning. *Journal of Communication, 51*(3), 498-513.

[17]Hunter-Hernandez, M., Costas-Muniz, R., & Gany, F. (2015). Missed opportunity: Spirituality as a bridge to resilience in Latinos with cancer. *Journal of Religion and Health, 54*(6), 2367-2375.

[18]Johnson, L. M., Zautra A. J., & Davis, M. C. (2006). The role of uncertainty on coping with fibromyalgia symptoms. *Health Psychology, 25*(6), 696-703. doi: 10.1037/0278-6133.25.6.696

[19]Jones, K., Simpson, G. K., Briggs, L., & Dorsett, P. (2016). Does spirituality facilitate adjustment & resilience among individuals and their families after spinal cord injury? *Disability & Rehabilitation, 38*(10), 921-935.

[20]Kramer, P. (1994). *Listening to Prozac: A psychiatrist explores antidepressant drugs and the remaking of the self listening to Prozac.* Penguin (USA).

[21]Livneh, H., & Antonak, R. F. (2005). Psychosocial adaptation to chronic illness and disability: A primer for counselors. *Journal of Counseling and Development, 83*, 12-20.

[22]Lockshin, M.D. (2017). *The prince at the ruined tower: Time, uncertainty, & chronic illness.* New York: Custom Databanks, Inc.

[23]Marmé, G. W., Marmé, M., & Stano, J. F. (2009). Dealing with uncertainty. In J. F. Stano, (Ed.), *Psychology of disability* (pp. 163-184). Linn Creek, MO: Aspen Professional Services.

[24]Marmé, M. (2017). Strength-based theory and practice: Perspectives and strategies that enhance growth, hope, and resilience for people living with chronic illness and disability. In J. K. Edwards, A. Young, & H. J. Nikels (Eds.), *Handbook of strengths-based clinical practices: Finding common factors* (pp. 125-148). New York: Routledge.

[25]Mishel, M. H. (1990). Reconceptualization of the uncertainty in illness theory. *Image: Journal of Nursing Scholarship, 22*, 256-262.

[26]Mishel, M. H. (1999). Uncertainty in chronic illness. In J. J. Fitzpatrick (Ed.), *Annual review of nursing research* (vol. 17, pp. 269-294). New York: Springer Publishing Company.

[27]Nanton, V., Munday, D., Dale, J., Mason, B., Kendall, M., & Murray, S. (2016). The threatened self: Considerations of time, place, and uncertainty in advanced illness. *British Journal of Health Psychology, 21*(2), 351-373

[28]Peters, A., McEwen, B. S., & Friston, K. (2017). Uncertainty and stress: Why it causes diseases and how it is mastered by the brain. *Progress in Neurobiology, 156*, 164-188.

[29]Rand, K., & Shea, A. (2013). Optimism within the context of disability. In M. Wehmeyer (Ed.), *The Oxford handbook of positive psychology and disability* (pp. 48-59). New York, NY: Oxford University Press.

[30]Roepke, A. M., & Seligman, M. E. P. (2014). Doors opening: A mechanism for growth after adversity. *The Journal of Positive Psychology, 10*(2), 107-115.

[31]Schlossberg, N. K. (1984). *Counseling adults in transition: Linking practice with theory*. New York: Springer Publishing Company.

[32]Seligman, M. E. P. (2011). *Flourish*. New York, NY: Atria Press.

[33]Wells, S. M. (2000). *A delicate balance: Living successfully with chronic illness*. Cambridge, MA: Perseus Publishing.

[34]Wong, Y. J. (2015). The psychology of encouragement: Theory, research, and applications. *The Counseling Psychologist, 43*(2), 178-216.

[35]Wright, L. J., Afari, N., & Zautra, A. (2009). The illness uncertainty concept: A review. *Psychiatric Pain Management, 13*(2), *133-138*.

[36]Yalom, I. D. (1980). *Existential psychotherapy*. New York: Basic Books, Inc.

This chapter is dedicated to Drs. G. W. Marmé and Joseph F. Stano, with gratitude for their inspiration on this topic and their insights into the development of the original version of this chapter.

Dr. Marmé provided the best of medical care to his patients in over 50 years of practice as a family practitioner. Beyond his skill as a physician, his care of patients and their families embodied a profound understanding and respect for the various ways that people "deal with uncertainty." When patients and their families saw him walk through the door, they were confident that he would find a way to the best solution possible and that, when good results were not to be found, he would see the patient and the family through whatever the future offered. He inspired confidence, faith, optimism, and hope. He provided encouragement, in addition to the most skilled of medical expertise.

Dr. Stano, throughout his careers as an educator and clinician, provided support to his clients, colleagues, students, and friends as they sought their own ways to address uncertainty in their lives. To know two such fine people guides me daily in my efforts to deal with uncertainty.

CHAPTER 8

LOSS, GRIEF, MOURNING, AND RESILIENCE

JAMIE MITUS

STEVE ZANSKAS

The onset of a disability may prompt a multitude of emotional reactions from the individual and the family. As the process of adjustment unfolds, feelings of loss, grief, and mourning may surface.[2,6,20,91] From the parents whose child is born with a developmental disability to the adult in mid-life who becomes deaf, these feelings manifest themselves in similar and different ways, given a host of factors related to the individual, the family, and the context in which they live.[66,75,103] Of particular importance, however, is the role resiliency plays in moving from feelings of loss, grief, and mourning to psychosocial well-being.

Several researchers have explored the experience of loss, grief, and mourning—most notably those concentrating on death and dying, and bereavement.[11,27,42,70,77] Several grief models are proposed within this area of research as a way to explain the process individuals experience when facing death directly or the death of a loved one. In an attempt to understand the adjustment process encountered by individuals with disabilities, some researchers are applying concepts from the bereavement literature to the disability population.[2,32,51,71,91,98] This has not occurred without some debate regarding the appropriateness of using these concepts to make inferences about individuals with disabilities.[1,15,48,66,70,71] Their suitability is questionable given the differences between the finality of death versus the ongoing nature of disability.[49] In the words of Reich, Zautra, and Guarnaccia, "Death itself is a discrete occurrence with few implications for the person's abilities to maintain adequate adjustment, … [individuals with disabilities] may face continuing and chronic burden associated with their stressful condition."[77, p. 64]

Regardless of the debate, some researchers still believe the bereavement literature offers a foundation upon which to build a strong basis of knowledge about the process of loss, grief, and mourning within the disability experience.[62,71,74,98] With this said, disability considerations are being incorporated within the scope of grief models to portray the nature of the disability experience more accurately.[50,64,70,74]

Transcending from grief and mourning to psychosocial well-being is another area explored within the rehabilitation literature. A trend toward exploring the role of resiliency on the adjustment process has emerged.[73,82] The belief here is that resiliency may hold significance in facilitating the movement from loss, grief, and mourning to psychosocial well-being.[66,73]

Early portrayals of resilience suggested resilient individuals are exceptional in their ability to adapt and adjust to loss.[58] Resilience research, however, indicates that resilience consists of an extensive array of ordinary behaviors that can be learned.[54,58,67,68,97] Maintaining good relationships, having an optimistic view of the world, keeping things in perspective, setting goals, taking steps to reach goals, and being self-confident are among the characteristics associated with resilience.[54] Originally considered a trait possessed by a few individuals, the construct of resilience has expanded to include the interaction of risk and protective processes that involve individual, family, & socio-cultural influences.[30,47,58,70,81,97,98] The recognition that resiliency can be acquired and used to facilitate the progression from loss to well-being presents rehabilitation counselors with an opportunity to assist their clients with their adjustment to the losses associated with disability.[47,48] The objective of this chapter is to review the process of loss, grief, and mourning in relation to disability and how resiliency facilitates movement towards successful adjustment and psychosocial well-being for the individual and the family.

LOSS, GRIEF, & MOURNING IN RELATION TO DISABILITY

Loss occurs when a person loses possession of something on which there was a certain level of dependency. The magnitude of the loss is greater when dependency is higher.[76] Within the context of disability, individuals may perceive loss resulting from a change in physical, cognitive, and/or emotional function, if they believe they no longer possess or have the same level of function as before.[2,41] A person with multiple sclerosis may perceive a loss of function related to walking if a wheelchair is now required for mobility. While function is seen as a primary loss related to the disability, associated secondary losses may also occur as in the case of change to the person's employment status, independent living, and/or social roles and relationships.

The experience of loss cuts across all types of disabilities. Individuals may interpret the magnitude of loss based on an evaluation of the former self compared to the current self,[2,74] with the disability serving as the distinct breaking point between the two selves.[12] Loss perceptions are also formed when comparisons of the self are made to the social norms under which a person lives. When seen as falling short of societal expectations, a sense of loss may develop in which missed opportunities are felt.[41] In the same way, family members of those with disabilities may engage in either type of evaluative process, setting in motion the potential to experience loss.[66,84] For instance, parents who upon learning their son or daughter has a disability, may feel a sense of loss about any future plans or dreams they envisioned for their child.[20,48] This perception of loss may, in part, stem from believing in societal norms that lower the expectations of individuals with disabilities in terms of the roles they are to assume in life.[86]

The presence of loss may bring about grief and mourning for some individuals with disabilities and their families.[2,23,41,66,90,102] As an emotional reaction to loss, grief and mourning are conceptualized as both universal and distinctive in nature.[15,76] That is to say, this reaction is thought to happen for most individuals confronting loss, but varies in presentation from one individual to the next. Defined as a normal process, grief and mourning allow the person to release with the loss any commitment to the relationship previously held.[66] The normalcy of this process is important to emphasize so as to prevent faulty assumptions that suggest the individual and/or the family are resistant toward accepting the disability. Such an assumption could lead to negative stereotyping.[20]

The magnitude of grief and mourning fluctuates from one individual to the next and is contextualized to the person's own biography.[2] Torpie,[93] an author on death and dying states, "Grief is proportional to the intensity of invested ties felt for loved objects and persons as a collective whole."[p. 120] In a similar vein, grief and mourning related to the disability experience are in some ways affected by the relative importance or investment given to the specific loss. To illustrate this point, an example of two individuals with amputations of the right arm above the elbow will be presented.

CASE STUDY
MATTHEW & GREGORY

Matthew is a concert pianist who has been playing since the age of four. His career is of great importance to him as he has invested his entire self-concept on his ability to play piano. Matthew is often quoted as saying, "my piano is my best friend; we complement each other exceedingly well."

Gregory is a construction worker who also values his work but does not identify himself solely by his trade. Although he prides himself on his physical capability, he places higher value on his social abilities. In fact, he has been considering a career change to become a teacher to align more closely with his social skills.

In this brief vignette, it becomes evident that Matthew has a larger investment in his ability to use his hands for his livelihood than Gregory does. Consequently, this could lead to a more intense grief and mourning process for Matthew despite the similarities of the disabilities. A similar experience may occur for family members, as well, where the importance given to the loss may affect the intensity of grief and mourning.

MATTHEW & GREGORY (Cont'd.)

Matthew is married to Ginger, who is also a concert performer. She and Matthew often practiced together which enriches their relationship. Since the amputation, Matthew has not played or performed. Consequently, Ginger feels a significant loss in her relationship with Matthew.

In contrast, Gregory's wife, Samantha, has worked as an Elementary school teacher. While the amputation has proven challenging for them, she is excited that he is now seriously considering a career change to become a teacher and is pleased that his disability can be easily accommodated so that he may pursue this goal. In the past, he has talked about becoming a teacher, but now he is starting to take steps towards realizing it. By shifting careers, Samantha feels they will have more in common, in turn strengthening their relationship.

In this scenario, both family members appear to experience loss but, specific to their respective relationships, the loss seems more pronounced for Ginger. In fact, Samantha foresees a gain to her relationship because of the amputation. For this reason, Ginger may experience a deeper level of grief and mourning than Samantha.

Within the scope of disability, loss can generally be organized into one of three categories: physical, psychological, and social loss.[2,11,29,35,62] Shown in Figure 1 are examples of loss associated with each category for the individual and, in some instances, for the family. For this chapter, attention will be devoted solely to psychological and social losses. Important to note, however, is that the three types of loss are not mutually exclusive in that they affect one another and, through an interactive relationship, influence the reactions of grief and mourning.

FIGURE 1

CATEGORIES OF LOSS

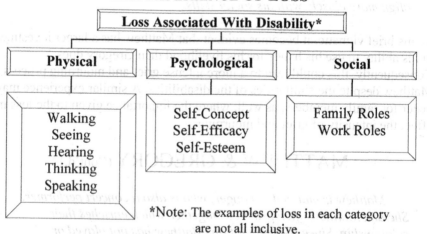

THE EXPERIENCE OF LOSS

Loss Associated With Disability*

Physical	Psychological	Social
Walking Seeing Hearing Thinking Speaking	Self-Concept Self-Efficacy Self-Esteem	Family Roles Work Roles

*Note: The examples of loss in each category are not all inclusive.

Psychological losses routinely discussed in the literature include loss of self-concept, self-efficacy, and self-esteem. Internally oriented, these losses can alter the manner in how individuals behave, think, and feel about themselves.[5] In contrast, externally-based social losses involve the person in relation to his/her social environment. Common experiences of social loss associated with the disability experience include family and work roles, among others. A loss of these roles may in some way limit or lead to a loss of social relationships in part because of social norms that essentially say individuals with disabilities are not expected to participate in society to the same degree as persons without disabilities.[11,86]

PSYCHOLOGICAL LOSS

Self-concept refers to the extent of awareness and insight individuals have of their limitations, attributes, or personal characteristics.[65] Loss of self-concept involves a shift in thought where individuals experience confusion about or no longer identify with one or more attributes that were previously crystallized within their self-image.[2] For example, a shift might be seen in someone who formerly identified as being outgoing but, with the onset of depression, has opted to spend more time alone. A change like this may prompt confusion for this person about whether he or she is still extroverted. When there are shifts as seen in the example here, an unraveling of the self-concept may occur, leading to uncertainty about one's own personal identity. In some instances, confusion may stem from the occurrence of "identity theft," a phenomenon that may occur for some individuals who are unable to speak or advocate for themselves as a result of the disability. In this case, others may define the person in a way that counters their own personal belief, enforcing decisions the individual might otherwise oppose. With the imposition of this new definition, personal identity as defined by the individual may be lost.[92] To illustrate this point, consider someone with aphasia. According to Thompson and Mckeever,[92] with the inability to communicate as effectively as before, others may transform this individual from a "person" into a "physical presence," who is now viewed as a burden to society instead of a contributing member.[92] This transformation takes place over time through the interactions of others with the individual. This confusion is further echoed by Alasweski, Alasweski, and Potter[2] who said the onset of a disability can, "undermine the taken-for-granted nature of the world."[p. 1072] When confusion occurs, there is a need to establish a new identity that allows the individual to create order to the self-concept again. For a full discussion on self-concept, refer to Chapter 5.

Other psychological losses include loss of self-efficacy and self-esteem. Self-efficacy encompasses the beliefs people have about their capabilities to achieve certain tasks that influence events in their lives.[5] When self-efficacy is strong, people are inclined to take on and master more challenging tasks. Self-esteem involves value judgments held by individuals about their attributes and capabilities, which influence feelings of self-worth.[65] When self-esteem is high, people tend to feel more positively about their self-worth.

Loss of self-efficacy and self-esteem may be more profound for individuals with disabilities. Reich, Zautra, and Guarnaccia[77] reported participants with disabilities in their study were more likely to lose self-esteem in comparison to participants bereaving the death of a loved one.[77] They were also more likely to experience feelings of helplessness and depression, suggesting a decline in self-efficacy. It was hypothesized these results occurred because individuals with disabilities experience loss daily, and the effects on their emotional health may be deeper in terms of altering self-concept in a negative way than for those in bereavement.[77] Alaszewski and colleagues[2] add that, for some individuals, continual reminders of the disability may lead to self-doubt about their abilities.

Other factors contributing to these losses may stem from lower expectations frequently placed upon individuals with disabilities.[86] For example, employers are inclined to believe individuals with disabilities will perform more poorly on the job. In fact, Colella and Varma[17] found a negative bias in the expectations of future job performance for individuals with disabilities. Such negative beliefs may be directly or indirectly communicated to, and subsequently internalized by, the person with a disability, leading to a loss of self-confidence and self-worth. Consequences such as these reiterate the importance of being able to reconstruct the self-concept following a disability to achieve psychosocial well-being.[6] For an in-depth discussion on self-esteem, refer to Chapter 5.

SOCIAL LOSS

> *"People with disabilities have the difficult task of challenging the personal, cultural and structural discrimination which conspires against forming any positive concept of self or autonomy. For some these cultural images may be internalized to produce negative perceptions of our personal identities and social roles defined and ascribed to us."*[11, p. 184]

Social loss for individuals with disabilities often comes in the form of roles within the family and work context. Individuals with disabilities are typically assigned to a group where lower expectations preclude them from full participation in these social roles.[11,86] An underlying assumption is that they are less likely to be socially active and involved within these roles. Such expectations lead to oppression, paternalism, and exclusion from full citizenship.[11,86] Individuals with congenital disabilities are often assigned to these roles at birth, while others who acquire a disability later in life are expected to relinquish old roles for those associated with the disability.

Pressures from society to take on certain roles, while resigning from others as a person with a disability, create struggles for the individual and the family. Bevan and Thompson[11] described this feeling of pressure in a woman with a spinal cord injury who experienced internal conflict between her social identity and the physical loss associated with the injury. Grieving this loss was complicated by the medical team who expected her and the family to adopt the "disabled" label they assigned to her as part of her identity. Not only did she struggle with the pressures to conform, but her family, who had known her in a different context prior to the spinal cord injury, also experienced a similar challenge.

Alterations in traditional family roles may occur for some individuals and their family, whether out of necessity or assumptions based on social norms.[20,48,62,74] Change in one person typically requires the entire family to adapt.[58] Whether disability affects the person who was the breadwinner, the primary decision maker, or the child caregiver, a transition period may evolve in which family roles are reassigned, requiring adjustment to the loss of old roles and the acquisition of new ones. The magnitude of shift in these relationships will determine the intensity of grief and mourning felt by the family, as well as the extent to which these roles were seen as detrimental to their relationships.[18,62] If family members are strongly tied to their previous roles and view them as supporting their relationships to one another, loss is likely to be greater.[74,75]

Concerns for the loss or shift in family roles may be experienced across various time orientations, including the present and the future as compared to the past.[23,90] In other words, family members may form expectations about their current and future roles that are in part based on the past. When those roles shift away from the established expectations because of a disability, the family may feel grief.

To illustrate this point, let us examine a working parent with a son in his senior year of high school who acquires a traumatic brain injury. Present concerns may relate to whether the son will be able to assume his role as a student, as well as the parent's ability to elevate the caregiver role while continuing to balance the worker role. As compared to the past, the parent may have expected the son to graduate on time while anticipating a decrease in the caregiver role in the near future. With the onset of the disability, these expectations in family roles may be called into question, thus creating a discrepancy in expectations between the present and the future with the past. The extent of these discrepancies may influence the degree of grief experienced by the family.

Relevant to the family is another phenomenon known as "double grief" associated with family members other than the parent or child with the disability.[102] In this case, other family members (e.g., grandparent, sibling) may experience loss on two levels. For example, a grandparent may experience direct loss associated with their role as a grandparent to their grandchild with a disability. Perhaps they envisioned being an active mentor to the grandchild, which they may still be able to do but on a more limited basis now. Indirectly, they may also feel the loss experienced by their own adult child who must transform the parental role to accommodate the needs associated with the child's disability. The grandparent may have envisioned for their own adult child the same type of parental experience they had, which may no longer be possible.

Work roles serve as another source of social loss. Individuals with disabilities often experience difficulties finding a job or reentering the working world as evidenced by the high unemployment rate of individuals with disabilities.[52] Consequently, there are limitations in the work roles they assume in society. For those who find jobs, occupational role entrapment may occur where they are relegated to lower-level positions typically stereotyped to people with disabilities.[86] This kind of entrapment, in many instances, underutilizes the individual's potential, thus leading to feelings of lost opportunity. Such a loss can be especially problematic for persons whose sole source of self-concept is grounded in their role as a worker. In Chamberlain's study, several participants reported having difficulties with self-esteem because of employment difficulties.[15] Work had provided them with a well-developed sense of identity prior to their disability. A quote from one of the participants illustrates the magnitude of this loss:

> *I used to be proud of my job and I earned a good wage. I'll never be able to work in that [executive] job again. Now I have a fraction of that money to live on. I have dropped from $25 per hour to less than $6. I have lost my identity, who will respect me now? No respect, no income; and that which I value so much – my mind – it doesn't work like it used to...*[p. 411]

The sense of pride this person felt about his job has disappeared due to changes within his work role. Also evident is the stress he feels from the loss of income associated with his change in employment. This can be especially stressful for the family if the individual served as the primary source of income in the household.[35]

THE EXPERIENCE OF GRIEF AND MOURNING

EMOTIONAL REACTIONS

Individuals with disabilities and their families may experience an array of emotions during the grief and mourning process. Emotional reactions commonly described in the literature include shock, anger, sadness/depression, guilt/regret, and anxiety.[35,66,75,103] Shock is typically identified as one of the first emotional reactions following the onset of a disability, when stability is replaced by vulnerability in the person's life. It is characterized by numbness and confusion, as well as depersonalization where disconnect from the self occurs.[50,62]

Anger often occurs in response to a direct threat to a sense of security in the world and is either internally directed towards the self or externally towards others.[62,103] When internally directed, anger may appear as self-criticism or self-blame.[50,62] Externally-oriented anger may be directed toward others believed to have caused the disability, as observed in Chamberlain's study of individuals with traumatic brain injury.[15] Several participants reported feeling angry toward the person responsible for their injury. This form of anger may be targeted toward people, objects, or certain aspects of the environment.[50]

Sadness is an emotional reaction signifying the person's acknowledgement of the disability. Although grief may be intensified here, this emotion is viewed as a stepping stone toward acceptance and is considered essential to the mourning process.[48] There is the potential, however, for sadness to transform into depression, a more severe emotional experience that may be counterproductive to the adjustment process.[48] For example, Adcock, Goldberg, Patterson, and Brown[1] reported that, in studies of persons with burns, depression contributed to longer hospital stays, more medical setbacks, and greater conflict within the family.

Guilt and regret serve as other emotional responses within the grief and mourning process that are usually founded on irrational beliefs.[35,48,62,74,103] In Chamberlain's study, regret was commonly expressed as a feeling among participants with traumatic brain injury, as well as their families.[15] This emotion was noted in comments where the participants expressed regret for being in the accident, as well as their parents wishing they could have prevented the accident from happening.[15] Family members who are unable to resolve their feelings of guilt may become overprotective, such that movement towards psychosocial well-being is increasingly challenged for the individual with the disability.[48]

Anxiety involves a heightened sense of fear where the individual or family may attempt to anticipate future danger related to the disability. Someone with a progressive disability, for instance, may experience anxiety when considering potential outcomes while undergoing medical tests or contemplating life changes.[50] In Westgren and Levi's[99] study of a woman with spinal cord injuries, anxiety was a common emotion prior to engaging in their first sexual contact since the injury. For many of the participants, they felt out of control and ambiguous about their "new" body image. With increased vulnerability, some individuals may find it challenging to trust others including family and friends.[45]

The manner in which these emotions are expressed will vary as both a product of the individual and the circumstances of the loss itself.[35] The nature of the physical, psychological, and social loss associated with the disability may also determine the type of emotional reaction experienced by the individual and/or the family. Below, we return to the case of Matthew to illustrate some of these emotional responses in relation to the various types of loss.

CASE STUDY
MATTHEW

Matthew's arm was amputated following an automobile accident one month ago. Having gone through extensive rehabilitation, he was recently fitted for a prosthetic. Matthew recalls the day of his fitting, which led to a wave of despair and the "blues" unlike any he felt before. This single event signified for him the permanence of his situation in that he would never have his "old" arm back. The arm itself, he thought, upsets him less than knowing he may have to give up his career as a concert pianist. When thinking about the uncertainty of his future and career, Matthew becomes extremely tense and feels his heart racing. It is often difficult for him to eat during these times. Sometimes he becomes extremely fixated in thought about what direction he will go, as performing is all he has ever known. What else could there possibly be? Body and soul, he is a concert pianist and has never envisioned himself in any other way.

Last night, Matthew's wife, Ginger, stopped by the hospital and told him she practiced with a mutual friend over the weekend in preparation for an upcoming performance. Matthew lashed out at her in frustration by raising his voice and saying, "You'll never do well in this performance; I don't even want to see it!" Later Matthew regretfully thought about his reaction toward Ginger, realizing the resentment he felt about her practicing with their friend. He thought, "it should have been me, not our friend." Suddenly a rush of fear enveloped him, realizing the nature of their relationship may change.

Would they ever be practice buddies again? This was so much a part of their relationship; would they have anything in common? Would she still love him if he couldn't play as he had before? While Matthew recognizes the strength of their relationship, he can't help questioning whether they will be able to withstand the changes taking place in their relationship since the accident.

DISCUSSION QUESTIONS

➤ What emotional reactions is Matthew experiencing in this scenario?

➤ What are some of the physical, psychological, and social losses triggering these emotions?

Stage Models of Grief and Mourning

Using stage models, several researchers have described the process of grief and mourning.[2,15,19,64] These models are intended to provide a framework for how this process unfolds in a sequential order with respect to the person's emotional response. Several models have been proposed in the literature, but most describe a similar process of grief and mourning incorporating many of the emotional reactions discussed earlier.[1,48,50,62,68,103] In the traditional sense, "these models describe discrete stages and present grief as linear and time bound, with resolution as a necessary and normal outcome."[48, p. 233]

While traditional stage models offer an important understanding of the grieving process, there are some considerations when applying them to the disability experience.[70,71,91] In their original form, stage models built in an expectation that the family, as well as the individual, would ultimately reach resolution after going through a series of stages in a linear and sequential order within a restricted timeframe.[48,66,103] This expectation derived from the idea that death is finite and, upon its occurrence, the person could begin moving forward toward the resolution of accepting the loss.

In the case of disability, loss can be experienced across the lifespan.[66] According to Chamberlain,[15] persons with disabilities may encounter situations throughout life that remind them of their loss, in turn triggering feelings of grief and mourning. In the case of someone with lupus, for example, periodic flare-ups may decrease the person's physical ability. Consequently, grief and mourning may reemerge parallel to the timing of the flare ups. Someone who acquired a spinal cord injury at the age of 18 may, upon turning 50, recycle through the grief process when reminded of a goal they had to run a marathon by then. In both scenarios, the individuals may recycle through some or all of the stages in any order.

Family members may also recycle through the stages of grief and mourning.[6] According to Davis and Schultz,[20] "grieving is ongoing whereby parents are progressively challenged by reminders of the discrepancy between what their child should be, and what their child is."[p. 369] Feelings of loss and grief may resurface upon certain milestones in life. For example, parents may be reminded of loss when setting up their child's individualized educational plan during high school or when seeking supportive housing as their child enters adulthood.

If stage models of grief and mourning are followed in the traditional sense, there is a higher risk for bias to occur toward individuals with disabilities and their families if they do not achieve the final stage of resolution, or cycle through all of the stages sequentially in a timely fashion.[48] Such bias may come in the form of assumptions that there is failure to accept the reality of the disability.[20] The ongoing presence of grief and mourning needs to be appropriately reflected in these models as a natural part of the process that extends across the lifespan.

More contemporary stage models of grief and mourning have accounted for many of the considerations described above as it pertains to loss. One of the well-known models specific to the disability experience is Livneh and Antonak's[50] Phases of Adaptation Model. Figure 2 provides an outline of the stages, which are described in detail in Chapter 1. While the emphasis is on adaptation, the eight-phase model describes various emotional reactions relevant to the grief and mourning process ultimately leading to adjustment and psychosocial well-being.[50,91]

FIGURE 2.

LIVNEH & ANTONAK'S (1997) PHASES OF ADAPTATION TO CHRONIC ILLNESS OR DISABILITY

Phases of Adaptation
Shock
Anxiety
Denial
Depression
Internalized Anger
Externalized Hostility
Acknowledgment
Adjustment

Also, important to note is the model's holistic perspective accounting for the affective, cognitive, and behavioral dimensions of the disability experience.[91]

THE MEANING-MAKING MODEL OF GRIEF AND LOSS

In recent years, there has been some concern regarding the heavy reliance on stage models to account for loss and grief among individuals with disabilities.[18,72,83] Some of these concerns relate to the limited empirical research associated with stage models.[72] Other models have been proposed to broaden the perspective of loss and grief. One model gaining popularity is Meaning-Making Theory, which states that the experiences people have are used to construct and maintain an understanding of who they are and what their purpose is in the world.[22,23] This understanding is further solidified when people share stories about their experiences with others.[23] When loss occurs as a result of a disability it is necessary for people to undergo a sense-making process that will do one of two things: (1) fit the implications of the loss within their current constructed identity of the self and the world, or (2) create new narrative that alters the self-identity and the world they live in. In this case, a reorganization of the belief system may be necessary for the individual to reconstruct a sense of purpose in the world.[36]

Finding the "silver lining" is also considered a part of the Meaning-Making Model in which the individual is able to see the benefits within the loss and, in turn, find new purpose.[23] According to Hibbard,[36] the perception of benefits seems to be more important than actually experiencing the benefits following a loss. Perceptions have been linked to shorter and less intense grief. As a model of adjustment, exploring the mean-making process among individuals with disabilities is showing promise in promoting better psychological well-being when dealing with loss.[22,90]

The first section of this chapter was intended to provide the reader with an understanding about the process of loss, grief, and mourning in relation to the disability experience. Evident from this overview is the variability of this experience from one individual to the next in that some people will go through more intense grief and mourning. What factors influence the depth of grief and the ability to move towards adjustment? The following section attempts to answer this question by exploring resiliency and showing the instrumental role it plays in facilitating movement toward adjustment and psychosocial well-being for the individual and the family.

THE ROLE OF RESILIENCY IN THE ADJUSTMENT TO DISABILITY

OVERVIEW OF RESILIENCE AND RESILIENCY

Despite our traditional strength-based approach, rehabilitation counseling professionals have engaged in minimal research about resiliency in relation to the losses experienced by individuals with a disability and their families. Recently, there has been increased psychological attention to the resilience of individuals following a traumatic injury.[10,14,24,36,89,101] However, the majority of research regarding resilience and resiliency has been conducted by either developmental psychologists using children, or by grief theorists examining the adult loss of a spouse.[7,54,55,58,97] As a result, rehabilitation counselors interested in the application of the process of resilience need to consult the literature from allied professions and extrapolate their findings to develop a conceptual framework. A frequently misunderstood construct, resilience has primarily been viewed as either a characteristic of exceptionally healthy people or as a pathological absence of grief.[7]

Disability studies scholars have argued that resilience as a construct is ableist and has the potential to marginalize people with a disability.[38,39,80,95] These authors support Ungar's[95] constructionist approach recommending professionals individually evaluate how risk impacts both access to and acquisition of resources. Similarly, Cardenas and Lopez[13] cautioned that, although promoting strategies to develop individual or familial resilience can be beneficial, these strategies are insufficient and are not a replacement for cultural and societal actions to improve the societal inequities often experienced by individuals who have experienced a disability or their families.[13] However, the influence of positive psychology has facilitated a paradigm shift in the perceptions of how individuals and their families respond to chronic illness and disability.[28,51,68,62,84]

A complex construct, resilience has lacked universal definition.[16,31,32,69] Resilience is commonly defined as "the capability of a strained body to recover" or "an ability to recover from or adjust easily to misfortune or change."[61] Resilience has been conceptualized as the human ability to adapt in the face of tragedy, trauma, adversity, loss, and ongoing significant life stressors.[68] As a construct with many dimensions, resilience cannot be reduced to a single characteristic or trait.[21,54,58,68,97] Although resilience cannot be reduced to a single characteristic, a review of the literature does reflect clusters or groupings of similar characteristics.

In order to improve the quality of research regarding the concept, many researchers have proposed standardizing the definitions and terminology.[31,54,58,78,97] For clarity throughout the chapter, we will adopt the recommended conventions and use the term resiliency when referring to a specific characteristic or personality trait and the term resilience when referring to the process of resilience.[54,58] Most researchers view resilience as "a dynamic process encompassing positive adaptation within the context of significant adversity."[54, p. 543] Two assumptions are inherent in this definition of resilience: (a) there is exposure to adversity or loss, and (b) there is an opportunity for constructive adaptation regardless of the severity of the loss or intrusion on one's life cycle. Although many people may possess characteristics associated with resilience, whether resilience is actually demonstrated can only be determined following a loss or an exposure to an adverse event.[55,67] The very nature of the construct requires resilience be operationally defined as an outcome which follows a loss with documentation of the factors that either contribute to or detract from adaptation.[55]

Researchers have also differentiated between the trajectories associated with recovery and resilience following adult trauma,[7,55] citing a functional and temporal distinction between the constructs. According to Mancini and Bonanno, the term *recovery* suggests a progression through the cycle of normal functioning; followed by an intervening loss and subsequent loss of function, grief, mourning; and an eventual return to pre-onset levels of functioning.[55] Complete recovery may occur quickly, or extend up to one or two years following a loss.[9] In contrast, the term *resilience* reflects an individual's or family's ability to maintain equilibrium and function following a loss.[55,63] Although the majority of resilient individuals experience a sense of grief or yearning following a loss, these experiences are temporary and do not preclude day-to-day functioning.

A COMPREHENSIVE MODEL OF RESILIENCE

Conceptualized in many ways since the construct's inception, Luthar, Cicchetti, and Becker[54] summarized the following concerns that have appeared in the literature about resilience as a psychological construct:

> ➤ vague definitions and terminology,

> ➤ differences in the function and the nature of the risks experienced among resilient individuals,

> ➤ the impermanence of resilience as a phenomenon, and

> ➤ general theoretical concerns.

Despite these concerns, the phenomenological and developing empirical evidence support the validity of resilience as a psychological construct.[7,26,54,56,58,78,100]

Richardson[78] identified three historical trends in the research about resilience and resiliency. Clinicians initially identified the developmental assets and protective factors based upon observations made in their clinical practice. Following the phenomenological descriptions of clinicians, researchers described resilience as a process of coping with stressors or loss that facilitates the identification and development of protective factors. The current research trend employs a postmodern view in which resilience is perceived as the force that drives a person to grow through adversity and life disruption.

Based upon his review of the literature, Richardson[78] developed a comprehensive model of the resilience process that is represented in Figure 3. This model reflects how individuals move through biological, psychological, and spiritual balance in response to disruptive life events. A person's readiness for reintegration determines which type of coping occurs. Insight and personal growth are attributed to one's repeated resilient reintegration. Individuals who remain in their "comfort zone," attached to past experiences, stagnate. Those individuals who experience a loss of motivation or hope as a result of chronic illness or disability experience chronic coping and loss. Dysfunctional reintegration, or coping, is characterized by destructive behaviors, such as substance use or other behavior. According to this model, resiliency begins when a person has adapted to one's life situation. It is important to note that resilient reintegration does not have to be immediate and may occur years after the onset of chronic illness, trauma, or disability. Richardson suggested counseling is useful to the extent that it assists clients to recognize their potential for growth, opportunities for recuperation, or continued loss as they are confronted with the disruptions of their life cycle. The path or trajectory taken by a client is a matter of choice, whether conscious or unconscious.

FIGURE 3

RICHARDSON'S RESILIENCE MODEL

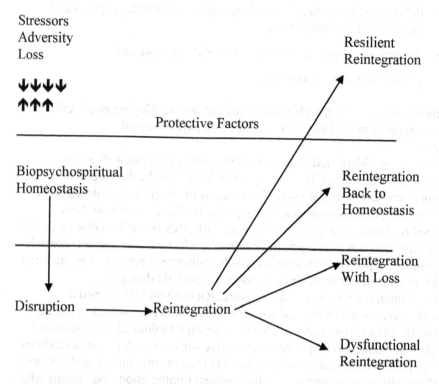

The bold downward-facing arrows represent the losses an individual confronts; the bold upward arrows represent the protective factors an individual possesses to cope with loss; the remaining arrows represent the path an individual takes after the onset of a chronic illness or disability.

GREGORY AND MATTHEW (Cont'd.)

Consider the previous case examples of Gregory and Matthew from the perspective of resilience. Both Gregory and Matthew have sustained traumatic injuries. The trauma has disrupted both men's sense of biopsychospiritual balance. Both Gregory and Matthew have the potential to reintegrate the meaning of their traumatic injuries. Despite the disruption of traumatic disability in both men's lives, one of the men appears to demonstrate more resilience and have greater potential for resilient reintegration.

DISCUSSION QUESTIONS

> In your opinion, which of the two men, Gregory or Matthew, appears more resilient to their traumatically sustained disability?

> What factors contribute to your opinion?

> Are both men eventually capable of demonstrating resilient reintegration? What would need to occur?

PROTECTIVE FACTORS

Resilient characteristics have frequently been referred to as protective factors or developmental assets.[78] Qualitative studies and clinical observations in developmental psychology have led to the development of an extensive list of protective factors. Garmezy[30] categorized these resiliency factors to include an individual's personality characteristics, having a supportive family environment, and other external support. A brief review of the results from phenomenological studies of resilient children has been provided to assist the reader to develop an understanding of the characteristics observed.

Following a 30-year longitudinal study of at-risk children that began in 1955, Werner and Smith[98] identified being female, hardy, adaptable, tolerant, socially responsible, and goal oriented as characteristics of resilient children, in addition to having communication skills, having self-esteem, and living in a nurturing environment. While studying inner-city youth, Rutter[81] had similar findings. Being female, having a cooperative temperament, a positive school environment, planning skills, self-efficacy, self-mastery, and at least one positive personal relationship with an adult were all characteristic of resilient children.

Garmezy[30] studied the children of parents who had been diagnosed with schizophrenia, for eleven years. The majority of children became competent adults. In addition to the characteristics noted in the previous studies, Garmezy found that the resilient children had high expectations, a positive outlook, problem-solving and critical thinking skills, and a sense of humor. The author concluded these characteristics fell within three broad categories: an individual's personality characteristics, having a supportive family environment, and other external support.

Research more closely related to the field of rehabilitation provides additional insight into the protective factors exhibited by individuals with a disability. Individuals and families have unique responses to losses or the stress associated with chronic illness or disability.[63] Turk[94] identified five factors associated with a person's positive adjustment to chronic illness: knowledge of the disability and treatment plan, coping resources, problem-solving attitude, sense of personal mastery, and motivation. Addressing adjustment from a more global perspective, Antonovsky[4] indicated protective resources included: physical, biochemical, material resources, cognitive-emotional, valuativeattitudinal, interpersonal-relational, and socio-cultural factors.

Miller[63] proposed a power resource model for coping with the losses and uncertainty associated with chronic illness and disability. The protective factors, or power resources, described by Miller include physical strength, psychological stamina and social support, positive self-concept, physical and emotional energy, knowledge of one's condition, motivation, and a belief system or sense of hope. According to this conceptualization, people's coping strategies can be used to offset insufficient power resources and, thereby, improve their ability to cope.

Resilient adaptation to loss has also been associated with flexibility.[8] Flexibility can be fostered through hope.[49,87,88] Hope reflects the client's perceived ability to identify goals, develop plans to achieve goals, and visualize a method of how goals can be attained.[25,87,88] Hardiness is another personality trait that contributes to an individual's resiliency to loss.[7,44,45,46,63] Kobassa[44,45,46] described hardiness as including three elements: the pursuit of meaning in one's life, the perception change represents an opportunity for growth, and the belief one can influence the life events experienced. Individuals with these beliefs appear to consider stressful situations as less distressing.[7,63] Hardiness, as a personality trait, appears to reinforce one's ability to tolerate the lack of control one experiences with loss.[63] Hardy individuals have also been described as being self-confident and capable of using available social support.[7,44,63] A primary source of social support is one's family. Livneh[51] advocated rehabilitation professionals consider the temporal nature of clinical and personal coping strategies impacting the psychosocial adaptation to chronic illness and disability.

FAMILIES AND RESILIENCE

Families, as the fundamental unit of social support, can play an important role in the rehabilitation process for individuals with disabilities. Research findings over the past decade have emphasized the positive dimensions of family resiliency and coping with disability, loss, or trauma.[40] Regrettably, rehabilitation counselors' focus on the individual might prevent them from recognizing the important roles families may play in rehabilitation planning.[28] The congruence or "fit" of a family's style of functioning with the type of onset (acute or gradual) is critical to resilient coping.[79] Families who are able to tolerate extreme emotional intensity, change roles and rules quickly, and identify and utilize resources initially have an advantage. Families that are less flexible and approach situations cautiously will have more initial difficulty, although they may also do well with support and counseling.[79]

Family resilience is not a static concept.[34,59] As reflected in the discussion of protective factors, family resilience is a developmental pathway that has multiple, and often unanticipated, routes to resilience.[7,55,59] Key components of the resiliency model that assist in explaining family behavior in response to stressors of illness or disability include the family's resources, their appraisal of the situation, and style of adaptation.[60]

Kinsella, Anderson, and Anderson[43] described the results of semi-structured interviews with 10 adult offspring and 10 adult siblings of individuals with mental illness. The children at risk who avoided pathology employed a variety of coping skills: constructive escape, seeking support from others, objectifying the illness, acquiring information about mental illness, and spiritual faith. Participants indicated they had also developed personal strengths because of their childhood and adolescent experiences with their parent's or sibling's mental illness. Fourteen of the participants described themselves as stronger and capable of managing adversity. These individual strengths included: independence or self-reliance, ability to create and accomplish, empathy, and an overall resiliency. An important finding from this study is that the younger the child, the more vulnerable the child appeared be to mental illness within the family.[43]

Parenting mediates the effects of both the protective factors and the risks experienced by children.[16] Hipke, Wolchik, Sandler, and Braver[37] examined predictors of resilience in children of divorce. Mothers participating in a preventive parenting program who were sad, frustrated, or felt helpless did not foster resilience in their children. A child's resiliency after divorce depended on their parents' mental health and ability to cope with the children's individual regulatory style.

McCubbin, Balling, Possin, Frierdich, and Byrne[59] identified six resiliency factors that helped families to manage and recover from the adversity of the diagnosis and active treatment phase for a child's cancer. Based on comprehensive interviews conducted with 42 parents in 26 families, identified the following resiliency factors: internal family rapid mobilization and reorganization; social support from the health care team, extended family, community, and workplace; and changes in appraisal to make the situation more comprehensible, manageable, and meaningful. Parents in this study emphasized the importance of teamwork, emotional availability, and each parent's affirmation of the other's contributions.

In a national survey, Marsh, Lefley, Evans-Rhodes, Ansell, and Doerzbacher[57] explored the potential for resilience among family members of people with mental illness. The sample included 131 immediate and extended family members. Participants were asked to describe any family, personal, or consumer strengths that had developed as a result of coping with a family member's mental illness. Family resilience was reported by 87.8% of participants. Personal resilience was reported by 99.2%, and consumer resilience by 75.6%. When asked, over three-fourths of participants answered they had experienced the process of recovery. Participants in the study cited the following resources as promoting positive change: the qualities of their family as a unit or of individual family members, including themselves and their relatives; participation in support groups; professional assistance; the assistance of friends, neighbors, and coworkers; religion; and hobbies.

Venters Horton and Wallander[96] studied the perceptions of hope and social support of 111 mothers of children who had cerebral palsy, spina bifida, or insulin-dependent diabetes. Their results indicated hope plays a significant role in the adjustment process. Hope was found to have both a direct and a mediating effect on stress. Mothers who expressed high levels of hope were found to be less distressed than mothers who were less hopeful. In addition, both the number of available social supports and the mother's expressed satisfaction with the available support were found to moderate maternal stress.

Although there has been limited research regarding family resilience in the field of rehabilitation counseling, several authors are worth noting. Koscuilek[47] examined family coping among 150 families with a member who had sustained a head injury. Three dimensions of family resilience were identified: individual-to-family versus family-to-community coping; family-respite versus head-injury-focused coping; and cognitive versus behavioral coping. Coping behaviors directed toward maximizing the fit between family and community resources were found to be a major positive factor underlying the families successfully coping with the losses associated with a head injury. Positive coping behaviors also included a family's focus on managing the care demands of the family member with a head injury and by those families who took direct behavioral action towards reducing the frequency and intensity of care demands.

Lustig[53] studied parents of 116 children with mental retardation and measured the dimensions of family sense of coherence, social support, family adaptability, family cohesion, and family adaptation. Most of the families in the study demonstrated resilience. Lustig indicated the rehabilitation counselor's goal is to assist families to develop the skills necessary to cope with future change. He suggested this goal could be accomplished by expanding external support using peer mentors or support groups and cognitive counseling approaches to increase or develop a sense of manageability, meaning, and optimism.

Conceptually, White, Driver, and Warren[100] noted that, although there was research examining treatment interventions for individuals who had sustained traumatic injuries, there was no research examining the role of resilience in the rehabilitation process. Subsequently, Griffin and associates[32] conducted a meta-analysis of the extant literature regarding resilience in families with a member who had experienced polytrauma. Based upon their analysis, these authors concluded that rather than a characteristic that a family possesses, resilience is a process through which a family proceeds.

Despite the promising findings regarding interventions to promote resilience, rehabilitation professionals should be aware that the extant literature regarding family resilience remains limited.[31,32] Gauvin-Lepage and associates[31] conducted a comprehensive review of the literature regarding family resilience following physical trauma. The authors noted the existing research is cross-sectional, lacks commonly accepted operational definitions of family resilience or a theoretical orientation, and often fails to consider the perspective of persons who have experienced trauma.

The focus of resiliency models is on understanding the strengths and capabilities that protect individuals and their families from the disruptions associated with unanticipated loss. In general, clients who have a disability need to have the power to manage their own care.[63] Empowerment strategies specific to the components of the resilience model are devoted to enhancing self-esteem, inspiring hope, overcoming energy deficits, and developing motivation and knowledge.[43,53,57,63] This strength-based approach would also appear to hold promise in facilitating positive rehabilitation and employment outcomes, the overall efficiency of rehabilitation counseling services, and the personal satisfaction of rehabilitation counselors.[28] The perspective that resilience is temporal and a process, rather than a characteristic an individual possesses, also appears to be relevant for professionals working with individuals in their adjustment to the grief and loss associated with acquired disability.[32,51]

IMPLICATIONS FOR COUNSELING

The role of the rehabilitation counselor is to assist individuals with disabilities experiencing grief and mourning to cope with their loss and prepare for future change. Within this capacity, they can cultivate potential to achieve both personal and professional goals to promote the person's psychosocial well-being. As part of the loss, grief, and mourning experience, there are four important implications for rehabilitation counselors.

> *First*, they need to recognize the multidimensionality and individuality of the grief and mourning process. There is a vast array of emotional experiences an individual and/or the family may experience when adjusting to a disability. It is important to avoid assumptions that these emotions will be the same across all their clients.

> *Second*, while many individuals with disabilities experience grief, it is important to know that the level of intensity will vary from one individual to the next and, in some instances, may even be absent.

> *Third*, stage models of grief provide a useful framework to refer to when addressing grief and mourning with clients, but it is essential to recognize the recycling and timeless nature of the process to avoid forming bias towards clients whose grief and mourning may reemerge.

> *Lastly*, rehabilitation counselors need to be sensitive to the family members of their clients who may also encounter grief and mourning. Recognizing that some family members are interdependent and influential with one another may have implications for the decisions their clients make about future plans.

Rehabilitation counselors should consider the role of resiliency when assisting individuals and their families to cope with loss, grief, and mourning associated with the disability. The construct of resilience has several implications for counseling individuals who have sustained a loss, are mourning, or grieving.[12, 55]

> Rehabilitation counselors need to recognize many people can cope effectively with the stress of experiencing loss following chronic illness or disability without formal treatment.

> Only those individuals who have developed clinically significant depression or prolonged difficulties functioning require psychotherapy.

> Since resilience can be learned, rehabilitation counselors need to consider the coping strategies of persons who exhibit resiliency and how they can be used to assist with the development of interventions for those requiring treatment.

When considering an intervention, Lustig[53] recommended rehabilitation counselors adopt an empowerment approach. Programs that empower individuals with a disability and their families would:

> treat adults as capable;

> build on strengths, rather than weaknesses; and

> promote the independence to make informed decisions.

Since resilience is a learned and modifiable behavior, rehabilitation counseling interventions that target clients' ability to identify resources, develop problem solving and coping skills, and reframe disabling conditions would be beneficial.[28,55,100]

Applying a family resiliency model, Marsh and colleagues[57] identified a number of recommendations for professionals working with families that have a family member with mental illness. The following suggestions have been adapted from these recommendations to assist rehabilitation counselors develop a more inclusive, systems approach to their work with individuals who have experienced loss as a result of chronic illness or a disability and their families.

➤ Rehabilitation counselors should apply competency or skill-based service models that emphasize the positive qualities of family systems in coping with chronic illness and/or disability.

➤ By working collaboratively with families, rehabilitation counselors can establish partnerships that build on the contributions of all parties, promote an atmosphere of mutual respect, involve families in decisions that affect them, and develop mutual goals for treatment and rehabilitation.

➤ When developing services or planning, consider the family's need for information about a family member's disability, the potential consequences for the family, and the anticipated treatment. Adopting this approach will facilitate the counselor's ability to promote skills for coping with the losses associated with a disability.

➤ As stated earlier, rehabilitation counselors need to acknowledge and address the unique needs of individual family members. Often, those who are most vulnerable suffer unless the counselor is willing to go beyond the shared family experience.

➤ Understanding that resilience is fostered by both the available number of supports and the individual's satisfaction with the available supports, rehabilitation counselors need to acknowledge the potential for family resilience, encourage resilient thinking and behavior, and reinforce resilience when it is observed, to strengthen both the family's internal working alliance, as well as the one between the family and professional.

REFERENCES

[1]Adcock, R. J., Goldberg, M. L., Patterson, D. R., & Brown, P. B. (2000). Staff perceptions of emotional distress in patients with burn trauma. *Rehabilitation Psychology, 45*(2), 179-192.

[2]Alaszewski, A., Alaszewski, H., & Potter, J, (2004). The bereavement model, stroke, and rehabilitation: A critical analysis of the use of a psychological model in professional practice. *Disability and Rehabilitation, 26*(18), 1067-1078.

[3]Anctil. T., O'Brien, M., L., Pecora, P., & Anderson-Harumi, C. (2007). Predictors of adult quality of life for foster care alumni with physical and/or psychiatric disabilities. *Child Abuse & Neglect, 31*(10), 1087-1100.

[4]Antonovsky, A. (1985). *Health, stress, and coping.* San Francisco: Jossey-Bass.

[5]Bandura, A. (1994). Self-efficacy. In V. S. Ramachaudran (Ed.), *Encyclopedia of human behavior* (Vol. 4, pp. 71-81). New York: Academic Press.

[6]Baxter, E., & Diehl, S. (1998). Emotional stages: Consumers and family members recovering from the trauma of mental illness. *Psychiatric Rehabilitation Journal, 21*(4), 349-355.

[7] Bonanno, G. (2004). Loss, trauma, and human resilience: Have we underestimated the human capacity to thrive after aversive events? *American Psychologist, 59*(1), 20-28.

[8] Bonanno, G., Papa, A., Lalande, K., Westphal, M., & Coifman, K. (2004). The importance of being flexible: The ability to both enhance and suppress emotional expression predicts long-term adjustment. *Psychological Science, 15*(7), 482-487.

[9] Bonnano, G., Wortman, C., Lehman, D., Tweed, R., Haring, M., Sonnega, J., Carr, D., & Nesse, R. (2002). Resilience to loss and chronic grief: A prospective study from preloss to18-months postloss. *Journal of Personality and Social Psychology, 83*(5), 1150-1164.

[10]Bonnano, G. A., Kennedy, P., Galatzer-Levy, I. R., & Lude, P. (2012). Trajectories of resilience, depression, and anxiety following spinal cord injury. *Rehabilitation Psychology, 57* (3), 236-247. DOI: 10.1037/a0029256

[11]Beven, D., & Thompson, N. (2003). The social basis of loss and grief: Age, disability, and sexuality. *Journal of Social Work, 3*(2), 179-194.

[12]Campbell-Sills, L., Cohan, S., & Stein, M. (2006). Relationship of resilience to personality, coping, and psychiatric symptoms in young adults. *Behaviour Research and Theory, 44*(4), 585-599.

[13]Cardenas, A., & Lopez, L. (2010). Analysis of matrix of resilience in the face of disability, old age, and poverty. *International Journal of Disability, Development and Education, 57* (2), 175-189. DOI: 10:101080/10349121003750760

[14]Catalano, D., Chan, F., Wilson, L., & Chiu, C. (2011). The buffering effect of resilience on depression among individuals with spinal cord injury: A structural equation model. *Rehabilitation Psychology, 56* (3), 200-211.

[15]Chamberlain, D. J. (2006). The experience of surviving traumatic brain injury. *Issues and Innovations in Nursing Practice, 54*(4), 407-417.

[16]Coleman, M., & Ganong, Lawrence. (2002). Editorial: Resilience and families. *Family Relations, 51*(2), 101-102.

[17]Collela, A., & Varma, A. (1999). Disability-job fit stereotypes and the evaluation of persons with disabilities at work. *Journal of Occupational Rehabilitation, 9*(2), 79-94.

[18]Collings, C. (2008). That's not my child anymore! Parental grief after acquired brain injury (ABI): Incidence, nature, and longevity. *British Journal of Social Work, 38*, 1499-1517.

[19]Davenport, D. S. (1981). A closer look at the "healthy" grieving process. *The Personnel and Guidance Journal, 59*(6), 332-335.

[20]Davis, D. J., & Schultz, C. L. (1998). Grief, parenting, and schizophrenia. *Social Science Medicine, 46*(3), 369-379.

[21]deRoon-Cassini, T. A., Mancini, A. D., Rusch, M. D., & Bonnano, G. A. (2010). Psychopathology and resilience following traumatic injury: A latent growth mixture model analysis. *Rehabilitation Psychology, 55*(1), 1-11. doi: 10.10.1037/a0018601

[22]deRoon-Cassini, T. A., St. Aubin, E. D., Valvano, A., Hastings, J., & Horn, P. (2009). Psychological well-being after spinal cord injury: Perception of loss and meaning making. *Rehabilitation Psychology, 54*(3), 306-314.

[23]Douglas, H. A. (2014). Promoting meaning-making to help our patients grieve: An exemplar for genetic counselors and other health care professionals. *Journal of Genetic Counseling, 23*, 695-700.

[24]Elliott, T. R., Hsiao, Y., Kimbrel, N. A., Meyer, E. C., DeBeer, B. B., Gulliver, S., Kwok, O., & Morissette, S. B. (2015). Resilience, traumatic brain injury, depression, and posttraumatic stress among Iran/Afghanistan war veterans. *Rehabilitation Psychology, 60*(3), 263-276. doi:.org/10.1037/rep000050

[25]Elliott, T., Witty, T., Herrick, S., & Hoffman, J. (1991). Negotiating reality after physical loss: Hope, depression, and disability. *Journal of Personality and Social Psychology, 61*(4), 608-613.

[26]Engle, P., Castle, S., & Menon, P. (1996). Child development: Vulnerability and resilience. *Social Science & Medicine, 43*(5), 621-635.

[27]Fasse, L., Sultan, S., Flahault, C., MacKinnon, C.J., Dolbeault, S., & Bredart, A. (2013). How do researchers conceive of spousal grief after cancer? A systematic review of models used by researchers to study spousal grief in the cancer context. *Psycho-Oncology, 23*, 131-142.

[28]Frain, M., Berven, N., Tschopp, M., Lee, G., Tansey, T., & Chronister, J. (2007). Use of the resiliency model of family stress, adjustment and adaptation by rehabilitation counselors. *Journal of Rehabilitation, 73*(3), 18-25.

[29]Gallagher, P., & Maclachlan, M. (2001). Adjustment to artificial limb: A qualitative perspective. *Journal of Health Psychology, 6*, 85-100.

[30]Garmezy, N. (1991). Resiliency and vulnerability to adverse developmental outcomes associated with poverty. *American Behavioral Scientist, 34*, 416-430.

[31]Gauvin-Lepage, J., Lefebvre, H., & Malo, D. (2015). Family resilience following a physical trauma and efficient support interventions: A critical literature review. *Journal of Rehabilitation, 81*(3), 34-42.

[32]Griffin, J. M., Friedemann-Sanchez, G., Hall, C., Phelan, S., & van Ryn, M. (2009). Families of patients with polytrauma: Understanding the evidence and charting a new research agenda. *Journal of Rehabilitation, Research, and Development, 46*(6), 879-892.

[33]Guest, R., Craig, A., Nicholson Perry, K., Tran, Y., Ephraums, C., Hales, A., Dezarnaulds, A., Crino, R., & Middleton, J. (2015). Resilience following spinal cord injury: A prospective controlled study investigating the influence of the provision of group cognitive behavior therapy during inpatient rehabilitation. *Rehabilitation Psychology, 60*(4), 311-321. doi: 10.1037/rep000052

[34]Hawley, D. (2000). Clinical implications of family resilience. *American Journal of Family Therapy, 28*, 101-116.

[35]Hayes, R. L., Potter, C. G., & Hardin, C. (1995). Counseling the client on wheels: A primer for mental health counselors new to spinal cord injury. *Journal of Mental Health Counseling, 17*(1), 18-30.

[36]Hibbard, R. (2013). Meaning reconstruction in bereavement: Sense and significance. *Death Studies, 37*, 670-692.

[37]Hipke, K. N., Wolchik, S. A., Sandler, I. N., & Braver, S. L. (2002). Predictors of children's intervention-induced resilience in a parenting program for divorced mothers. *Family Relations, 51*(2), 121-129.

[38]Hutcheon, E., & Lashewicz, B. (2014). Theorizing resilience: Critiquing and unbounding a marginalizing concept. *Disability & Society, 29*(9), 1383-1397. doi: 10.1080/09687599.2014.934954

[39]Hutcheon, E., & Lashewicz, B. (2015). Are individuals with disabilities and their families resilient? Deconstructing and recasting a well-intended concept. *Journal of Social Work in Disability & Rehabilitation, 14*, (1), 41-60. doi: 10.1080/1536710X.2015.989560

[40]Jacques, R. (2006). Family issues. *Psychiatry, 5*(10), 337-340.

[41]Keany, K. C. M., & Glueckauf, R. L. (1993). Disability and value change: An overview and reanalysis of acceptance of loss theory. *Rehabilitation Psychology, 38*(3), 199-210.

[42]Keyes, K., Pratt, C., Galea, S., McLaughlin, K. A., Koenen, K. C., & Shear, M. K. (2014). The burden of loss: Unexpected death of a loved one and psychiatric disorders across the life course in a national study. *The American Journal of Psychiatry, 171*(8), 864-871.

[43]Kinsella, K. B., Anderson, R. A., & Anderson, W. T. (1996). Coping skills, strengths, and needs as perceived by adult offspring and siblings with mental illness: A retrospective study. *Psychiatric Rehabilitation Journal, 20*(2), 24-32.

[44]Kobassa, S. C., Maddi, S. R., & Kahn, S. (1982). Hardiness and health: A prospective study. *Journal of Personality and Social Psychology, 42*, 168-177.

[45]Kobassa, S. (1979a). Personality and resistance to illness. *American Journal of Community Psychology, 7*, 413-423.

[46]Kobassa, S. (1979b). Stressful life events, personality, health: An inquiry into hardiness. *Journal of Personality and Social Psychology, 37*, 1-11.

[47]Kosciulek, J. (1994). Dimensions of coping with head injury. *Rehabilitation Counseling Bulletin, 37*(3), 244-258.

[48]Kurtzer-White, D., & Luterman, D. (2003). Families and children with hearing loss: Grief and coping. *Mental Retardation and Developmental Disabilities, 9*, 232-235.

[49]Lent, R. W. (2004). Toward a unifying theoretical and practical perspective on well-being and social adjustment *Journal of Counseling Psychology, 51*(4), 482-509.

[50]Livneh, H., & Antonak, R. F. (1997). *Psychosocial adaptation to chronic illness and disability.* Gaithersburg, MD: Aspen Publication.

[51]Livneh, H. (2016). Quality of life and coping with chronic illness and disability: A temporal perspective. *Rehabilitation Counseling Bulletin, 59*(2), 67-83. doi: 10.1177/0034355215575180

[52]Louis Harris and Associates. (2000). *Closing the gap.* Washington, DC: National Organization on Disability. Retrieved from www.nod.org/content.cfm

[53]Lustig, D. (1997). Families with an adult with mental retardation: Empirical family typologies. *Rehabilitation Counseling Bulletin, 41*(2), 138-157.

[54]Luthar, S., Cicchetti, D., & Becker, B. (2000). The construct of resilience: A critical evaluation and guidelines for future work. *Child Development, 71*(3), 543-562.

[55]Mancini, A., & Bonanno, G. (2006). Resilience in the face of potential trauma: Clinical practices and illustrations. *Journal of Clinical Psychology, 62*(8), 971-985.

[56]Mannion, E. (1996). Resilience and burden in spouses of people with mental illness. *Psychiatric Rehabilitation Journal, 20*(2), 13-23.

[57]Marsh, D. T., Lefley, H. P., Evans-Rhodes, D., & Ansell, V. I. (1996). The family experience of mental illness: Evidence for resilience. *Psychiatric Rehabilitation Journal, 20*(2), 3-12.

[58]Masten, A. (2001). Ordinary magic: Resilience processes in development. *American Psychologist, 56*(3), 227-238.

[59]McCubbin, M., Balling, K., Possin, P., Frierdich, S., & Byrne, B. (2002). Family resiliency in childhood cancer. *Family Relations, 51*(2), 103-111.

[60]McCubbin, H. I., Thompson, A., & McCubbin, M. A. (1996). *Family assessment: Resiliency, coping and adaptation.* Madison, WI: University of Wisconsin.

[61]Merriam-Webster Online Dictionary. (2008). Resilience. Retrieved from http://www.merriam-webster.com/dictionary/

[62]Mills, B., & Turnbill, G. (2004). Broken hearts and mending bodies: The impact of trauma on intimacy. *Sexual & Relationship Therapy, 19*(3), 265-289.

[63]Miller, J. (2000). *Coping with chronic illness: Overcoming powerlessness* (3rd ed.). Philadelphia: F. A. Davis Company.

[64]Miller, F. (1996). Grief therapy for relatives of persons with serious mental illness. *Psychiatric Services, 47*, 633-637.

[65]Miyahara, M., & Piek, J. (2006). Self-esteem of children and adolescents with physical disabilities: Quantitative evidence from meta-analysis. *Journal of Developmental and Physical Disabilities,18*, 219-234.

[66]Murray, J. A. (2001). Loss as a universal concept: A review of the literature to identify common aspects of loss in diverse situations. *Journal of Loss and Trauma, 6*, 219-241.

[67]Murray, C., & Doren, B. (2013). Resilience and disability: Concepts, examples, cautions, and prospects. In M. L. Wehmeyer (Ed.), *The Oxford handbook of positive psychology and disability* (pp. 182-197). New York: Oxford.

[68]Newman, R. (2005). APA's resilience initiative. *Professional Psychology: Research and Practice, 36*, 227-229.

[69]Newton-John, T., Mason, C., & Hunter, M. (2014). The role of resilience in adjusting to chronic pain. *Rehabilitation Psychology, 59*(3), 360-365. doi: 10.1037/a0037023

[70]Niemeier, J. P., & Burnett, D. M. (2001). No such thing as 'uncomplicated bereavement' for patients in rehabilitation. *Disability and Rehabilitation, 23*(15), 645-653.

[71]Neimeier, J. P., Kennedy, R. E., McKinley, W. O., & Cifu, D. X. (2004). The loss inventory: Preliminary reliability and validity data for a new measure of emotional and cognitive responses to disability. *Disability and Rehabilitation, 26*(10), 614-623.

[72]Niemeier, J. P. (2008). Unique aspects of women's emotional responses to disability. *Disability and Rehabilitation, 30*(3), 166-173.

[73]Oaksford, K., Frude, N., & Cuddihy, R. (2005). Positive coping and stress-related psychological growth following lower limb amputation. *Rehabilitation Psychology, 50*(3), 266-277.

[74]Osborne, J., & Cyle, A. (2002). Can parental responses to adult children with schizophrenia be conceptualized in terms of loss and grief? A case study analysis. *Counseling Psychology Quarterly, 15* (4), 307-323.

[75]Padrone, F. J. (1994). Psychotherapeutic issues with family member of persons with physical disabilities. *American Journal of Psychotherapy, 48*(2), 195-207.

[76]Reed, A. W. (1974). Anticipatory grief work. In B. Schoenberg, A. C. Carr, A. H. Kutscher, D. Peretz, & I. K. Goldberg's (Eds.), *Anticipatory grief* (pp. 346-357). New York, NY: Columbia University Press.

[77]Reich, J. W., Zautra, A. J., & Guarnaccia, C. A. (1989). Effects of disability and bereavement on the mental health and recovery of older adults. *Psychology and Aging, 4*(1), 57-65.

[78]Richardson, G. (2002). The metatheory of resilience and resiliency. *Journal of Clinical Psychology, 58*(3), 307-321.

[79]Rolland, J. (1994). *Families, illness, & disability: An integrative treatment model*. New York: Basic Books.

[80]Runswick-Cole, K., & Goodley, D. (2013). Resilience: A disability studies and community psychology approach. *Social and Personality Compass, 7* (2), 67-78. doi: 10.1111/spc3.12012

[81]Rutter, M. (1985). Resiliency in the face of adversity: Protective factors and resilience to psychiatric disorder. *British Journal of Psychiatry, 147*(598-611).

[82]Rybarczyk, B., Edwards, R., & Behel, J. (2004). Diversity in adjustment to a leg amputation: Case illustrations of common themes. *Disability and Rehabilitation, 26*(14/15), 944-953.

[83]Sapey, B., (2004). Impairment, disability, and loss: Reassessing the rejection of loss. *Illness, Crisis, and Loss, 12*(1), 90-99.

[84]Seligman, M., & Csikszentmihalyi, M. (2000). Positive psychology. *American Psychologist, 55,* 5-14.

[85]Serrano-Ikkos, E., & Lask, B. (2003). The psychosocial correlates of transplant survival. *Journal of Cystic Fibrosis, 2,* 49-54.

[86]Smart, J. (2001). *Disability, society, and the individual.* Austin, TX: ProEd.

[87]Snyder, C. R. (2000). The past and possible futures of hope. *Journal of Social and Clinical Psychology, 19*(1), 11-28.

[88]Snyder, C. R., Lehman, K., Kluck, B., & Monsson, Y. (2006). Hope for rehabilitation and vice versa. *Rehabilitation Psychology, 51*(2), 89-112.

[89]Sullivan, K., Edmed, S., Allan, A., Smith, S., & Karlsson, L. (2015). The role of psychological resilience and mTBI as predictors of postconcussional syndrome symptomatology. *Rehabilitation Psychology, 60*(2), 147-154.

[90]Thannhauser, J. E. (2014). Navigating life and loss in pediatric multiple sclerosis. *Qualitative Health Research, 24*(9), 1198-1211.

[91]Thomas, K. R., & Siller, J. (1999). Object loss, mourning, and adjustment to disability. *Psychoanalytic Psychology, 16*(2), 179-197.

[92]Thompson, J., & Mckeever, M. (2012). The impact of stroke aphasia on health and well-being and appropriate nursing interventions: An exploration using the theory of human scale development. *Journal of Clinical Nursing, 23,* 410-420

[93]Torpie, R. J. (1974). The patient and prolong terminal malignant disease: Experiences from a radiation therapy center. In B. Schoenberg, A. C. Carr, A. H. Kutscher, D. Peretz, & I. K. Goldberg (Eds.), *Anticipatory grief* (pp. 119-123). New York, NY: Columbia University Press.

[94]Turk, D. (1979). Factors influencing the adaptive process and chronic illness. In I. Sarason, & C. Spielberger (Ed.), *Stress and anxiety* (Vol. 6, pp. 291-311). New York: John Wiley & Sons

[95]Ungar, M. A. (2004). Constructionist discourse on resilience: Multiple contexts, multiple realities among at-risk children and youth. *Youth & Society, 35,* 341-365.

[96]Venters Horton, T., & Wallander, J. (2001). Hope and social support as resilience factors against psychological distress of mothers who care for children with chronic physical conditions. *Rehabilitation Psychology, 46*(4), 382-399.

[97]Walsh, F. (2002). A family resilience framework: Innovative practice applications. *Family Relations, 51*(2), 130-137.

[98]Werner, E., & Smith, R. (1992). *Overcoming the odds: High risk children from birth to adulthood.* Ithaca, NY: Cornell University Press.

[99]Westgren, N., & Levi, R. (1999). Sexuality after injury: Interviews with women after traumatic spinal cord injury. *Sexuality and Disability, 17*(4), 309-319.

[100]White, B., Driver, S., & Warren, A. (2008). Considering resilience in the rehabilitation of people with traumatic disabilities. *Rehabilitation Psychology, 53*(1), 9-17.

[101]White, B., Driver, S., & Warren, A. (2010). Resilience and indicators of adjustment during rehabilitation from a spinal cord injury. *Rehabilitation Psychology, 55*(1), 23-32.

[102]Woodbridge, S., Buys, L., & Miller, E. (2008). Grandparenting a child with a disability: An emotional rollercoaster. *Australian Journal on Ageing, 28*(1), 37-40.

[103]Wordon, J. W. (2001). *Grief counseling and grief therapy: A handbook for the mental health practitioner* (3rd ed.). New York: Springer Publishing Company.

CHAPTER 9

MULTICULTURAL
CONCEPTS OF DISABILITY

ROXANNA N. PEBDANI

Culture is one of the many things that make us who we are. Our culture influences how we dress, how we speak (or what language we speak), how we interact with people, how we think, and how we interpret events, among many other things. There are countless varying definitions of culture, and a recent review of some these definitions concluded that culture, broadly, is a "social construct vaguely referring to a vastly complex set of phenomena."[46, p. 300] For the purposes of this chapter, we will be defining culture with a slightly more thorough definition: "a set of attitudes, behaviors, and symbols shared by a large group of people and usually communicated from one generation to the next."[71, p. 4]

Often, when we discuss culture, our minds immediately go to a discussion of race or ethnicity. However, culture is much larger than these two individual attributes. Culture can be related to race, sex, sexual orientation, socioeconomic status, religion, disability status, and many others. There is military culture, culture related to particular colleges and universities, and even culture related to a particular city where a person lives, or a sports team with which they are affiliated. Within these cultures, people belong to different subgroups in each culture, called cultural groups. These are groups of people who adhere to a set of cultural norms or have similarities based on their group membership.[25] These cultural groups may be based on race or ethnicity, sexual orientation, disability status, etc.

Understanding culture is particularly important because a person's culture influences one's thoughts and attitudes, particularly related to the construct of interest–disability. According to Banks,[8] culture is one of the lenses we use to interpret disability and the impact it will have on a person's life and on the lives of one's family members and community. A person who is HIV positive in the United States will have a different experience than someone with the same diagnosis in South Africa. A man who has sustained a spinal cord injury may have different experiences from a woman who has sustained the same level of injury. Someone from a higher socioeconomic level will likely have a different disability experience from someone from a lower level. Therefore, it is essential we look at the bigger picture when discussing multicultural concepts of disability, so that we can see how belonging to different cultural groups can interact with a person's disability status.

This chapter will address cultural differences and how these affect individuals with disabilities in different ways. We will begin with a discussion of intersectionality, or the idea that each of our separate identities (e.g., race, sex, disability status, etc.) work together to formulate who we are,[69] followed by a discussion of cultural groups. The chapter will present cultural differences that can impact cross-cultural understanding, and then disability culture will be explored. The chapter will conclude with a section on implications for working with people with disabilities.

IDENTITIES AND CULTURAL GROUPS

Individuals have multiple identities–relating to race, sex, sexuality, and beyond. Cultural identity is how closely individuals consider themselves as belonging to certain cultural subgroups.[37] In the following pages, we will discuss cultures and identities as related to race, sex, sexual orientation, socioeconomic status, disability, religion, and military service. We will also discuss cultural groups for each topic. However, first we must start with a broad framework for understanding difference: intersectionality.

INTERSECTIONALITY

Intersectionality, how a person's different identities interact, is a growing way to approach looking at identities in a multicultural context. For example, when a person has multiple identities with high incidence of disability, they may be more likely to acquire a disability over the course of one's lifetime. Research shows that both being female and having low educational attainment increase an individual's likelihood of having a disability;[77] therefore a woman with low educational attainment will be more likely to have a disability than her male counterparts, especially when compared with men who have advanced degrees. This connection is an example of intersectionality, since we are looking at the relationship between multiple identities. Given what we know about different identities and their impact on disability, it is important that we look at how these identities interact with one another to influence a person's life.

Disability. Disability status, at its core, is whether or not an individual has a disability. However, as with all of these categories, this only touches the surface. This includes type of disability, its level of visibility, its impact on the individual, and its progression, among other things, this is addressed further in Chapter 2. We do know that disability is related to race,[6,31,40,74] sex,[11,26] socioeconomic status,[19,23,73] and many other personal factors, as will be discussed in this chapter.

Race. Race is a socially constructed concept that can be defined as "a group of people distinguished by certain similar and genetically transmitted physical characteristics."[74, p. 5] Racial categories can vary from country to country and are defined by society. In the United States, for example, the U.S. Census considers five racial identities in its recording of the racial composition of the country.[78] These categories include White, Black or African American, American Indian and Alaska Native, Asian, and Native Hawaiian and other Pacific Islander. They also include a separate category for people who are Hispanic. Recently, the U.S. Census has begun to include the option of two or more races in their categorization, as well.

Broadly, we know there are disparities in prevalence of disability based on race. With respect to health-related quality of life (HRQoL), Asians rated their health status the best, followed by Whites, African Americans, Hispanics, and

American Indian/Alaskan Natives.[17] Traditionally, people who are American Indian or Alaska Native have the highest prevalence of disability, as well as the earliest onset of disability, although many times this ethnic group is collapsed in the data due to low numbers. In a study of American Indians and Alaskan Natives, Goins and colleagues[31] found that members of this cultural group are more likely to experience functional limitations and difficulties in self-care. This study also found that women who were of American Indian/Alaska Native descent, were older, had lower levels of education and lower household income, were either unemployed or single, and who lived in a large metropolitan area, were more likely to have a disability.

Much of the research on race and disability has focused on the differences between African Americans and Whites. Research shows that African Americans have shorter life expectancies and spend larger parts of their lives with chronic health problems.[23,56] African Americans are also less likely to have health insurance[18,22] and are less likely to receive important health care treatments and follow-up.[18,79] African Americans are more likely to have diabetes, hypertension (high blood pressure), stroke, kidney conditions, bladder conditions, stomach ulcers, vision impairments, and difficulties in activities of daily living.[38,39,70] In a study using the 2012 National Health Interview Survey, there were statistically significant racial/ethnic differences in disability status; 10.2 % non-Hispanic whites, 14.8 % non-Hispanic African Americans, 8.1 % Latino, and 6.7 % other racial minorities had severe disability.[32] Hispanic individuals, like African Americans, are less likely to have health insurance.[18,22] Hispanic individuals, however, have the lowest rate for hypertension, a primary cause of heart disease (the leading cause of death in the U.S.), while African Americans have the highest rate.[57]

Sex. Sex, not to be confused with gender, is a biological characteristic that defines one as female or male–a person's XX or XY chromosomes.[83] Therefore, a person's sex is determined chromosomally, and by sex organs. Gender, on the other hand, can be defined as "attitudes, feelings, and behaviors that a given culture associates with a person's biological sex."[1, p. 2] A person's gender may or may not conform (align with) an individual's biological sex (their XX or XY chromosomes or their physical indicators of biological sex).

Sex can have an impact on a person's disability status. Broadly, disability is more common in women who are of European, African, or Asian descent–our first example of intersectionality (the relationship between two cultural identities–in this case race and sex). Latinas are also more likely to have a disability than their male counterparts. Research also shows disparities in survival rates for women with disabilities. For example, women of color are more likely to die sooner than their male counterparts after a diagnosis of HIV/AIDS.[11] Women receive fewer treatment options and later interventions across many disability categories, including renal disease, cardiovascular disease, and arthritis; men may be underdiagnosed with conditions considered to be "female diseases," like depression and osteoporosis.[66]

There are also concerns about abuse for women with disabilities. Women with disabilities are more likely to be abused than their male counterparts.[21,75] A recent study found that women with specific disabilities (physical and sensory) were more likely to have been abused as children.[7] This study also found the majority of abuse these women experienced as adults came from their intimate partners, and that women who had children were less likely to report this abuse.

Sexual orientation. Sexual orientation is a concept that relates to sexual attraction. Sexual orientation is "to whom one is sexually and romantically attracted."[1, p. 6] People who are attracted to individuals of the same gender would be considered homosexual or lesbian, while individuals who are attracted to people of the opposite gender would be considered heterosexual. Individuals who are attracted to members of both genders are called bisexual.

People with disabilities, however, are often viewed as asexual. Those who are granted the notion of a sexual existence are typically assumed to be heterosexual.[16] Prior to federal protection for marriage equality in 2015, same sex couples encountered difficulties many couples in heterosexual marriages did not face when a disability is acquired. Same-sex partners were not allowed hospital visitation rights, the same rights as spouses for medical and end-of-life decisions, and were not entitled to survivor benefits. The Supreme Court (*Obergefell v. Hodges,* 576 U.S.) decision granted marriage equality across the country, but some states are seeking to overturn this decision to regain states' rights.

Socioeconomic status. Socioeconomic status is not solely how much money an individual makes through income, although that is a part of what makes up an individual's socioeconomic status. Also involved is the individual's level of educational attainment and their occupation.[2] Research has consistently shown that people with disabilities are more likely to live below the poverty level[23] and less likely to be employed.[15]

Research also shows that a person's socioeconomic status has a large impact on disability. Individuals who live in poverty are less likely to have health insurance than those who do not,[23] and are less likely to receive medical treatment in general.[57] Those who do have health insurance are less likely to use the health insurance they have.[82] People who live in poverty also have higher incidences of certain disabilities and illnesses; experience more food insecurity; are more likely to be impacted by health factors, such as smoking and obesity; and live in inferior housing, with poor ventilation, mold, and infestations of rodents and insects, all which contribute to health complaints such as auto-immune and respiratory conditions.[44]

Religion. While religion may not have a direct impact on disability prevalence, it certainly has a relationship with disability. The most common religion in the United States is Christianity with 70.6% of Americans self-identified as Christians in 2014.[63] Other popular religions in the U.S. include Judaism, Islam, Buddhism, and Hinduism, along with several Native American religions. There are also a growing number of atheists and agonistics in the U.S.

While religion does not necessarily change one's likelihood of acquiring a disability, there are relationships between religion and disability; unfortunately, there is little research in this area.[47] People with disabilities may see religious organizations as a source of support, and may use religion as a coping mechanism,[47] including sense of community. Individuals tend to turn to religion as the level of disability increases, and can use it for both positive and negative coping.[48] That said, given the diversity of religions and growing proportion of non-religious individuals in the U.S., it is important we be aware of how a person's religious beliefs (or absence of religious beliefs) can affect him or her when discussing disability.

Military service. Military service is not generally included in lists of cultural identities; however, it is an important one in the world of disability. Military culture is a topic of which most civilians are unaware. Veterans likely consider their military service to be an important part of their lives, including those who acquired a disability during their service.[81] Each branch of the military has their own culture (i.e., Army, Air Force, Navy, Coast Guard, and Marines), however there are overarching themes throughout military culture, as well.

The number of troops surviving war-related injuries is becoming increasingly larger due to advances in medicine and body armor.[54] During war, the number of military members who are separated (discharged) from the military due to disability increases significantly.[62] In 2012, the top five reasons for separation from the Army were back pain, osteoarthritis, posttraumatic stress disorder, foot and ankle/lower extremity problems, and psychiatric disorders.[62] However, when looking at members of all military branches, the top three reasons for disability designation were tinnitus, hearing loss, and posttraumatic stress disorder.[54]

Mental disorders are the number-one cause of hospitalization in active duty military, with more hospitalizations for women than men.[4] In a 2005 study, Hoge and colleagues[43] found that almost 10% of active duty military members who were hospitalized for psychiatric problems were medically-separated from the military. The increase of both physical and mental health-related disabilities present in veterans means that military culture in disability is becoming increasingly important to those of us who work with individuals with disabilities.

While this is by no means an exhaustive list of cultural identities that exist in the United States, this does provide a helpful framework about disability in a multicultural context. With an understanding disability related to these topics, one should be able to understand the importance of intersectionality when working with individuals with disabilities. Still, this discussion of identity is focused on culture in the United States; when working with people from other countries, professionals need to be aware of many other things.

WORLD CULTURES

In the late 1960s and early 1970s, a researcher named Geert Hofstede began conducting research on cultural dimensions across country lines.[42] He used this data to develop five dimensions of culture. Hofstede posited that cultures fall on one end or another of the continuum of these dimensions. Over time, he validated these dimensions on over 50 countries around the world, and other studies have continued to validate this model. The five dimensions he developed were: individualism versus collectivism, masculinity versus femininity, power distance, uncertainty avoidance, and long-term versus short-term orientation. More recently, Hofstede added a sixth dimension, indulgence versus restraint. While Hofstede's work was initially developed to help businesses understand cross-cultural communication at work, his research has been used broadly within the social sciences. Using his six dimensions of culture, we can look at disability in different countries from a wider lens.

Individualism versus collectivism. According to Hofstede's model, individualism versus collectivism is the extent to which a person is expected to value caring for the self vs. caring for the family. The idea of "putting oneself first" would be an example of individualism, while instead focusing on the benefit of the family would be collectivism.[42] The United States ranks very high on individualism, along with other Anglophone top four countries like Australia, Great Britain, and Canada; Latin American countries tend to be more collectivistic.[41] Hofstede's work also showed that, in individualistic cultures, people with depression or schizophrenia tend to be isolated, and disability, in a broad sense, is something that an individual must work to overcome.

Research is somewhat split on the impact of individualism versus collectivism on disability. Some suggest higher rates of disability in individualistic cultures,[55] while others suggest individualistic cultures provide less help to people with disabilities.[35] Some research suggests that individualism is somewhat related to stigma against people with disabilities.[65] On the contrary, Meyer[55] suggested that, in individualistic cultures, people with disabilities are more likely to be integrated into society and be awarded equal rights to individuals without disabilities. This may be because individualistic societies value human rights for all group members.[41] However, in collectivist cultures, people with disabilities are more likely to be segregated and avoided[55] and they may not have the same level of rights that other members of the collectivist society are afforded.[41] The suggestion that disability is a source of shame in collectivist cultures is especially significant given the importance of group belonging in these cultures.[41,55] It is also significant given the importance of the aging population in collectivist societies—where families are expected to care for their aging family members who will likely acquire a disability as they age.

Masculinity versus femininity. Masculinity versus femininity is the extent to which a culture adheres to historically masculine or feminine norms.[42] For example, does the society value being competitive (masculine) or cooperative

(feminine)? Are gender roles split (masculine) or is there an opportunity for them to overlap (feminine)? High levels of masculinity occur in Japan, Austria, Venezuela, Italy, and Switzerland, while higher levels of femininity occur in Sweden, Norway, the Netherlands, Denmark, and Costa Rica.

Feminine countries tend to value caring for others, which makes feminine societies more positive for people with disabilities.[60] Latin American countries, on the other hand, have varying levels of masculinity and femininity. On the one hand, Latino/as tend to be agreeable and supportive towards individuals in need (feminine orientations), however the Latin concept of *machismo* is more masculine.[3] In feminine cultures, collaboration is important, as is quality of life. Feminine cultures value giving help to those in need, and work is less important than family.[41] There are both feminine and masculine dimensions of culture that can make life easier for people with disabilities living in feminine cultures.

Power distance. Power distance is the idea of hierarchy.[42] Are members of this culture comfortable with an unequal distribution of power, or do they expect all members of a group to be treated more-or-less equally? Are members of this society comfortable with human inequality? To what extent do they accept the idea that some people have more (e.g., prestige, wealth, power) than others?

Cultures that tend to score high on scales of power distance include Malaysia, Guatemala, Panama, Philippines, and Mexico.[41] Those that score low are Austria, Israel, Denmark, New Zealand, and Ireland. According to Zea et al.,[84] Latino/a cultures tend to be more hierarchical, which is demonstrated in disability as having a hierarchical relationship with health care providers. Cultures that have higher power distance orientations value equality over freedom, though cultures with low power distance tend to believe that people deserve equal individual rights.[41] Cultures with high power distance orientations are more likely to place blame on the individual, while those from low power distance countries will place blame on the system. Individuals from high power distance-oriented countries tend to have more negative opinions of people who are elderly; regardless, they respect and fear older individuals. Cultures with both low power distance orientations and high-power distance orientations have the potential for positive and negative impacts on disability.

Uncertainty avoidance. Uncertainty avoidance relates to control.[41] How comfortable are members of this culture with the idea of not having control of a situation, or to what degree do they need control to be comfortable. Oliver and Cravens[60] posited a need for control in a culture presents itself as a want to minimize disability. Countries with high levels of uncertainty avoidance include Greece, Portugal, Guatemala, Uruguay, and Belgium.[41] On the opposite end of the spectrum, countries with low levels of uncertainty avoidance include Singapore, Jamaica, Denmark, Sweden, and Hong Kong. Countries with low levels of uncertainty avoidance tend to be more tolerant of diversity, which can be positive for people with disabilities.

Long-term vs. short-term orientation. Long-term versus short-term orientation is essentially how people of a culture focus on the current versus the distant or progressive.[42] Do they focus on tradition and how things have historically been done, or do they look towards the future and try to make changes in society despite tradition? Countries with strong long-term orientations include China, Hong Kong, Taiwan, Japan, and South Korea.[41] These cultures may have a stronger focus on status, while short-term orientations care less about social status. Cultures with short-term orientations expect tolerance for those who are different; on the other hand, cultures with long-term orientations believe that people in society should be equal. Aspects of both long-term and short-term cultures can be positive for people with disabilities.

Indulgence vs. restraint. Indulgence versus restraint is the idea that some cultures are more focused on the immediate (e.g., having fun, enjoying life) and other cultures are focused on delaying gratification.[42] Given the dimension of indulgence versus restraint is relatively new (developed in 2010), there have been fewer studies on this dimension, and therefore less information about how the dimension relates to disability. With time, the body of literature will grow. For now, it is important to understand the differences along this continuum dimension.

With this knowledge, one can view disability through different cultural frameworks. We do not have to know exactly how one country or another view disability, but can use this broad knowledge to frame disability in different cultures. Knowing about these cultural dimensions and learning of a person's orientation towards these dimensions can help professionals interpret cultural views of disability.

DISABILITY CULTURE

If we look back at the definition of culture framing this chapter: "a set of attitudes, behaviors, and symbols shared by a large group of people and usually communicated from one generation to the next,"[71] it may stand to reason people with disabilities can share attitudes, behaviors, and symbols, communicated from generation to generation, leading to the development of a disability culture. However, while many disability scholars argue there is a presence of disability culture, others disagree. Some disability rights activists and scholars argue that since disability can happen to anyone across people of any race, age, gender, socioeconomic status, and so on, there is no unified disability culture.[28] This argument, though, has largely been refuted and many disability rights activists and scholars assert disability culture does exist. Within this, the extent to which a person with a disability may identify with disability culture will vary.[10] Disability culture, therefore, remains an important topic in disability rights and within the academic areas of disability studies and rehabilitation counseling.

Many scholars have attempted to define disability culture, resulting in varied definitions of this construct. Entire manuscripts have been written on the definition of disability culture. Two common definitions from disability activists and scholars appear most pertinent. Steven E. Brown,[13] a disability rights activist and scholar, investigated multiple definitions of disability culture from many different countries. He then developed his own definition:

> *People with disabilities have forged a group identity. We share a common history of oppression and a common bond of resilience. We generate art, music, literature, and other expressions of our lives and our culture, infused from our experience of disability. Most importantly, we are proud of ourselves as people with disabilities. We claim our disabilities with pride as part of our identity.*[p. 23]

Carol Gill,[30] also a disability rights activist and disability studies scholar, explained disability culture by saying:

> *The elements of our culture include, certainly, our longstanding social oppression, but also our emerging art and humor, our piecing together of our history, our evolving language and symbols, our remarkably unified worldview, beliefs and values, and our strategies for surviving and thriving.*[p. 166]

These definitions share similarities with one another and with our overarching definition of culture. According to both authors, one of the underpinnings of disability culture is *resilience* (or, in Gill's words, *surviving and thriving*). Similarly, both scholars present a unifying theme of oppression for people with disabilities, which is consistent with the thoughts of other scholars.[9,28] Brown's definition focuses on disability pride, which is consistent with other definitions of disability culture, as well–in fact, Gill's broader outline of disability culture also includes pride.[28] This may be interpreted as seeing disability as a source of difference, not a source of shame.[9] Gill's idea of disability culture, as having a united worldview, relates to Barnes and Mercer's[10] observation that people with disabilities share a common identity, and often share common interests.

Brown, Gill, and others[9,10] presented disability arts as a major part of disability culture. This includes visual art, dance, music, poetry, literature, and beyond. Beginning in the 1970s, there has been a growing movement referred to as the disability arts movement.[9] According to some, disability arts allows people with disabilities the opportunity to unite, facilitates the development of a cultural (and perhaps political) identity, and leads to positive representations of disability in society.[9,49]

Similarly, musical artists with disabilities are becoming more prevalent in pop culture. The disability rights movement spurred many disability rights-

related songs, which gained popularity as the movement grew.[14] Related to this is disability dance. While wheelchair dancing is not a new concept for people who use wheelchairs, dance troupes featuring individuals with disabilities have become more prevalent in the United States. Dance companies like Infinity Dance Theatre in New York and AXIS Dance Company (a traveling company), have dancers with and without disabilities performing routines together to diverse audiences with and without disabilities.[53] DanceAbility International catalogues mixed-abilities dance groups around the world and does outreach and education on inclusive dance.[22]

Finally, disability literature has been a central part of disability culture since its inception, and has become a focal point of disability studies. There are notable memoirs of people living and thriving with disability in most bookstores. Other literature has evolved. *The Disability Rag,* was initially started in 1980 as a newspaper for the Independent Living Movement, was transformed into a book in the mid-1990s, and later a web site in the late 1990s.[64] Contemporary disability literature can be found in the multitude of online blogs, websites, e-zines, and visual media available on the Internet, reaching a broader and more diverse global audience.

DEAF CULTURE

While it would seem that disability culture would be an inclusive one, given the linguistic differences between people who are deaf or hard of hearing and people who can hear, some members of the Deaf community have found disability culture to be marginalizing.[36] People who are deaf face the same discrimination people with other disabilities face (e.g., housing, employment, education).[12,29] However, they also experience negative stereotypes from members of the hearing community,[59] which could lead to discrimination from the disability community, as well.

The Deaf community and scholars within make a distinction between the concepts of Deaf and deaf. When referring to a lack of hearing (the biological component), we use *lowercase d* deaf. However, when discussing the social aspect, issues of culture, and cultural identity, we use *capital D* Deaf. Scholars often use the word D/deaf to indicate that they are talking about both people who are deaf and Deaf culture.[34,52] While the socially constructed view of deafness is that being D/deaf is a disability, a loss, and a limitation,[50] Deaf culture asserts that being deaf is not a disability, but instead a problem within society.[52]

Similar to disability culture, there is not one unified definition of Deaf culture. One definition comes from Dr. Barbara Kannapell, whose definition of Deaf culture included "a set of learned behaviors of a group of people who are deaf and who have their own language (American Sign Language), values, rules, and traditions."[51] Others view Deaf culture or Deaf identity as having pride in D/deafness, valuing sign language as a form of communication, believing that people who are D/deaf are equal to people who are hearing.[36]

Central to all of Deaf culture is the idea that being D/deaf is a source of pride and the challenges associated with being deaf are a problem of society, not one of being D/deaf.[52]

Perhaps the best example of this comes from hundreds of years on Martha's Vineyard (through 1950) during which time there was a large concentration of people who were deaf.[68] Martha's Vineyard is a large island off the coast of Cape Cod in Massachusetts. During this time, one in 150 island residents were deaf for genetic reasons. Because there was such a high prevalence of people who were deaf, everyone who lived on the island was able to sign, which meant everyone on the island could communicate with one another. Nora Ellen Groce wrote a book about the people on the island who were deaf.[33] Using oral histories, she was able to learn about the culture of the island and the lives of its inhabitants. In many of her meetings, she found communication between people who were deaf and hearing was so natural that many hearing interviewees could barely remember which of the islands inhabitants were deaf. Eventually, most of the islanders who were deaf left the island to attend residential schools for children who were deaf, leading to a decrease in the deaf population on the island. Almost simultaneously, the island grew as a popular vacation destination, and sign became less common on the island. Eventually, all the deaf inhabitants either left the island or died. However, the ease of communication prior to the popularization of the island–when linguistic barriers were removed–demonstrates the social context in which Deaf culture is held and exemplifies the idea that the implications of being deaf come from society, not from a lack of hearing.[52]

On the other side is the debate concerning cochlear implants. People who are not members of Deaf culture, including physicians and other medical professionals who work with people who are D/deaf, frequently suggest cochlear implants as a treatment for deafness.[80] Cochlear implants are often the preferred method of treatment for children who are born deaf to parents who are hearing. Cochlear implants are a way to medically treat deafness, using an electrode put in the cochlea to simulate vibration and transmit electrical energy to the brain, allowing a person to hear. There are many arguments against cochlear implants in the Deaf community. The first argument is that medical treatment to "cure" D/deafness, at its core, sends the message that people who are Deaf should be fixed and are of less worth than people who are hearing.[36] Another argument is that children who receive cochlear implants lose their ability to be members of Deaf culture, but also are not fully members of hearing culture. Most importantly, members of Deaf culture believe that children who are D/deaf are the future of their culture, and therefore cochlear implants have the potential to lead to a cultural genocide.[36,51]

Deaf culture is one of the strongest and most visible of disability cultures. In fact, until recently, Deaf culture was the most widely known subset of disability cultures. More recently, the Neurodiversity Movement has also

become a common dialogue when discussing the broader concept of disability culture.

THE NEURODIVERSITY MOVEMENT

The Neurodiversity Movement began on the Internet in the 1990s,[20,61] and has grown into a civil rights movement for people with both neurological and neurodevelopmental disorders (i.e., attention deficit-hyperactivity disorder, bipolar disorder, epilepsy, autism spectrum disorders).[27] The concept of neurodiversity is founded on two main ideas. First, autism spectrum disorders and other neurological conditions are, at their core, a natural variation. The second idea is that there is value to neurodiversity and to recognizing and accepting that people vary in their neurological makeup.[45] While the Neurodiversity Movement broadly consists of people with any type of neurological disorder, much of the movement focuses on individuals on the autism spectrum.

Similar to Deaf culture, the Neurodiversity Movement fights against the idea that neurotypicality (or not having a neurological disorder) is the ideal, and argues that autism and other neurological disorders are part of a person's identity and not something to be cured.[5,45,61] This tends to be in direct opposition to how many parents of children with neurological disorders view their disorders.[20,61] Parents of children with neurological disorders often seek a cure, looking for ways to reduce symptomology and to bring their child closer to the "norm."[5,20] In seeking a cure and attempting to reduce symptomology, parents of children with neurological disorders often work with therapists to deliver treatment to change behaviors.[72]

Because of this, self-advocacy has become a large part of the Neurodiversity Movement.[61] The tried and true "Nothing About Us Without Us" slogan of the Disability Rights Movement–implying that independence and autonomy are of the upmost importance–has been adopted by the Neurodiversity Movement[67] and transformed into "By Autistics For Autistics."[61] Self-advocates oppose many of the treatments given to people on the spectrum, especially those aimed at changing behavior they consider to be harmless, but therapists or non-movement members see as abnormal.[20,61]

Self-advocacy has become important in reducing the stigma against people who are neurodiverse, stigma that comes from society, parents, therapists, and organizations working to support people on the autism spectrum. While people on the spectrum have become more prevalent in film and television,[24] their characters still tend to be very stereotypical in their portrayal (i.e., all characters with autism having savant skills). Self-advocates have also taken umbrage with advocacy and awareness campaigns they see as painting people on the spectrum in a bad light.[58]

Ultimately, disability culture is a complex topic with varying individual identities. There are multiple definitions of disability cultures, and even sub-cultures within disability culture itself. Deaf culture is a well-known disability

263

culture, and the Neurodiversity Movement is gaining prominence within the disability community. Each culture has its own art, music, poetry, and literature, and each have their own rules, values, and communication styles. Being aware of these differences is important for anyone working with people with disabilities.

IMPLICATIONS FOR WORKING WITH PEOPLE WITH DISABILITIES

The implications of culture for individuals who work with people with disabilities in any field are extensive. This can include people who work as rehabilitation counselors, special education teachers, school counselors, mental health counselors, physical therapists, occupational therapists, nurses, doctors, and many more. Having a broader understanding of culture allows someone working with individuals with disabilities to work more productively with people who may be different from themselves. Understanding culture allows us to better understand ourselves and others. Intersectionality, the idea that we have many cultural identities interact with one another, allows us to see culture in a different light. We can use intersectionality to view and understand cultural differences in new ways. It is highly unlikely counselors will work with those who match them on all attributes of diversity; nor is that desired. Understanding our own identities and how they interact is the first step to understanding the identities of others.

Intersectionality also allows us to understand how these identities interact with one another to influence disability status. For some people, this will mean higher rates of disability depending on characteristics like race, sex, and socioeconomic status. Similarly, members of some groups are less likely to have health insurance and less likely to receive quality health care. Professionals who are aware of these disparities can help advocate for proper treatment for their clients or patients.

While much of the conversation on culture in the United States tends to be focused on our country's culture, practitioners who work with people with disabilities must be prepared to work with clients of all backgrounds, including global cultural identities. Hofstede's framework allows a way to conceptualize different cultures and worldviews. Using this information can help people who work with individuals with disabilities, especially counselors, think about their client's culture and how it affects the client's outlook on life and interactions with other people. Hofstede's polar representations of worldview also allows professionals to explore where they fall on this cultural continuum–and how that affects their work with clients who are culturally different.

Finally, disability culture is an essential concept when working with people with disabilities in any setting. We must be aware of disability culture and how it affects a person with a disability. Contrary to mainstream culture that might

view disability as a source of shame, disability is a source of pride within disability culture; perspective professionals should seek to appreciate and cultivate within clients. Similarly, being aware of other aspects of disability culture (e.g., art, music, dance, and literature), including Deaf culture (e.g., language, communication rules, pride), allows a professional working with people with disabilities a unique view into the world of disability, and share in the traditions of this cultural heritage.

CONCLUSION

People who work with clients with disabilities should remain aware of culture as it relates to people with disabilities. This means understanding intersectionality, understanding worldviews, and understanding disability culture–but it is not limited to these topics. People who are competent in working with individuals of other cultures remain aware of their own culture and how it influences their work with others. As it is impossible to learn everything about all cultures, people who wish to be competent in working with people from other cultures should work to become lifelong learners. Lifelong learners are people who make a concerted effort to build their knowledge related to culture and disability through different avenues of learning. This learning can be done by reading the news, reading memoirs, watching documentaries, attending community events, becoming friends with people from different cultures, and generally seeking out information about other cultures wherever it can be found.

REFERENCES

[1]American Psychological Association. (2011). Definition of terms: Sex, gender, gender identity, sexual orientation. Retrieved from https://www.apa.org/pi/lgbt/resources/sexuality-definitions.pdf

[2]American Psychological Association. (2015). Disability & socioeconomic status. Retrieved from http://www.apa.org/pi/ses/resources/publications/disability.aspx

[3]Arciniega, G. M., Anderson, T. C., Tovar-Blank, Z. G., & Tracey, T. J. G. (2008). Toward a fuller conception of Machismo: Development of a traditional Machismo and Caballerismo Scale. *Journal of Counseling Psychology, 55*(1), 19-33.

[4]Armed Forces Health Surveillance Center. (2015). Hospitalizations among members of the active component, U.S. armed forces, 2014. *Medical Surveillance Monthly Report, 22*(4), 11-17.

[5]Baker, D. L. (2011). *The politics of neurodiversity: Why public policy matters.* Boulder, CO: Lynne Rienner Publishers.

[6]Balcazar F. E., Suarez-Balcazar Y., Taylor-Ritzler T., & Keys C. B. (Eds.). (2010). *Race, culture, and disability*. Sudbury, MA: Jones & Bartlett.

[7]Ballan, M. S., Freyer, M. B., Marti, C. N., Perke, J., Webb, K. A., & Romanelli, M. (2014). Looking beyond prevalence: A demographic profile of survivors of intimate partner violence with disabilities. *Journal of Interpersonal Violence, 29*(17), 3167-3179. doi:10.1177/0886260514534776

[8]Banks, M. E. (2003). Disability in the family: A life span perspective. *Cultural diversity and ethnic minority psychology, 9*(4), 367-384. doi:10.1037/1099-9809.9.4.367

[9]Barnes, C. (2003). *Effecting change; Disability, culture and art?* Paper presented at the Finding the Spotlight Conference, Liverpool Institute for the Performing Arts.

[10]Barnes, C., & Mercer, G. (2001). Disability culture: Assimilation or inclusion? In G. Albrecht, K. Seelman, & M. Bury (Eds.), *Handbook of disability studies* (pp. 515-534). Thousand Oaks, CA: SAGE Publications, Inc.

[11]Beatty, L. (2003). Substance abuse, disabilities, and black women: An issue worth exploring. *Women & Therapy, 26*(3/4), 223-236.

[12]Bowe, F. G., McMahon, B. T., Chang, T., & Louvi, I. (2005). Workplace discrimination, deafness and hearing impairment: The national EEOC ADA research project. *Work, 25*, 19-25.

[13]Brown, S. E. (2002). What is disability culture? *Disability Studies Quarterly, 22*(2), 34-50.

[14]Brown, S. E. (2008). "Hear us shout:" Music celebrating disability pride and liberation. *Review of Disability Studies: An International Journal, 4*(2). Retrieved from http://rdsjournal.org/index.php/journal/article/view/262

[15]Bureau of Labor Statistics. (2015). Persons with a disability: Labor force characteristics summary. Retrieved from http://www.bls.gov/news.release/disabl.nr0.htm

[16]Campbell, M. (2017). Disabilities and sexual expression: A review of the literature. *Sociology Compass, 11*. Advanced online publication. doi: 10.1111/soc4.12508

[17]Centers for Disease Control and Prevention. (2013). Health-related quality of life — United States, 2006 and 2010. *MMWR, 62*(Suppl 3), 105-111.

[18]Centers for Disease Control and Prevention. (2015). *Black or African American populations*. Retrieved from http://www.cdc.gov/minorityhealth/populations/REMP/black.html

[19]Centers for Disease Control and Prevention. (2015). *Summary health statistics: National Health Interview Survey, 2015*. Retrieved from https://ftp.cdc.gov/pub/Health_Statistics/NCHS/NHIS/SHS/2015_SHS_Table_P-1.pdf

[20]Chamak, B. (2008). Autism and social movements: French parents' associations and international autistic individuals' organizations. *Sociology of Health & Illness, 30*, 76-96.

[21]Curry, M. A., Hassouneh-Phillips, D., & Johnston-Silverberg, A. (2001). Abuse of women with disabilities: An ecological model and review. *Violence Against Women, 7*(1), 60-79.

[22]DanceAbility International. (2012). *International links & resources.* Retrieved from http://www.danceability.com/links.php

[23]DeNavas-Walt, C., Proctor, B. D., & Smith, J. C. (2011). Income, poverty, and health insurance coverage in the United States: 2010. *Current Population Reports: Consumer Income.* Retrieved from http://www.census.gov/prod/2011pubs/p60-239.pdf

[24]Draaisma, D. (2009). Stereotypes of autism. *Philosophical Transactions of the Royal Society B: Biological Sciences, 364*(1522): 1475-1480.

[25]~~.~~ ferson, C., Lalive, R., & Fehr, E. (2008). The coevolution of cultural groups and ingroup favoritism. *Science, 321*, 1844-1849.

[6]Feldman, S. I., & Tegart, G. (2003). Keep moving: Conceptions of illness and disability of middle-aged African-American women with arthritis. *Women & Therapy, 26*(1/2), 127-142.

[27]Fenton, A., & Krahn, T. (2007). Autism, neurodiversity and equality beyond the 'normal.'. *Journal of Ethics in Mental Health, 2*(2), 1-6.

[28]Galvin, R. (2003). The paradox of disability culture: The need to combine versus the imperative to let go. *Disability & Society, 18*(5), 675-690.

[29]Gaona, E. (2015). Deaf and those who use wheelchairs face added discrimination in rental housing market. Retrieved from http://www.nvrc.org/2015/07/deaf-and-those-who-use-wheelchairs-face-added-discrimination-in-rental-housing-market/

[30]Gill, C. J. (2009). The psychological view of disability culture. In R. M. Baird, S. E. Rosenbaum, & S. K. Toombs (Eds.), *Disability: The social, political, and ethical debate* (pp. 163-169). New York, NY: Prometheus Books.

[31]Goins, R. T., Moss, M., Buchwald, D., & Guralnik, J. M. (2007). Disability among older American Indians and Alaska Natives: An analysis of the 2000 census public use microdata sample. *The Gerontologist, 47*(5), 690-696.

[32]Goyat, R., Vyas, A., & Sambanoorthi, U. (2016). Racial/ethnic disparities in disability prevalence. *Journal of Racial and Ethnic Health Disparities, 3*(4), 635-645.

[33]Groce, N. E. (1985). *Everyone here spoke sign language.* Cambridge, MA: Harvard University Press.

[34]Hamill, A. C., & Stein, C. H. (2011). Culture and empowerment in the Deaf community: An analysis of Internet weblogs. *Journal of Community & Applied Social Psychology, 21*, 388-416.

[35]Hampton, N. Z., & Xiao, F. (2007). Attitudes toward people with developmental disabilities in Chinese and American students: The role of cultural values, contact, and knowledges. *Journal of Rehabilitation, 73*(3), 23-32.

[36]Harvey, E. R. (2013). Deafness: A disability or a difference. *Health Law and Policy Brief, 2*(1), 42-57.

[37]Hays, D. G., & Erford, B. T. (2014). *Developing multicultural counseling competence: A systems approach.* Boston: Pearson.

[38]Hayward, M. D., & Heron, M. (1999). Racial inequality in active life among adult Americans. *Demography, 36*(1), 77-91. doi:10.2307/2648135

[39]Hayward, M. D., Miles, T. P., Crimmins, E. M., & Yang, Y. (2000). The significance of socioeconomic status in explaining the racial gap in chronic health conditions. *American Sociological Review, 65*(6), 910-903.

[40]Helgeson, V. S., & Zajdel, M. (2017). Adjusting to chronic health conditions. *Annual Review of Psychology, 68*, 545-571.

[41]Hofstede, G. (2001). *Culture's consequences: Comparing values, behaviors, institutions, and organizations across nations* (Vol. 2nd ed.). Thousand Oaks, CA: Sage Publications.

[42]Hofstede, G., Hofstede, G. J., & Minkov, M. (2010). *Cultures and organizations: Software of the mind.* (Vol. Revised & Expanded 3rd ed.). New York: McGraw-Hill.

[43]Hoge, C. W., Toboni, H. E., Messer, S. C., Bell, N., Amoroso, P., & Orman, D. T. (2005). The occupational burden of mental disorders in the U.S. military: Psychiatric hospitalizations, involuntary separations, and disability. *American Journal of Psychiatry, 162*, 585-591. doi:10.1176/appi.ajp.162.3.585

[44]Institute for Research on Poverty. (2013). *Poverty fact sheet #3: Poor and in poor health.* Retrieved from https://www.irp.wisc.edu/publications/factsheets/pdfs/PoorInPoorHealth.pdf

[45]Jaarsma, P., & Welin, S. (2012). Autism as a natural human variation: Reflections on the claims of the Neurodiversity Movement. *Health Care Analysis, 20*(1), 20-30. doi:10.1007/s10728-011-0169-9

[46]Jahoda, G. (2012). Critical reflections on some recent definitions of "culture". *Culture and Psychology, 18*(3), 289-303. doi:10.1177/1354067X12446229

[47]Johnstone, B., Glass, B. A., & Oliver, R. E. (2007). Religion and disability: Clinical, research and training considerations for rehabilitation professionals. *Disability and Rehabilitation, 29*(15), 1153-1163.

[48]Koenig, H. G. (2012). Religion, spirituality, and health: The research and clinical implications. *ISRN Psychiatry, 2012,* article ID 278730, doi:10.5402/2012/278730

[49]Kuppers, P. (2014). *Studying disability arts and culture: An introduction.* New York, NY: Palgrave MacMillan.

[50]Lane, H. (2002). Do Deaf people have a disability? *Sign Language Studies, 2,* 356-379.

[51]Laurent Clerc Deaf Education Center. (n.d.). *American Deaf culture.* Retrieved from http://www3.gallaudet.edu/clerc-center/info-to-go/deaf-culture/american-deaf-culture.html

[52]Levy, N. (2002). Reconsidering cochlear implants: The lessons of Martha's Vineyard. *Bioethics, 16*(2), 134-153.

[53]Martin, L. (2014). Dancing with disability: A look at the Infinity Dance Theater. *NEA Arts Magazine.*

[54]McNally, R. J., & Frueh, B. C. (2013). Why are Iraq and Afghanistan War veterans seeking PTSD disability compensation at unprecedented rates? *Journal of Anxiety Disorders, 27,* 520-526. doi:10.1016/j.janxdis.2013.07.002

[55]Meyer, H. D. (2010). Framing disability: Comparing individualist and collectivist societies. *Comparative Sociology, 9,* 165-181. doi:10.1163/156913210X12548146054985

[56]Mullahy, J., & Wolfe, B. (2001). Health policies for the non-elderly poor. In S. Danzinger & R. Haveman (Eds.), *Understanding poverty* (pp. 278-313). New York: Russell Sage Foundation.

[57]National Center for Health Statistics. (2017). *Health, United States, 2016: With chartbook on long-term trends in health.* Hyattsville, MD: Author.

[58]Nicolaidis, C. (2012). What can physicians learn from the Neurodiversity Movement? *American Medical Association Journal of Ethics, 14*(6), 503-510.

[59]Nikolaraizi, M., & Makri, M. (2004). Deaf and hearing individuals' beliefs about the capabilities of deaf people. *American Annals of the Deaf, 149,* 404-414.

[60]Oliver, E. G., & Cravens, K. S. (1999). Cultural influences on managerial choice: An empirical study of employee benefit plans in the United States. *Journal of International Business Studies, 30*(4), 745-762.

[61]Ortega, F. (2009). The cerebral subject and the challenge of neurodiversity. *BioSocieties, 4,* 425-445.

[62]Patzkowski, J. C., Rivera, J. C., Ficke, J. R., & Wenke, J. C. (2012). The changing face of disability in the U.S. Army: The Operation Enduring Freedom and Operation Iraqi Freedom effect. *Journal of the American Academy of Orthopaedic Surgeons, 20*(1), S23-S30. doi:10.5435/ JAAOS-20-08-S23

[63]Pew Research Center. (2015). *America's changing religious landscape.* Retrieved from http://www.pewforum.org/2015/05/12/americas-changing-religious-landscape/

[64]Ragged Edge Online. (2007). *A little history about this website.* Retrieved from http://www.raggededgemagazine.com/departments/ragland/003044.html

[65]Rao, D., Horton, R. A., Tsang, H. W. H., Shi, K., & Corrigan, P. W. (2010). Does individualism help explain differences in employers' stigmatizing attitudes toward disability across Chinese and American cities? *Rehabilitation Psychology, 55*(4), 351-359. doi:10.1037/a0021841.

[66]Regitz-Zagrosek, V. (2012). Sex and gender differences in health. *EMBO Reports, 13*(7), 596-603.

[67]Robertson, S. M., & Ne'eman, A. D. (2008). Autistic acceptance, the college campus, and technology: Growth of neurodiversity in society and academia. *Disability Studies Quarterly, 23*(4).

[68]Romm, C. (2015). The life and death of Martha's Vineyard sign language. *The Atlantic.* Retrieved from https://www.theatlantic.com/health/archive/2015/09/marthas-vineyard-sign-language-asl/407191/

[69]Schulz, A. J., & Mullings, L. (2006). *Gender, race, class, and health: Intersectional approaches.* San Francisco: John Wiley & Sons, Inc.

[70]Shin, P., Jones, K., & Rosenbaum, S. (2003). *Impact of high health center penetration in low-income communities.* Washington, DC: George Washington University Medical Center, Center for Health Services Research and Policy.

[71]Shiraev, E., & Levy, D. A. (2012). *Cross-cultural psychology: Critical thinking and contemporary applications* (5th ed.). New York, NY: Routledge.

[72]Silverman, C. (2012). *Understanding autism: Parents, doctors, and the history of the disorder.* Princeton, NJ: Princeton University Press.

[73]Simpson, L., Owens, P., Zodet, M., Chevarley, F., Dougherty, D., Elixhauser, A., & McCormick, M. C. (2005). Health care for children and youth in the United States: Annual report on patterns of coverage, utilization, quality, and expenditures by income. *Ambulatory Pediatrics, 5*, 45-46.

[74]Skiba, R. J., Poloni-Staudinger L., Gallini S., Simmons A. B., & Feggins-Azziz R. (2006). Disparate access: The disproportionality of African American students with disabilities across educational environments. *Exceptional Children, 72*, 411-424.

[75]Smith, D. L. (2008). Disability, gender and intimate partner violence: Relationships from the behavioral risk factor surveillance system. *Sexuality and Disability, 26*, 13.

[76]Smith, L., Hatcher, J., & Wetherheimer, R. (2002). The association of childhood ashtma with parental employment and welfare receipt. *Journal of the American Medical Women's Association, 57*, 11-15.

[77]United Nations Enable. (n.d.). *Factsheet on persons with disabilities.* Retrieved from http://www.un.org/disabilities/documents/toolaction/pwdfs.pdf

[78]U.S. Bureau of the Census. (n.d.). *Race.* Retrieved from https://www.census.gov/quickfacts/fact/table/US/PST045216

[79]Vaccarino, V., Rathore, S., Wenger, N., Frederick, P., Abrahmson, J., Barron, H.,...National Registry of Myocardial Infarction Investigators. (2005). Sex and racial differences in the management of acute myocardial infarction, 1994 through 2002. *New England Journal of Medicine, 353*, 671-682.

[80]Valente, M., Hosford-Dunn, H., & Roeser, R. J. (2008). *Audiology treatment* (2nd ed.). New York: Thieme Medical Publishers, Inc.

[81]Veterans Administration. (n.d.). Understanding military culture. *Community provider toolkit: Serving veterans through partnership.* Retrieved from http://www.mentalhealth.va.gov/communityproviders/military_culture.asp - sthash.Wq0qk3KZ.dpbs

[82]Weinick, R., Byron, S., & Birerman, A. (2005). Who can't pay for healthcare? *Journal of General Internal Medicine, 20*, 504-509.

[83]World Health Organization. (n.d.). *Defining sexual health.* Retrieved from http://www.who.int/reproductivehealth/topics/sexual_health/sh_definitions/ en/

[84]Zea, M. C., Quezada, T., & Belgrave, F. Z. (1994). Latino cultural values: Their role in adjustment to disability. *Journal of Social Behavior and Personality, 9*(5), 185-200.